Robert Harrop

Bolingbroke

A political study and criticism

Robert Harrop

Bolingbroke
A political study and criticism

ISBN/EAN: 9783337068936

Printed in Europe, USA, Canada, Australia, Japan

Cover: Foto ©Suzi / pixelio.de

More available books at **www.hansebooks.com**

BOLINGBROKE

A POLITICAL STUDY AND CRITICISM

BY

ROBERT HARROP

LONDON
KEGAN PAUL, TRENCH & CO., 1, PATERNOSTER SQUARE
1884

CONTENTS.

CHAPTER I.

CHAPTER II.

CHAPTER III.

CHAPTER IV.

CHAPTER V.

CHAPTER VI.

CHAPTER VII.

BOLINGBROKE,

A POLITICAL STUDY AND CRITICISM.

CHAPTER I.

I.

THE events of the autumn and winter of 1688, in putting an end to the long contest between the sovereigns of England and their Parliaments, established the system of government under which we live. A new dynasty was called to the throne by a resolution of the estates of the realm, and undertook the administration with powers carefully limited by their enactments. The monarchy was made a component part of an aristocratic constitution, and an aristocratic legislature the ruling power in the State.

Parliamentary government is government by party attachments—by bodies of men united together with a view of promoting the general good by their corporate action and on certain common principles. These bodies have never taken permanent and definite forms. The "common principles" which distinguish a political party are never condensed into fixed articles of belief. They are the product of the changing circumstances of the time acting on certain inherited traditions; and just as in nature the same generic type, when thrown into new conditions of life, develops new varieties with different wants and habits—varieties hardly to be recognized sometimes as members of one family—so in the world of politics circumstance gives to every body of principles its distinguishing colour and discriminating effect, and men called by the same party name in successive generations will be found pursuing the most dissimilar objects, and professing in the pursuit the most opposite sentiments. The High Churchmen, for instance, of the reign of Queen Anne and the first Georges were just as sound Tories as the followers of Lord Eldon a hundred years later. They were intent on bringing back the old discarded polity in Church and State which embodied some of the most cherished traditions of Toryism. The overthrow of that polity had brought with it many evils—long years of war, a great increase in the public burdens, the consolidation of party government on a narrow and corrupt basis ; and the High Church leaders, fastening as was natural on the vulnerable parts of the new system, pressed for a policy of isolation in foreign affairs, a strict economy in the public services, and a radical change in the methods of parliamentary management—advocated, in short, in the interest of such high Tory doctrines as monarchy by right of birth, caste privilege, and sacerdotal ascendency, those very measures of peace, retrenchment, and reform which the Tory of the next generations denounced as the rankest Liberalism. It was the same with their Whig opponents. In their equally natural anxiety to strengthen by every kind of external bulwark a liberal plan of government which made the will of the nation as expressed in Parliament supreme, deposed the landed interest, and reduced the Crown and the Church to the position of handmaids of the State, they instituted that very policy of repression and proscription which the follower of Lord Eldon spent his life in justifying—organized corruption into an elaborate system which it has cost their descendants many years of labour to root out, multiplied places and pensions for the convenience of their party friends, harassed their party rivals with tests and penalties, expended the public money in the purchase of nomination boroughs, subsidized foreign powers to "guarantee" our domestic institutions, and bribed members of Parliament to support them. Each of the great parties has preserved under all changes of front its essential aims : the Whig, when most arbitrary and oppressive, having in view the ultimate and indefeasible authority of the people he governed ; the Tory, when most prone to radical changes, taking his stand on the principle of the divine right of governments. But neither party has been awed by the mere phantom of political consistency, or has hesitated, when the objects of pursuit have been in keeping with the general tenor of its policy, to seek them by measures altogether at variance with its most characteristic professions. The friends of freedom and self-government, in the ferment of Jacobite enthusiasm which followed the accession of the Hanover line, deprived the electors of their voice in affairs as the readiest means of saving the representative system. The hereditary enemies of popular rights, a hundred and fifty years later, debased the suffrage in the hope of striking a vein of Imperialism in the ignorance and passions of the multitude.

Walpole first brought to perfection our present system of party management. Coming into power with signal advantages—the Crown for the moment effaced, and all his political rivals discredited—he had full leisure to establish that scheme of veiled Republicanism which was the Whig ideal and is the modern practice. He knew that his party represented in its constitutional policy the ideas and principles of the Revolution ; and he set himself to carry out the objects of the Revolution by strengthening his party influence. He inspired domestic politicians with his own love of parliamentary government, with its attendant blessings of order and personal liberty and lenient administration, much as he inspired foreign potentates with his own love of peace, by showing how favourable these things were to their material interests ; and just as he ruled George I. and George II., so he ruled the House of Commons, not by corruption in the vulgar sense, not by seducing men from their allegiance or their pledges, but by playing on the various foibles and desires of men elected to support his policy but without fixed principles to keep them true, by proving to them how their personal objects could be best obtained through the ascendency of his party, and by drilling them in the methods by which that ascendency could be best preserved.

The success of Walpole in confirming party divisions and in fixing parliamentary government on party lines determined the nature of the opposition with which his authority was assailed. The most formidable of his opponents, the head of a complex faction of moderate Tories and disaffected Whigs drawn together by a common dislike of Walpole and a common desire for his removal, developed a rival system, which was intended to serve as the basis for their joint action. It united certain elements from the ostensible creed of both. But it may be described in the main as an attempt to reverse the constitutional methods of the great Whig minister while professing to respect his public objects. Walpole governed by party organization. Bolingbroke denounced party government as fatal to the whole spirit of an autocratic constitution. Walpole magnified the power and the responsibilities of the House of Commons, which, under his impulse, was gradually taking into its own hands all the functions of government. Bolingbroke sought to reduce Parliament to its old position of a mere consulting body, and to exalt the prerogative of a patriot king hindered by no constitutional restraints from freely exercising his individual judgment. Walpole pushed the principle of ministerial responsibility to the furthest point by making every public act of the hereditary ruler the work of a trusted parliamentary statesman, and the whole government strictly answerable to the chief minister, as the foremost representative of the prevailing party in Parliament. Bolingbroke would have made the Revolution sovereign in person once more the moving spring in the machine, and ministers, as in the old days, a body of agents and advisers chosen by his authority and working under his direction.

Thus in the rivalry of the two statesmen the two rival systems, monarchical and parliamentary, came into final conflict. A generation passed away. The House of Commons, under too strict ministerial guidance, became more and more exclusive till it ceased to be in any real sense a representative body. The accidental combination of parties collected under the standard of " Patriotism " was dissolved. The Whig methods were extended and degraded. The Tory principle was stripped of its democratical varnish. That system which in its pure form was to have been a true aristocracy of birth and merit, pursuing the general good under the control of a legislature freely chosen by the people and including every variety of franchise, degenerated into a government of privileged orders, reforming as little as possible, desiring official station as a means of lucrative dignity rather than active usefulness, and keeping themselves in power by the influence of wealth and close connections. The rival system which Bolingbroke revived, the system of monarchy bound but not fettered by constitutional limitations, wisely apprehensive of public opinion, securing a loyal obedience to its measures through their inherent honesty and rectitude and freedom from party bias, did not degenerate; for it has never existed except on paper. Like other attempts to create a common standing-ground for inconsistent principles—like the *via media* of Anglo-Catholicism, for instance, midway between the real religions of Popery and Protestantism, it is hardly capable of being professed, acted on, or maintained in any large sphere of operation; presupposing in the hereditary sovereign an amount of personal wisdom and a degree of personal disinterestedness which, while human nature remains the same, it is hopeless to look for.

At length, about the beginning of George III.'s. reign, under the advice chiefly of an astute and cold-blooded Scotch lawyer, who had been the colleague of Pelham and the pupil of Bolingbroke, the worst parts of the two systems, each now false to its leading idea, were joined together. The parliamentary methods of Pelham were employed for the purpose of carrying out the autocratic objects of Bolingbroke. The despotic polity which Bolingbroke advocated was re-established under the cloak and by the instrumentality of the constitutional forms which he denounced. It was the merit of George III. and his advisers to see that parliamentary institutions had struck root; that the Whig aristocracy, with the liberal ideas and principles they represented, could not be got rid of except by using against them the machinery of the Whig constitution; and that a representative body powerful over the nation, but no longer responsible to the nation, was at once the most effective and the least invidious weapon for overthrowing representative government. By dexterously playing off one parliamentary faction against another ; by binding to their interest the self-seeking politicians generated in the corruption of the parliamentary system ; by an unscrupulous use of the means of influencing members which the parliamentary methods of Walpole had brought to perfection, they succeeded in emancipating the court from the control of Parliament, while still leaving Parliament, in appearance, what the Revolution had made it—the ostensible master of the State.

From this union of ignoble methods with personal objects in government sprang the narrow and exclusive Toryism of the great French war, which erected privilege into an idol. Under this system the monarchy relapsed into the semblance of its old position. Its interests being now identified with those of the ruling caste, it no longer cared to make its influence felt in any sustained pressure on affairs. Government continued to rest, as in the time of Walpole, on organized party support. But the two remaining features of the old constitution, suppressed under Walpole's ascendency, reappeared—a Church establishment supported in its intolerance by the State as the sole repository of religious truth, yet deriving from the State all its pretensions to authority ; and a governing class of landlords, monopolizing power in virtue of some inherent superiority attaching to the possession of soil, and exercising it mainly in the effort to keep up rents and hamper commercial enterprise.

As an engine of government, this system had many merits. It sanctified the principle of authority ; it guaranteed the stability of institutions ; it developed the administrative capacities of the nation, and secured an efficient political training for its rising talent. Prescription gathered round its very abuses—its sanguinary code, its Church pluralities, its rotten boroughs, its vicious court. At length the high notions of liberty, of which it was the negation, and which had formed the redeeming element in the creed of patriotic Toryism, discarded by the political heirs of Bolingbroke, found a refuge amongst the shattered remnant of the Whigs, instructed by adversity, purified by desertions, and penetrated by the philosophical teaching of the two past generations; filled them with a new hatred of the rule of race over race, of class over class, and of religion over religion; impelled them to track out and assail privilege in all its various strongholds; and incited them to the efforts which in our time abolished slavery, reformed the legislature, and destroyed the Irish Church.

In the following pages an attempt is made to portray the public character and career of one of the most eminent party leaders and greatest political writers of the past century; to trace in his policy the final effort of the old monarchical system to reassert itself at the expense of parliamentary government; to show how, in the form in which he had designed it, this effort failed; and how, in place of the old system, parliamentary institutions, fixed on too narrow and corrupt a basis, offered themselves and were seized upon as the instruments of despotic authority.

II.

Henry St. John was born at Battersea in 1678. He was sprung from a younger branch of the St. Johns of Bletsoe, an ancient Wiltshire family, of which one member had in the reign of James I. been created Earl of Bolingbroke. They were, as Clarendon complained, a "mutinous race," with a fatal tendency to combine the principles of the Roundhead with the manners of the Cavalier. At the breaking out of the great Rebellion, they had been fitly represented by a young patrician with many of the social qualities of the brilliant kinsman whose story we have to tell. He had been raised to the House of Lords by Charles I. in his father's lifetime, but had found the ties of public duty stronger than those of interest and gratitude, had quitted his boon companions, had joined the parliamentary forces, and on the field of Edgehill had testified with his blood his devotion to civil liberty. He was slain in covering the retreat, and the court historian appropriately ends his narrative of the young patriot's fate with the congenial slander that he received his death-wound in the act of "running away."

The family mansion at Battersea, in which St. John was born, was at this time the residence of his grandfather, Sir Walter St. John, a cousin of the young Republican soldier who fell at Edgehill. Sir Walter seems to have been a genial, hen-pecked country gentleman of charitable instincts, a Tory at heart notwithstanding his surroundings, whose schools, still existing in the parish, have kept his memory green. His married son and daughter-in-law lived with him, after the patriarchal custom of the time. The latter, Bolingbroke's mother, was a lady of the noble house of Rich. Of her little is known; but his father, a man of some note in his day, was a true scion of the St. Johns, a thorough club-man and man of the world, a duellist, a gambler, who, born under the protectorate of Cromwell, survived far into the reign of George II., who earned the viscount's coronet bestowed on him by George I. by near half a century's faithful service of the "cause of freedom," and who distinguished himself amongst all his brother legislators by his ardent pursuit of pleasure. Swift, to whom Lord St. John's Whig and Low Church principles were even more offensive than his loose habits of life, speaks of him with immense contempt as an old beau of the Restoration, an old lounger at coffee-houses, an old fribble, and so forth. But to have been abused by Swift is, after all, one of the soundest titles to respect in a politician of Queen Anne's reign.

The most prominent member, however, and the undisputed head of the little household, still remains to be mentioned. This was St. John's grandmother, Joanna St. John, the wife of Sir Walter, and the daughter of that dark and melancholy Oliver St. John, himself a cadet of the House of Bolingbroke, who defended Hampden before the Exchequer Chamber, and bore the chief part in framing and passing into law the Act for Strafford's attainder. He was, perhaps, the ablest of all the Long Parliament leaders, the man who, with the exception of Cromwell, left the most enduring mark on passing events; and in his daughter were reproduced many of the great qualities of the Republican lawyer and diplomatist. She essayed to mould her grandson's character in its early plastic years. Under her stern Puritan rule, his childhood passed in austere seclusion. His rudiments were taught him by her favourite chaplain, afterwards a famous dissenting preacher, whose meeting-house at the time of the Sacheverell riots was burnt by the High Church mob. For their relaxation the family studied, when the labours of the day were over, the commentaries of another worthy evangelical divine, a shining light of Puritanism, whose distinction it was that he could preach a hundred and seventeen different sermons on the hundred and seventeenth Psalm. St. John never forgot those sermons. His father could escape to the theatre or the Mall on pretence of public business. But no such excuse was open to a youth of his tender years ; and it was Manton's sermons, as Bolingbroke used often afterwards to tell his friends with a shudder, that first made him a High Church-man, "that he might never hear them read or read them

more." * At last the poor lad was rescued and sent to
Eton. But the gloomy decorum of the Battersea household still overshadowed him ; and this readiest and most
persuasive of orators, this most brilliant talker in an age
when conversation was studied as an art, the most finished
gentleman in a society where charm of manner was cultivated to its highest perfection, the "all-accomplished St.
John," left there the reputation of being a dull boy, by
no means a match in parts for his schoolmate and companion Walpole. From Eton he was transferred, it is said,
to Christchurch, then the natural resort of youths of high
connections, whatever their politics, but rapidly becoming
under Aldrich and Atterbury a mere hotbed of Toryism.†

With this mixed ancestry, half-Roundhead, half-Cavalier,
with the rusty Calvinism of his earliest teachers varnished
over with a thin layer of scholarship and philosophy,
St. John came up to London, fresh from a household of
precisians, and with the example of a dissolute father
to guide him, at a time when the reaction against the
tyranny of the saints had not yet spent itself, and when
the morals of Rochester and Sedley still gave the tone
to fashionable life. A young patrician suspected of Puritan
leanings was, in a manner, bound to wipe out the imputation by more than common profligacy. What school and
college had begun, foreign travel completed. The years
1698 and 1699 were spent by St. John in wandering through
France and Italy. Of his movements, little definite has
come down to us. It is believed that he passed most of
his time at Paris, then appealing to the young Englishman
with all the charms of novelty ; that he formed a close
friendship there with Prior, the secretary to the British

---

* Bolingbroke to Swift, July 28, 1721.

† So says tradition. There is, however, no authentic record of St. John's
presence at Oxford till 1702, when, visiting the city in the train of Queen
Anne, he received an honorary degree.

legation, and not the best companion for a youth of St. John's habits ; and that through his kinsman Lord Jersey, ambassador to the court of France, he was initiated into the delights and exposed to the temptations of the Parisian coteries. When he returned home at the beginning of 1700, it was with a perfect mastery of French, with a sprinkling of Italian, with manners in the highest degree refined and polished, with his convictions unsettled and his moral nature undermined—with all the graces and all the vices of a courtier. It was hoped by his friends that marriage might steady him, and in the spring of his return he underwent that ceremony at their request. The lady selected for him—it was again Lady St. John's choice— was Frances Winchcomb, daughter and co-heiress of Sir Henry Winchcomb, of Bucklersbury, in Berkshire. At the general election, which took place in the autumn of the same year, he was returned for the family borough of Wootton Basset, which his father relinquished to him.

III.

St. John entered Parliament at a critical time in the history of English politics. The full import of the change which the Revolution had made in the relative position of the Crown and the House of Commons was but little understood, and nothing can to a modern eye seem more un- sightly or more pregnant with public dangers than the state of parties :—with a sovereign on the throne of strong will and high capacity, who essayed to govern as well as reign ; with an untrusted ministry tottering from internal weakness and forced upon him by hard necessity ; with a House of Lords dominated by the Revolution Whigs, less by the force of numbers than of intellect and statesmanship ; and with a High Church and High Tory Commons far more aristocratic in temper than the Lords, far more imbued with the special ideas of the landowning class, but distracted by faction, disaffected to that form of government of which it was the leading factor, uncertain how and in what direction to assert the supreme authority which it possessed, and ready in its eagerness for change of some kind to fall under the guidance, at one moment, of extreme Jacobites, and at another of extreme Republicans.

It was mainly composed of country gentlemen, the heirs of the old historic Cavaliers. A sense of the imminent dangers which threatened the supremacy of their Church and their own class privileges had driven these rural magnates into rebellion. In defence of that supremacy and those privileges, they had made themselves consenting instruments in remodelling the old constitution, in establishing a new form of government based on those very principles of civil and religious freedom against which their fathers had taken arms. It was conduct altogether opposed to the best traditions of their party. It was opposed to the express instructions of that Church on whose behalf and in whose interests, mainly, those traditions had been forsaken. Already it was being visited, as it seemed, with an appropriate retribution. The Church had been rescued from the dangers which threatened her on the side of Rome. She was safe in the exclusive possession of her dignities and her emoluments. But still her exclusive privileges had been impaired. The public worship of her Puritan rivals had been placed under the equal protection of the law. Under the shelter of a free system, Protestants who rejected her communion were rapidly growing into power and wealth, asserting their true position, becoming dominant in municipal councils, founding schools and colleges which might at no distant day prove dangerous competitors to Westminster and Trinity. The State, secured on one side from the intrusion of those Popish recusants whom King James, by virtue of his dispensing power and to the extreme wrath of the true English gentleman, was thrusting into the public offices, the army, and the bench of justice, was fast becoming, under the reformed Government, a prey to classes hardly less offensive—to Dutchmen, to Presbyterians, to speculators enriched by " trade."

The public burdens, again, incurred in defending a change of polity which brought to the country gentleman such doubtful blessings, had increased fourfold ; and this increase, less from any unfairness in the incidence of taxation than from the thriftless habits of his class, was felt as a peculiar hardship by the proprietor of land. When, in the first years of the new government, as a basis for the increased assessment which the expenses of the State required, it had been necessary to revalue the landed property of England, Parliament, as was natural in an assembly composed of landowners, had taken especial care to provide that the new burdens should fall lightly on the landed interest, and that the new descriptions of wealth which mercantile enterprise was creating should bear their share. Thus, through commissions consisting of the principal country gentlemen in every county, the proprietors of land, unlike all other classes, had been suffered to assess themselves. The price of the commodity which they produced had been artificially kept up by bounties on the exportation of English grain. Large additional burdens had been laid on imports. The dividends of public companies had been heavily taxed. Stamp and other duties had been imposed ; whilst by far the chief part of the extraordinary charges of the war, charges which in former reigns had fallen exclusively on realized and therefore mainly on landed property, had been met by borrowing money on the security of special funds, funds carefully selected as pressing as evenly as possible on all classes.

By all these financial changes the landed interest had benefited at the expense of rival bodies. But the country gentleman, as a rule, lived up to the verge of his income. He required the whole of his year's rents to provide for his year's expenses. He felt any new public burden as something taken away from the conveniences and comforts of his life. He was quite unable, too, from sheer want of means, to avail himself of those increased facilities for the employment of their surplus earnings which the increasing liabilities of the State gave to the professional and the commercial classes, and which enabled the merchant, the tradesman, and the man of business to take back with one hand in the shape of additional income what they gave with the other in the shape of augmented taxes. He saw, in fact, with no little disgust, that the merchant, the tradesman, and the man of business were actually thriving under that system which weighed him down, and that in the impulse which the change of polity had given to every kind of progress he was losing ground, through the rivalry of new men and the creation of new forms of wealth, even in his own party strongholds—in the county which his ancestors had represented, in the borough at his park gates where his tenants and dependants lived. It was natural that these things should make him sore. To the country gentleman, indeed, the Revolution had brought with it hardly anything but evil. The religious supremacy of his Church, the political supremacy of his class, his own social position and worldly prosperity, were all menaced by new dangers, dangers which he had but dimly if at all foreseen when, not without doubts and misgivings, he had reluctantly assented to it.

Hitherto his attempts to remedy these evils had failed. He had hoped, when the war was over, that by disbanding the regular army and resuming the exorbitant grants which King William (at a season of such national distress !) had carved out of the hereditary dominions of the Crown and bestowed on his mistress and boon companions, the land-tax, which pressed so heavily on himself and his fellows, might be brought back to something like its old figure. He had hoped that by rigidly excluding all pensioners and placemen from the House of Commons, and by requiring every member who sat there to possess a substantial estate in land, the territorial interest to which he belonged, exposed now to so many rivalries, might be restored to something like its old predominance.

But these hopes had been disappointed. The army, though reduced in numbers, still remained, in the eyes of the country gentlemen, an expensive incumbrance on the nation, and a standing peril to the interests they valued. The attempt to vacate the obnoxious grants of public land lavished on the Orkneys and Portlands, amidst such unexampled public burdens, the courtiers had defeated by an adroit manœuvre. The Place Bill and the Regulation of Elections Bill had indeed been passed through Parliament. But by a stretch of the royal preroga-tive, on which none of his successors have ventured, and which was altogether opposed to the spirit of the reformed polity, they had been vetoed by the King. In truth, King William, with his great gifts, his knowledge, his energy, his strong passions, was but ill qualified to play the part of a constitutional sovereign. On first coming over he had striven, as he thought, to be "impartial," to divide the great departments as evenly as might be between Whigs and Tories, subject to the condition that his cabinet council should present a faithful miniature of his

Parliament. When it appeared that this old plan of mutual distrust and covert antagonism among the servants of the Crown, though excellently fitted for enabling the sovereign to determine in the last resort the tendencies of government, was altogether unsuited to the new order of things, in which this function belonged to the chosen representatives of the nation, it was with many misgivings that the Prince had suffered himself to lapse into the hands of a homogeneous ministry. He was far too shrewd not to see that the new system, a system essential to the proper working of parliamentary government, would for that very reason withdraw from the sovereign most of that personal authority which he had hitherto exercised as the moderating influence in divided counsels; and it was only because, at the moment when he first made it, the change would strengthen his hands by bringing into his service men all of whom were prepared to support his policy and carry out his objects that he was induced to take a step which his judgment disapproved. For King William was just as fond of power, just as impatient of restraint, just as prone to magnify the kingly office, as any of his predecessors. When, therefore, the opinion of the country turned, when his Whig ministers lost, as we should say, the "confidence" of Parliament, when a House of Commons bitterly opposed to them and their common objects was sent to Westminster, instead of making his administration and his policy reflect the changing moods of his legislature with the delicate precision of modern times, King William, intent on his high aims and reluctant to discard servants whom he had learnt to trust, had sought to clog the wheels of Parliament, to use the constitutional advisers furnished to him by Parliament as a means of violently wrenching the State into a course which Parliament and the nation condemned

C

The result had been three years of faction and anarchy, for which the King and his Whig ministers must be held responsible, and which had tended all the more to exasperate the Tory landlords against a parliamentary sovereign and parliamentary government. One by one, by criminal prosecutions, by votes of censure, by threats of impeachment, by combined rushes, so to speak, of the dominant party, which shook the very foundations of the State, the Whig junto had been driven from office. Rochester, the old minister of James II., and Tankerville, the old lieutenant of Monmouth, such are the vicissitudes of fortune, now found themselves directing, in the interest of Cavaliers and High Churchmen, the councils of William of Orange. When, early in February, 1701, the new Parliament met, though the King was known to be sulky and the minister unreliable, the triumph of the country gentlemen seemed complete. In the first division in which they tried their strength, Harley, their candidate for the Speakership, was chosen over his Whig competitor by a majority of two to one.

The history of the next few years may be best studied in connection with the character and career of this man. It is the history of disappointed hopes on the part of the High Church gentry, of the gradual strengthening of the influences that bore against them, and the gradual drifting of power to the Whig chiefs more from the force of circumstances than from any efforts of their own to grasp it. In shaping events to these ends, Harley bore a great part. He was what was then known as a Trimmer. He never continued to act cordially for any length of time with any large body of men. He went with them up to a certain point and then stopped short. A statesman of those days generally regarded his own and his country's interests as bound up with the interests of his party. Harley was an exception to this rule. He once said of himself, with some justice and with more point than his style usually displays, " I have no inclination to any party; I have no obligation to any party; I have no antipathy to any party." * In his youth, a Presbyterian and an Exclusionist, in his early manhood, a thorough-paced supporter of the Revolution while the success of the Revolution seemed doubtful, and a rancorous persecutor of Jacobites so long as the return of James seemed likely, he became, after the peace of Ryswick, an inveterate critic of the Revolution government. This threw him into the society of Tories; he rose to be a leader of the country party, and he learnt to talk with sufficient readiness the dialect of his new friends. But he was a Tory by accident and association, not from conviction. The prejudices and exaggerations of the party moved his resentment. He had no sympathy with the sacerdotal leanings of its members, or with the high monarchical doctrines which they derived from the lessons of priestly counsellors. In his heart he still carried Whig principles to the extreme of what we should now call Radicalism. He was in favour of peace, retrenchment, and unfettered industry. He was opposed to standing armies. He advocated the principle of " non-intervention " in continental affairs, except when the material interests of the kingdom were distinctly threatened. He desired to see the House of Commons entirely independent at once of royal and of ministerial control; he claimed for that House an intrinsic superiority over its two cognate branches; and he insisted on its right to know beforehand, and to freely criticize, both the foreign and the domestic policy of the State. Where he chiefly differed from the recognized Whig statesman, was in his dislike to that principle of party government with which the Whigs were now

* Harley to Godolphin, November 5, 1706.

beginning to be identified; in his opposition to the new-fangled cabinet system, with its secret action and joint responsibility, the nature and effect of which he altogether misunderstood; and in his desire to revive and invest with new authority the old superseded Privy Council. With little of the statesman and nothing of the orator, he had an influence in parliamentary circles which no statesman or orator of that time exceeded; for he had developed an unrivalled skill in the lower parts of politics, in the mystery of parliamentary management, in the art of discovering the weak side of every character, acquiring its confidence, and playing upon its foibles. But he used this skill, not as Walpole afterwards did, for the purpose of welding a great party majority into an efficient instrument for carrying out, under the guidance of its own chosen leaders, the policy on which the nation, in electing that Parliament, had set the stamp of its approval, but in devising checks on the executive power, and in organizing secret resistance to the ministers of State, whom he still persisted in regarding as in some degree the enemies of the people they served. The consequence was that every party in its hour of need profited by his exertions, and that every party in its hour of triumph suffered by his perfidy. For, like many men of Puritan descent and training, he concealed an extreme propensity to artifice and intrigue under an outward show of grave and austere decorum.

Up to this point Harley had urged and directed the Tory onset. He now interposed to keep from the victorious party the fruits of their success. Nor was this difficult; for the country gentlemen, who formed by far the larger half of the supporters of the new ministry, had been sailing under false colours. In their hearts they held opinions which it was impolitic, indeed illegal, openly to avow. In opposition, therefore, being set against a pure

Whig administration, they had allied themselves with democrats, had talked the language of democrats, and supported the designs of democrats. This was just the conjuncture favourable to the influence of a man like Harley, a democrat at heart, a Tory by accident, a trimmer by profession ; and to the course which he then took England owes a debt of gratitude which ought not to be forgotten. For it was owing to the peculiar skill and tact which Harley displayed in operating on the various sections of a Tory Parliament that the two great questions which at this time occupied the public mind were settled on principles assuredly not Tory.

These two questions were of vital moment to the security of the Revolution settlement. Since the death of the young Duke of Gloucester in the preceding year, there had been no parliamentary heir to the Crown, except the Princess Anne. At the same time, the success of the French King's intrigues at Madrid had threatened, by uniting France and Spain, to untrim the balance of power, place the whole of Western Europe at the mercy of the Bourbons, and make the restoration of the hereditary line by French arms in the highest degree probable.

Now four-fifths of the country gentlemen were Jacobites. They looked forward to the restoration of the hereditary line when purged of its religious errors. They were in favour of government by royal prerogative in the interest of the clergy and landed gentry. They were opposed to every scheme of foreign policy which should, under the plea of preserving the balance of power in Europe, throw external difficulties in the way of re-modelling their own domestic institutions into conformity with these views ; and they chafed bitterly under the burdens cast upon them in the attempt to establish such a scheme. Yet under Harley's dexterous management the Act of Settlement was passed, finally disinheriting the hereditary line. By Harley's exertions the prerogative was fenced round with new restrictions and limitations altogether opposed to the spirit of an autocratic polity. Under Harley's leadership bills were carried into law attainting the legitimate heir, and imposing on all public men the duty of formally abjuring him as an impostor. Nay, such was the influence of this consummate master of compromise and conciliation, that the very party which had already forced King William to recognize the Bourbon claim to Spain, the party of hereditary right, the party of prerogative, the friends of peace and retrenchment and an isolated foreign policy, were brought to consent to measures of which the object was to dismember Spain in the interest of the Austrian line, which made England the moving spirit in a mighty coalition, and which—at the cost of tripling her annual burdens and adding more than thirty millions to her public debt—saved her parliamentary constitution by identifying it with the ambitions of half the great Powers of Europe.*

If King William had died six months earlier, it is probable that the High Tories would have won the game and that a memorable page in our history would never have been written. But events played into his hands.

---

* The Act of Settlement, though supported by the Whigs, was not, strictly speaking, a Whig measure. It was drawn in the interest of that Tory-Radical opposition to the Whig junto, the leading members of which were now in office. It *declared* the Princess Sophia, "as a Protestant," to be the next in succession to the Crown ; and it entailed the Crown on her and her heirs, "being Protestants." In other words, it made Catholicism a sort of natural and, as it were, self-evident bar to the throne like idiocy, and thus saved, in appearance, the favourite High Church doctrine of indefeasible hereditary right. The restricting clauses, on the other hand, by which the prerogative was limited, were far more stringent and far more enfeebling to the executive government than the Whig junto approved, and were designed to carry into effect the "radical principles" on which the joint opposition to the Whig junto had been founded. The two most important of them were repealed as soon as the pure Whigs returned to power.

Great as was the exhaustion of England, strong as was her aversion to a burdensome foreign policy, she was still bent on preserving her national independence. She had been moved to anger when Lewis, in defiance of all his pledges, annexed the Spanish monarchy, and garrisoned with his troops the long line of Flemish fortresses from Luxemburg to Antwerp. But when, later on in the same year, James II. died at St. Germains, and Lewis, once more in defiance of his pledges, recognized the Jacobite Pretender as King of Great Britain, the slumbering embers burst into flame. In the heat of patriotic resentment, financial distress and political discontent were alike forgotten ; and the whole nation stood forth against the perjured oppressor.

William seized his opportunity with the skill of a practised diplomatist. The Grand Alliance against the House of Bourbon was constructed. The English Parliament was dissolved. The English ministry was remodelled. The King's speech from the throne, a masterly State paper long cherished as the last word of solemn warning addressed to all Protestant nations by the foremost champion of Protestantism, was drawn up by his old Chancellor Somers, the trusted depositary of his counsels, and the faithful guardian and exponent of his policy during the critical years that followed. In a few months the great soldier and statesman was no more. The old ministers were replaced. The Whig chiefs were jealously excluded from the new Privy Council. In the new Parliament, elected in the summer of 1702, their scanty following was overwhelmed in the rush of loyal Toryism, welcoming the advent of a sovereign only one degree removed from the line marked out by God. But the policy of the State never lost the ply which William in his latest moments had given to it. War was proclaimed against France and Spain. Marlborough, whom the King had designated as

his successor in the command of the allied armies, and
employed to put the finishing touches to the fabric of the
Grand Alliance, was named by the new Queen to be the
captain general of her forces. By Marlborough's influence,
the shrewd and temperate Godolphin, now bound to
himself by close personal and domestic ties, was preferred
as first minister to the recognized chief of the dominant
faction. And it was Marlborough's judgment and winning
address which prevailed with the two Secretaries of State,
both of them high Tories, to abandon the foreign policy
identified with Tory traditions, and consent that England
should enter the war, not as a mere ally, a mere Portugal
or Denmark, whose function was complete when her petty
tribute of arms or gold had been paid in, but as the
animating spirit and motive power of the great confederacy.*

A minister who subordinates party traditions to his
conceptions of public duty must expect to be roughly
treated by party. But the position of the first Tory
advisers of Queen Anne was altogether unprecedented.
They had the ungrudging confidence of the sovereign,
who had just mounted the throne with the hearty goodwill of Englishmen, and who in her temper, in her religious

---

* One effect of the Puritan rebellion had been to change the foreign policy
of England. By nature, by geographical position, by the commercial occupations and free inquiring spirit of her rising classes, England was especially
marked out as a leader in the great Northern confederacy of progressive and
emancipated Europe. The foreign policy of Elizabeth had been marked by
steady adherence to this principle. But the Stuarts, coquetting with Catholicism
at home, had leaned with all the weight of Government to Catholicism abroad.
The country had always opposed to this policy a resistance more or less vain.
The Parliament of 1621 had been dismissed for advising James I. to join the
continental Protestants against Spain. When the Government became
Puritan, the foreign policy of Elizabeth was revived. Under Cromwell,
England became not merely a partner in the general Protestant interest of
Europe, but the maker and leader of the combination; and the policy of
William and the Revolution Whigs was the policy of Cromwell, and Elizabeth
applied to the different circumstances of their time.

feelings, and in her intellectual capacity, exactly typified their national characteristics. In the House of Commons they had an immense party following; and the House of Commons, if it had only known the extent of its own authority, and used its power with decency and moderation, was the foremost body in the State, the body justly entitled to determine and prescribe the national policy. Yet the policy of the State was, in fact, determined and prescribed by a little knot of men who were not members of the House of Commons, who had no voice or share in the executive government, who had no right of access to the person of their sovereign, whom the sovereign in fact distrusted and disliked, whom her ministers regarded with jealousy even in the act of seeking and accepting their counsels, whom the House of Commons had just impeached and tried to ruin; and the leader of this little band was not, as might be supposed, some great noble powerful from high descent and vast possessions, but a poor lawyer and adventurer, the son of an attorney in a provincial town. Marlborough and Godolphin, having adopted a policy from Somers and the Whig junto, began to look to Somers and the Whig junto for help in carrying it out, and to bid for that help by new concessions. Meanwhile, the country gentlemen, the rank and file of the ministerial party, mutinous and discontented but not yet openly hostile, caring nothing for the objects which their leaders were pursuing, intent on objects with which their leaders had small sympathy, devoted all their energies to faction and mischief. Their great delight was baiting the House of Lords, that House of Lords to which, through their own folly and perverseness, the centre of political power was gravitating.

It was in this work, which was pursued session after session with unflagging industry, that Henry St. John won his spurs as a debater. As he afterwards frankly acknowledged,[*] he knew nothing at this time of politics, and was moved partly by a spirit of boyish frolic, partly by the belief that in the ranks of the country gentlemen there was a better opening and more chance of advancement for an enterprising speaker than amongst the grave and experienced Whigs. He set himself to expose the organized hypocrisy of official Toryism by showing what unofficial Toryism could achieve. In his very first session, notwithstanding his Whig connections, he put himself ostentatiously forward in the impeachment of the Whig junto for the offence of concluding a partition treaty, on which in his subsequent years he founded his own foreign policy as minister. In his second, notwithstanding his Puritan antecedents, he not only supported but took a large share in framing the Occasional Conformity Bill, a measure admirably fitted no doubt to perpetuate the authority of his party friends, but conceived in the very spirit of the Test Act and the Conventicle Act ; and when this outrageous attack on the vital principle of the new polity had been warded off by the Whig lords, he appeared in the Painted Chamber as spokesman for the party of sacerdotal privilege. He was one of seven commissioners nominated by the House of Commons to overhaul the accounts of the late war and cook up a charge of peculation against the Whig Chancellor of the Exchequer. In the year after the Queen's accession, a Jacobite plot was discovered in Scotland. Somers and Halifax, provoked at the hesitation of the Secretary of State, took the matter out of the hands of the Queen's Government, ordered the culprits into the custody of Black Rod, appointed a Whig committee to interrogate them, and directed that no one whatever should have access to the prisoners till they had

* "Letters on History," Works, ii. 425.

appeared for examination at the bar of the House of Lords. These proceedings, strong proceedings it must be confessed on the part of a parliamentary opposition and in a matter with respect to which Parliament—the offence having been committed in Scotland—had no sort of jurisdiction, roused the friends of ministers in the Commons to a state of frenzy. A counter-committee was at once formed there to search the records and frame an address of sympathy to the Queen. St. John was made chairman; and the characteristic address which he drew up, pledging her faithful Commons to defend her prerogative "against all invasions whatever," may be still read in the journals, and had the merit at least of eliciting from the great Whig jurisconsult one of the most masterly of his State papers. Again, in the well-known case of the Aylesbury men, in which St. John made his first reported speech, a heavy blow was dealt by the same skilful hand at the exasperated country gentlemen. The claim of the representative body, ascribing to itself an exclusive jurisdiction in election matters, and denying the right of the voter to vindicate his qualification before the law—a claim perfectly defensible in itself, but put forth with offensive acrimony and supported with unseemly violence—led to another embittered controversy between the Houses, in which the superior judgment, temper, and urbanity of the peers were again signally displayed.

In each of these matters it would be easy to frame a plausible, and in some, perhaps, a valid defence for the action of the House of Commons. Its leaders put themselves in the wrong by their utter want of dignity and decorum and self-restraint, by the very failings which to the end of his long life distinguished St. John in controversy. Perhaps no Englishman has ever united more happily the various qualities of mind and person which go to form a consummate orator ; nor, if the concurring testimony of friends and foes alike is to be credited, was the pre-eminence of Marlborough in the field more unquestioned in that age than the pre-eminence of Bolingbroke in the senate. Yet with all his fine gifts and the ascendency they won him, no one was ever less qualified to be a guide and ruler of men. For with the rare physical and mental endowments of the orator he had the orator's temperament, his nervousness and sensibility, his passion and his unscrupulousness. The bitter words in which Clarendon once described a famous parliamentary leader of his time may be applied with far more fitness to St. John. He had indeed " a head to contrive, a tongue to persuade to, and a hand to execute any kind of mischief." In his own pointed language he "showed the Tories game and encouraged them with his halloo."

IV.

From this position of huntsman to the pack of High Church squires and rectors, St. John was promoted in the spring of 1704 to be a member of this transition Government. He owed his preferment to the influence of Harley. It was Harley's object throughout the whole of this reign to keep in power a Government in which neither party should altogether preponderate, a Government which, varying its composition as the constituencies changed their opinions, should represent, like Sir William Temple's ideal Privy Council, the House of Commons in miniature. His object at the moment was to depress the High Church interest, which he considered too strong ; and his manner of effecting this object was thoroughly characteristic, characteristic of his wise aims and his crooked politics.

Thus with a view of destroying the Occasional Conformity Bill, which as then drawn would have made the Church party omnipotent at all borough elections, and which in the interest of free government had been once remodelled and once rejected by the more tolerant House of Lords, he suggested to Bromley, who had the measure in charge, the expediency of "tacking" it to a bill of supply, and of thus forcing the Liberal peers into the dilemma of either consenting to a vast proscription of the Dissenters or of refusing to Government the supplies necessary for carrying on the war. The High Church leader fell headlong into the snare; and the result was precisely what the shrewd parliamentary tactitian who laid it foresaw. A schism was at once formed in the ranks of the High Church party. Just as had happened fifteen years before, when the Whigs on their side, then in a great majority in the House of Commons, had made a somewhat similar attempt to secure, this time under cover of a retrospective penalty inflicted on their party opponents,[*] an unjust monopoly of electoral power, the more sober and moderate members of the body revolted, and refused to follow their chiefs in a step which they condemned as factious. The attempt to unite the two bills was rejected in the House in which the Church party was supreme. Its leaders, abandoned by their most respectable followers and humiliated in the eyes of the nation, took to quarrelling amongst themselves. The ministers, relieved for a time from their querulous and exacting support, were free to devote their energies to the great work they had in hand; and an unconstitutional measure was laid on the shelf for two Parliaments.

Another of Harley's schemes for weakening the Church party and bringing a wider support to ministers was

---

[*] The clauses added by Howard and Sacheverell to the Corporation Bill of 1690.

equally successful. This was to disclose privately to Marlborough a movement set on foot by some of the High Tory leaders for procuring through the secretary, Lord Nottingham, a reconstruction of Government in their interest. Marlborough, thus forewarned, took the initiative, under the Speaker's advice, by prevailing on the Queen to dismiss two subordinate ministers—Lord Jersey from the office of Chamberlain, and Sir Edward Seymour from that of Comptroller. Thereupon Nottingham, irritated at the removal of his colleagues, resigned. The vacant places were filled up according to Harley's recommendation. His friend, Sir Thomas Mansel, a moderate Tory, succeeded Seymour; Lord Kent, a moderate Whig, succeeded Jersey. Harley himself, without at first resigning the Speakership, was made Secretary of State. But his master-stroke was to procure the post of Secretary at War for the rising hope of the stern and unbending High Churchmen, the young orator who had declaimed so eloquently against bloated armaments, and urged such unanswerable reasons for making the war entirely maritime. St. John was then in his twenty-sixth year. Ambition prevailed over party connections formed chiefly with an ambitious object ; and he became the right hand man of the Whig general, both in Parliament and at Whitehall.

St. John's history during the next four years is merged in the larger history of the Godolphin administration. The genius of Marlborough drove back the French and Bavarians from the Danube to the Rhine, saved the Empire from destruction, re-established the liberties of Europe, and raised the fame of England to a height which it had never reached before. Part of the blaze of glory which surrounded the successful general was reflected upon the ministry of which he was in fact the virtual head ; and so far as a subordinate member of that ministry on whom no small share of its administrative labours had fallen, and who had discharged his duties with eminent skill and energy, is entitled to claim credit for the great achievements of his leader, St. John may twine about his brow some part of the laurels of Ramillies and Blenheim.

One result, however, of the success of the ministerial policy was to depress the ministerial faction, or at least that large portion of it which was intent on transferring the theatre of war to the Spanish main, and which welcomed every new victory in Germany or Flanders with wry faces. At the general election of 1705, fifty of the most acrimonious and intolerant High Churchmen, the "tackers," as they were opprobriously called, lost their seats. The Low Church party obtained for the first time in ten years a clear majority in both Houses. It was necessary to make a definite arrangement with them. Compliments were exchanged in the Lords between Somers and Godolphin. One by one the friends of the Whig chief returned to power. Cowper, their best debater, received the Great Seal. Addison, their best leader-writer, was made Under-secretary of State. A year later Sunderland, the staunchest and most ardent of the Whig junto, replaced the Tory Hedges.

The effect of these changes was, without any avowed change of policy, to give the opposition leaders at length a paramount influence in Government. In the earliest of them, notwithstanding the clamour they excited amongst its ordinary supporters, Harley had been an active and willing instrument. His dinner-table, then one of the pleasantest in London, had been at the service of Godolphin for smoothing the social relations of the new ministers ; whilst his zealous co-operation in the election of a Whig Speaker, and in furthering the Whig plan for the securing of the Protestant succession, even in the absence of the parliamentary heir, had done much to soften the antipathy with which the leaders of that party had regarded him. But when it appeared that the change of men in which he had borne so large a part was the prelude to an entire and, in his view, an unconstitutional change of system ; when, under the advice of the incoming ministers, the Privy Council was purged by the dismissal of all the Queen's old and trusted Tory councillors ; when the two clauses in the Act of Settlement were repealed which he had himself inserted as essential to his favourite scheme of government with limited and divided responsibilities ; when, in a word, it became abundantly clear to him that what the heads of the Whig connection wanted was not simply an increased share and voice in the administration proportioned to their increasing numbers in Parliament, but the undisputed power of directing the State towards the ends and by the sole instrumentality of that dominant party which now prevailed there ;—from that moment the weight of Harley's influence was shifted into the opposite scale, and Marlborough and Godolphin began to experience the same perfidy from which Nottingham and Rochester had already suffered. In the winter of 1707, the accomplished Trimmer began his famous intrigue for undoing the effect of his own work, for outwitting the dominant faction and supplanting the too submissive Tory ministers by bedchamber tactics, an intrigue which Swift, then visiting London on one of his periodical hunts after preferment, extols—and this, too, in a letter to a Father of his Church —as the "greatest piece of court skill known in our time." For the moment the attempt failed. In company with St. John and Harcourt, Harley was, after a sharp struggle, dismissed from office. But the ministers had yet to reckon with his wily and dauntless spirit.

V.

A few weeks after Harley's fall, Queen Anne, replying to an address of congratulation from the House of Lords on the recent failure of a projected French invasion (an invasion which had brought clearly to light, it may be remarked in passing, the evils of the old system of divided responsibility*), made use of words which created no small stir amongst the coffee-house politicians ; for they were taken as signifying a new purpose on the part of the chief minister, a recantation of his Tory principles, and an intimation that his Government should be thenceforth in name and character what it had long been in policy, a Whig Government.

But the triumph of the party was shortlived, and, even during the few months that it lasted, more apparent than real. The administration of Godolphin, even at the height of power and fame, when its great military and legislative achievements were fresh in the public mind, had struck no root either at court or in the nation. It was what was called in the language of the time an " arbitrary cabal," a parliamentary ministry depending on party allegiance, and built on the sandy foundation of popular support. In the period which began in 1700 and ended in 1705, power had belonged to the Whigs but not place. Events had played into their hands, had shown

---

* The management of the navy was the weak place in Godolphin's ministry. Naval battles were indeed won, as at Malaga, Barcelona, and Toulon ; and the fleet under Shovel and Leake was all powerful in the Mediterranean. But small French squadrons and isolated cruisers issuing from Dunkirk, St. Malo, or Brest, were the scourge of the channel ; and the naval marine of France, though greatly inferior to the English in numbers, was almost always able to make its attacks in superior force. The anxiety of the Whigs to remedy this by a complete reorganization of the admiralty, and the " want of respect " it showed to Prince George, her husband, then Lord High Admiral, was one main cause of the Queen's dislike to them.

D

the superior fitness of their policy to the circumstances of their time, and had imposed on their party rivals the necessity of seeking and accepting their assistance. In an authority so exercised by the inherent force of statesmanship and capacity for affairs, and in an assembly the deliberations of which were not open to the public eye, there was nothing invidious, nothing that could offend against the national sense of loyalty.

But in the five years that followed, the condition of things was changed. After the election of 1705, the Whigs had a great parliamentary majority in both Houses, with at first only a few scattered and ill-supported representatives in the administration of the Queen. It was not reasonable to expect that they, the appointed trustees of the national welfare, should be content with their old position of unofficial responsibility ; and they bent all their energies towards making good and improving the footing they had gained.

The domestic history of these years is, therefore, on the surface, the history of a struggle for place. It was not, no doubt, the mere cupidity of self-seeking politicians for the emoluments and influences of office, but the legitimate ambition of statesmen, conscious of great powers and desirous to promote in the most effectual manner the policy they had at heart. King William had sought to preserve that local civil liberty which, when united with order, was the birthright of the English people, by "embodying it," to use the words of Burke, "in the political liberty, the order, and the independence of nations united under a natural head." In the Prince's estimation the second of these combined objects in importance took precedence of the first, justified the adventure by which the first was attained, and went far to console him for the incidents that accompanied and the results that followed from it—for that diminution of the kingly prerogative and that elevation of Parliament to supreme power to which he was naturally as hostile as had been either of his predecessors. In the opinion of the Whig statesmen, on the other hand, the relative importance of the two was reversed. They valued the general freedom of Europe ; they supported the measures taken for assuring it ; they consented to the sacrifices which those measures involved, mainly because they regarded " the political liberty, the order, and the independence of nations " as an essential guarantee for their own local civil liberty, and for the parliamentary institutions on which that liberty depended.

But they agreed with King William that the two were in fact inseparable, and furthered with all their energies his schemes for uniting them. They enlarged the scope of the war to the limits of his original purpose. They discarded the notion unwillingly forced upon him of dismembering the power of Spain, accepted the Austrian claim in full, and united it with the Hanoverian claim to England as the conjoined objects of the Grand Alliance. They protected the parliamentary settlement of the English Crown by a wide system of foreign guarantees. They secured that settlement at the same time against the chief domestic danger which threatened it by incorporating England and Scotland under a common administration, a union which William had earnestly desired and repeatedly pressed upon them. They devised and carried through Parliament an ingenious scheme, by which the provisions of the Act passed in 1701 were made to execute themselves, without vexing the Queen in her last moments with the unwelcome presence of the successor marked out by law. That was a time when the great body of the Anglican Church was openly disaffected to the new system, and when the loyalty of its rulers and overseers was a matter of vital importance to the State. Accordingly an engagement was extorted from the Queen, after a sharp struggle, that no Bishop should be appointed without the knowledge and consent of her ministers, and a previous understanding that his influence in Parliament and in the nation should not be used against their policy. The public opinion of those days, the influence still lingering round the traditions of the old monarchy, would not have permitted the victorious statesmen to exact, in the face of a hostile court, that complete and immediate change in the formation of the Cabinet Council which follows under a free constitutional system a change in the relative strength of parties. Each of the great fortresses of State had to be besieged and captured in its turn, much as Marlborough was reducing the strongholds of Flanders and Brabant, until by the close of 1709 all the chief Whig leaders—Somers, Wharton, Orford, Cowper, Sunderland—had returned to office as the result of a protracted campaign of parliamentary strategy and party organization.

It was the effect of these successive contests that weakened the Government. Prolonged as they were, month after month, they caused no little ill blood between the Treasurer and his new colleagues ; they increased the repugnance with which the Queen had always regarded the now dominant party ; they associated Marlborough and Godolphin with the victors in the struggle as objects of her dislike ; and they produced on the public mind the impression that she was becoming a prisoner in their hands. The Whig leaders, on their side, naturally resented the delays they had been made to suffer, and the shifts and manœuvres to which they had been driven, made no sufficient allowance for Godolphin's difficulties, ascribed to mere cupidity on his part what was due almost entirely to his waning credit at court, and in their private correspondence angrily denounced the chief minister under whom they served as a man "incapable of doing any right thing with a good grace." Godolphin on the other hand, conscious that he had done his best for them, was indignant at their suspicions. He was astonished, too, at their blindness. For he saw that the invidious pre-eminence they were claiming in its councils was impairing the stability of his Government and imperilling the success of the very objects they had at heart.

And if the overwhelming presence of the Whig junto and the means taken for securing it were felt as a grievance by Godolphin, a shrewd and experienced statesman, whose aims in the main coincided with theirs, who was bound to them by ties of interest, whose administration had been saved by their exertions and rendered illustrious by their policy, what must they have seemed to Queen Anne, a Tory both by training and conviction, brought up to value the prerogative as an essential part of government? In her view it was a direct usurpation, in the interest of one set of men, of functions which belonged to herself, which she was bound to exercise for the benefit of all parties, and, so far as might be, in accordance with her own personal beliefs. She expressed these views with perfect clearness in her correspondence. "Why should I," she writes to Godolphin, so early as August, 1706, in answer to one of the first of his demands—"Why should I, who have no end, no interest, no thought but the good of my country, be made so miserable as to be brought into the power of one set of men?" "You press that there may be more of this party in place of trust to help to carry on the business this winter; and you think if this is not complied with, they may not be hearty in pursuing my service in Parliament. But will not men of sense and honour promote the good of their country, though everything is not done as

they desire?" "Throwing myself in the hands of a party
is a thing I have always been desirous to avoid. Maybe,
some may think I would be willing to be in the hands
of the Tories, but whatever people may say of me, I do
assure you I am not inclined, nor ever will be, to employ
any of those violent persons that have behaved themselves
so ill to me. All I desire is my liberty in encouraging and
employing all those that concur faithfully in my service,
whether they are called Whigs or Tories, not to be tied
either to one or the other ; for if I should be so unfortunate
as to fall into the hands of either, I shall not imagine
myself, though I have the name of Queen, to be in reality
anything but their slave, to my personal ruin and the
destruction of all government."

The experience of five generations has at length reconciled our parliamentary sovereigns to these "miseries"
inseparable from their position. It has taught them how
the system of party responsibility as now understood and
practised elevates the throne above the strife of politics,
and gives it new dignity as the arbiter and exponent of the
national will. But in justice to Queen Anne it must be
remembered that the modern practice, under which the
dominant majority in Parliament, as the embodiment of
prevailing opinion, absorbs all power and patronage in the
State, was then a distinct and, in the eyes of many, an
unconstitutional innovation, contrary, as Bolingbroke justly
said, to the "ancient and strict forms of our Government."
Like all such innovations, it had to struggle and gradually
force its way to recognition in the face of traditional
prejudices. High in the Queen's confidence was her
favourite prelate and spiritual director, Archbishop Sharp.
In all matters of difficulty he was her chief confidant and
adviser. And he was in many respects well fitted for
this office. For his Tory and sacerdotal proclivities were

accompanied with a sobriety of judgment which preserved him from the excesses of his party, and with an independent spirit which extorted the respect even of opponents. At the height of the Catholic reaction under King James II. he had, though one of the royal chaplains, distinguished himself by preaching against the pretensions of the Church of Rome.   In the midst of the Revolution, when the throne had been declared vacant, he had in the very presence of the House of Commons distinguished himself by preaching against the right of Parliament to depose the sovereign. He had scrupled to succeed any of the High Church prelates deprived for a too strict adherence to their common principles. But he had done nothing to perpetuate the schism ; he had in fact supported the plan of William's Government for a comprehension even with Dissenters, and at length had accepted a mitre from his hand.

The same independence and the same moderation accompanied him through life. Though zealous for the Occasional Conformity Bill and closely connected with the Tory leaders, he had strongly condemned their scheme for forcing it on the Whig peers, tacked to a bill of supply. More than once, indeed, when warmly pressed by the Queen to support in Parliament some High Church measure, he had refused ; and these refusals, testifying as they did to his manly spirit and his entire freedom from the vices of the ecclesiastical courtier, gave added weight to his judgment when, deeply imbued as was natural with the old notions of government, he now assured her that her personal prerogative was an essential part of the State polity, and that for her manner of exercising it, though the fiction of ministerial responsibility protected her from punishment in this world, she would assuredly be held accountable before the throne of Heaven. Such an injunction, coming from a man so eminent, given as he tells

us " with many hard words," and accompanied by a prayer
that " God would inspire her with courage " * to assert the
authority He had committed to her, could hardly fail to
confirm the Queen in her prepossessions and destroy all
remnant of confidence in her legitimate ministers.

It was in these circumstances that she turned for help
to Harley. Completely estranged from Godolphin and his
set, resenting in the highest degree the dictation she had
experienced at their hands, she had, even before his fall,
taken Harley into her special favour. His deference and
suavity of manner disarmed her feminine criticism. Differing with her on many points, his views on party government exactly tallied with hers. He sympathized with her
in her distress. He showed her how easily her difficulties
might be avoided and her old authority re-established.
Let her revert to the old constitutional plan of governing
with a divided council. Let her choose for her servants,
as far as possible, moderate men not deeply pledged to the
extremes of either side. Let her give the balance of power
to the prevailing faction ; but let her keep in places of
trust a sufficient number of the vanquished party to act
as checks on their successful rivals and preserve the
traditions of the defeated policy. Above all, let her have
no secret cabal, no government within the government, to
anticipate decisions which should be the result of discussion
and mutual compromise.

After Harley's removal, in February, 1708, in order to
contrive interviews with the discarded minister a certain
amount of finesse was necessary ; and here the Queen had
recourse to the weapons with which nature has endowed
her sex. A favourite waiting-maid, who had been introduced into the palace by Lady Marlborough herself, but
who was also a distant kinswoman of Harley's and a

* " Life of Archbishop Sharp," by his son, i. 319,

warm supporter of his objects, was selected by the Queen
to play the part which Chiffinch had filled in the intrigues,
political as well as amorous, of her father and her uncle.
During many months the intercourse proceeded without
remark. Every part of the long correspondence which
the Queen maintained with her chief ministers, every
dilatory plea put in to avoid compliance with their demands,
every appeal touchingly made to their forbearance, every
stratagem ingeniously contrived for thwarting them, was
drafted, inspired, dictated, or devised by Harley. To the
student of modern politics her letters are most interesting ;
for they are penetrated with the constitutional theories
of an eighteenth century Stockmar.

In the intrigue which he now set on foot for rescuing
the Queen from party thraldom, it was no part of Harley's
object to change the policy of the State. He had indeed
a constitutional dislike to war ; and he is known to have
resented the recent vote of Parliament, demanding the
entire restitution of Spain by the House of Bourbon, as
tending to make the return of peace more difficult. But
he was pledged to the main lines of the Whig foreign
policy as completely almost as Godolphin. His opinions,
though not exactly Whig, were far removed from Toryism ;
and though he had since his fall been reconciled to the
High Church leaders, he was not anxious, through the
return of their friends to power, to waive in their favour,
as must then have happened, his claim to the chief authority. The Parliament, again, was Whig ; it was admirably
organized in support of the Whig party ; to dissolve it,
when it had still more than two years to run, would have
been a high-handed, an imprudent, and probably an unsafe
measure ; for there was as yet no evidence of a change
in the opinions of the nation generally or of any dissatisfaction with the conduct of affairs. When he assured both

Somers and Cowper, as he did more than once as soon as whispers of his intrigues began to circulate, that a "Whig game was intended at bottom," there is no reason to doubt that he was, from his own point of view, sincere, or that his original purpose went further than a change in the methods and composition of Government ;—the removal of Godolphin, of Sunderland, of the family connections of Marlborough ; the substitution of ministers more agreeable personally to the Queen, and more amenable to her influence ; the abandonment of the system of governing by party committees, which he condemned as foreign to the whole scheme of the English polity ; and the transfer of power in matters of State to the entire Privy Council. These were Harley's views. His desire was, as he had told Godolphin some months before, to make the Queen herself the "centre of union" among politicians as in the old time ; he doubted, he said, the possibility of bringing the nation to consent to any other Government but hers ; and he "dreaded the thought" of running from the extreme of one side to the extreme of the other, as each in its turn became triumphant in Parliament, as tending to embitter the strife of factions, and withdraw all steadiness and continuity from the action of the State.*

VI.

With these objects Harley now set himself to form out of those politicians, whom the intemperance of the High Church leaders, the exclusiveness of the Whig junto, and the devouring ambition of Marlborough had estranged

---

* Harley to Godolphin, September 10, 1707. Compare Harley to Godolphin, August 15 and November 16, 1706; and Harley to Marlborough, September 6th and November 12th of the same year ("Hardwick Papers").

from their old connections, a new party which should look to the sovereign in person as its chief; and in this work he was largely assisted by two peers of high standing and influence, who, five years later, when the movement threatened to result in the unqualified triumph of Toryism, contributed by a bold enterprise to defeat it. Of these, the stronger in character, though the weaker in parts and the least known to our generation, was Charles Seymour, Duke of Somerset, sixth in descent from the great Lord Protector. The authority which Seymour exercised amongst his brother nobles, an authority bearing no small resemblance to that of Harley in the House of Commons, was due in part to his position as the second temporal peer, but chiefly to his independence of party ties, and to the conviction that he regulated his public conduct by a different and, in the opinion of many, a higher standard of public service. The politics of his family were Tory. It was as a Tory that he entered public life. Scarcely had he done so when he was called upon to choose between two fundamental principles of the Tory creed—unquestioning obedience to the authority of the Crown, respect for the rights of the Church as by law established and for the Protestant constitution of the realm. Somerset made his choice without hesitation. Putting aside the admonitions of his friends, disobeying the express commands of his sovereign, he refused, though a member of the royal household, to take part in a State ceremony which he held to be illegal, and was not only dismissed—that was to be expected—but deprived of his military commission, and, after a time, of his lord lieutenancy.

The insult would have driven a weaker man into complicity with the extreme Reformers; and it had the effect of disengaging Somerset from his old party con-

nections. He acquiesced without difficulty in the great
parliamentary vindication of the right of the nation to
self-government. He was in favour indeed, at first, of
leaving with James the kingly title; but Parliament having
decided for a complete change of system, he loyally
accepted the settlement made by law, played a distinguished part at the coronation of the parliamentary
sovereigns, and upheld through all vicissitudes the Revolution polity.   No suspicion of Jacobite intrigue rests
upon his memory.   Such, indeed, was the whiteness of
his record in this respect, that when, after the rebellion
of 1716, treason was charged against his son-in-law, Sir
William Wyndham, he pleaded as a set-off his own
unbroken loyalty, and claimed the release of his Jacobite
kinsman as only a fair acknowledgment of his own un-
faltering opposition to Jacobitism.

It was the rejection of this claim that finally drove
Somerset from public life.   In the time of Queen Anne,
his position, his character, and the friendship which had
existed almost from childhood between his wife and the
Queen, gave the Duke an immense influence in the palace.
To gain over such a man was indeed a triumph for
Harley's diplomacy.   For Somerset was no courtier; he
was never tempted to maintain his private influence at
the cost of the public service, or forgot out of deference
for the royal wishes the paramount interests of the State.
At the memorable council of February 9, 1708, when
Godolphin and Marlborough, irritated at Harley's intrigues
against them and failing to obtain the Queen's consent
to his dismissal, had virtually retired from the Government,
and the favourite Secretary of State, notwithstanding their
absence, was proceeding, with the Queen's full sanction,
to open the business of the day, virtually as her chief
minister, it was Somerset who interposed, interrupted the

speaker in spite of her frowns, and with a curt scornful sentence crushed his budding pretensions.   The fallen ministers were replaced.   Harley and his friends were removed.   The Government became entirely Whig ; and the policy of the State was confirmed in the direction which the Whig leaders had marked out for it.

It is impossible now to know the full reasons which led the Duke, after rendering so great a service to the Whig cause, suddenly to change his course and become a main instrument in furthering the very scheme which in its earlier stages he had risked the Queen's favour to frustrate.   His colleagues in their anger ascribed his conduct to pure ambition, to the desire of taking on himself, with no other qualification than a title and a pedigree, the leading part in politics. *   And it is not unlikely that Somerset, all whose actions were influenced by an inordinate pride of birth, resented the manner in which new men, mere barons of King James's and King William's creation, domineered over the House of Lords. He was impelled, it is certain, by no desire to change either the foreign or the domestic policy of the realm. For as soon as it became evident that the movement would result, not merely in the humiliation of one faction, but in the exaltation of its rival, in ruin to the political system with which the first was identified, in danger to the parliamentary settlement which, in common with the defeated ministers, he had so long and so consistently upheld, then Somerset at once drew back, went with the Whig statesmen into vigorous opposition,† instructed the constituent bodies under his influence to choose members hostile to the new Government at the very election in which it first appealed to the confidence of the nation in

* Godolphin to Marlborough, March 7th and April 17, 1710.
† Without resigning his place in the household.

its favour,* arranged the terms of that coalition between
Nottingham and Somers, which was formed to maintain
the old policy and reinstate the old councillors, did his
utmost to resist the treaties of peace, concerted with his
former colleagues the means of frustrating the ambitious
schemes of Bolingbroke, and when at length the crisis
came and the fate of England hung in the balance, interposed once more to save the State.

Closely allied with Somerset was a peer of greater
renown, matchless in grace of manner, polished by books
and travel, and long familiarity with courts, but inferior
to his friend in strength, dignity, and elevation of character, Charles Talbot, Duke of Shrewsbury. The essential
difference between the two men is well marked by the
different motives impelling them to the similar course they
took. The conduct of Somerset was that of a man of
narrow intellect and little political insight, but inflexibly
honest, and animated, even when most mistaken, by a
high sense of public duty. Shrewsbury was a man of fine
understanding and good impulses in the main, but fickle,
vain, and sensitive, constantly impelled by passion and
by resentment at fancied slights into courses which were
at variance with all his professions, of which he disapproved
even in the act of entering on them, and from which he
had neither the boldness nor the address to extricate
himself without dishonour.

He began life as a Revolution Whig. He had signed
the invitation to the Prince of Orange ; he had mortgaged
his estate to defray the charges of the Prince's expedition ;
and though under thirty had been Secretary of State
in his first composite ministry. But he had resented with
the heat of youth King William's well-meant attempt at

---

* St. John to Drummond, October 13, 1710; Swift's Works, v. 183 (Scott's
edition).

governing by the old device of mingling together the two contending factions, and had listened in his anger to the insidious overtures of Jacobite suborners. In 1694 the Whig party became supreme in the State, and Shrewsbury returned to office as their principal leader. Soon, however, his treason, already known to the King, was publicly disclosed by Fenwick; and after that day of disgrace and humiliation, to his refined and keenly sensitive nature, political life became insupportable. His health and his spirits failed. He deserted and abandoned his post, rejected even the glittering bait of the Lord Treasurership—never offered by William to any other of his subjects—obtained the King's reluctant consent to travel, and after wandering for a while finally settled at Rome. A new reign opened. A new Government from which all his old colleagues were excluded was formed. A new war for the deliverance of Europe from tyranny and priestcraft was begun. The fate of England depended on the struggle. But still Shrewsbury lingered beyond the Alps, leading the life of a virtuoso, filling the galleries of his political friends with the masterpieces of Italian art, and corresponding with them about the "styles" of Correggio and Guido Reni.

At last, in the summer of 1706, moved by their expostulations, he returned just as the Whig statesmen, having secured a strong footing in Parliament, were beginning their hard fight for supremacy in the closet. It was because King William had refused to yield up the whole executive power into their hands that Shrewsbury had quarrelled with him sixteen years before. The Whig leaders, remembering this fact, conscious of their high purposes and of the momentous issues depending on the struggle, expected, and not unnaturally, that their old chief, even if not disposed to any active exertions, would at least support and co-operate with them in this renewal of their old demand. But his nature, always weak and irresolute, had been unnerved by ill-health and by domestic anxieties. It wanted, as his friend Lord Halifax delicately and generously put it, something of that " base alloy " necessary to fit a man in revolutionary times for the rough handling of politics. The Duke was encumbered, too, with an Italian marchesa, under whose endearments he was pining away, and whose disreputable connections hung like a millstone round his neck. He was less than ever fitted to be a pilot in extremity.

When the struggle was over and the victory won, he claimed from the dominant party the office of Lord Lieutenant of Ireland. It was a post, he said, where a man had just business enough, enough to hinder him from falling fast asleep, but not enough to keep him unpleasantly wide awake. But the Whigs, conscious of the precariousness of their position, were determined to confide this great department to stronger and more trustworthy hands. The bolder Wharton was preferred to him. There is no doubt that Shrewsbury felt keenly this humiliation, which happened just at the moment when he was first made privy to Harley's design. In his anger he consented to betray, at the instance of Somerset, the party of which he had once been the honoured chief, as sixteen years before he had betrayed, at the instance of Middleton, the sovereign whom he served, who had distinguished him with his personal friendship and loaded him with constant kindnesses.

It is probable that other magnates of the Whig party looked with no disfavour on a scheme which would remove Godolphin from the treasury and confine Marlborough to his military command. It is certain that the adventure, even in its later development, had the cautious approval of the Privy Seal, Newcastle, and the hearty co-operation of the brilliant and unprincipled Argyle. Argyle, indeed, like Somerset, soon repented his defection, and did his best to atone for it. A soldier, an orator, a fine gentleman, renowned in all the walks of public and private life, but fickle in his attachments and jealous in his temper, he was impelled no doubt at the moment by envy of the fame of Marlborough. In truth, Marlborough's greatness, his cupidity and ambition, the vast amount of public money absorbed by his connections, his own ill-judged and dangerous project for securing to himself by patent a life-grant of his various offices, and the audacious attempt of his son-in-law Sunderland to anticipate Sir Robert Peel, and expel from the Queen's bedchamber, by a vote of Parliament if necessary, every female adherent of the opposite faction, excited alarm and indignation against the Government, even amongst men not unfriendly to its policy. On the side of the Tories, Atterbury, whose turbulent and factious spirit had forced him into the front rank of politics, undertook to manage and keep in check the rampageous High Churchmen. Their older leaders looked with no great favour on a scheme which would deprive them of so much influence, whilst their two most rising speakers were at the moment out of Parliament. Harcourt, unseated on an election petition, was pushing his fortunes at the bar ; and St. John, deprived of the family borough by his grandfather's death, was rusticating and philosophizing in Berkshire. But it was not by parliamentary opposition that Godolphin's power was to be overthrown ; and Harley, a host in himself, was indefatigable in the art of whispering, which he so well understood. His rôle was to disarm the suspicions of the Whig magnates, and his meshes were spread even in the recesses of the Whig cabinet; for he assailed through one distinguished

emissary the Lord Chancellor, through another the Lord
Lieutenant, through a third the Lord President, the very
model and impersonation of Whiggism. By the beginning
of 1710 the plot was ripe. Nothing remained but to cut
down and gather in the abundant harvest, when an event
happened which gave at first an immense impulse to
Harley's project, but ended by deranging all his plans.

VII.

Nearly every great reflux of public opinion from the
Liberal to the Conservative party has been the work, directly
or indirectly, of the Anglican priesthood ; and a careful
observer could hardly fail to detect that such a reaction
was now at hand. The notion that the Government leaders
were bent not merely on impairing the just authority of
the Crown, but on withdrawing from the Church its
exclusive rights and privileges, was deeply rooted in the
mind of every rustic vicar. It dated from the time when
Marlborough and Godolphin, intent on securing support
against their own unruly followers, had become unsound
on the great question of Occasional Conformity, a question
on which the supremacy of the Church in civil administration so largely depended. At both Universities the ministerial opponents of the "tack" had been mobbed and
insulted by the gownsmen. The Lower House of Convocation had warmly taken up the cause. It had even reiterated
the High Church doctrine of passive obedience to divinely
appointed rulers, and solemnly condemned a sermon
preached by Hoadley against the sacerdotal principle.
A year later, when the alliance of ministers with the Whig
statesmen was complete, Rochester, the favourite champion
of the High Church party, had been put forward to obtain

a parliamentary confirmation of this theory—that under a Government dominated by Whigs the supremacy of the Church, and with it all legitimate authority in the nation, must be " in danger." A great debate had taken place. The Queen, whose secret sympathies were well known, had been brought down to the House of Lords to witness the expected triumph of her friends. But the attack had collapsed somewhat ignominiously; and ministers, assuming the offensive in their turn, had carried the war across the frontier by making the expression of this belief a penal offence, and by denouncing all who held it as " enemies of the Queen and kingdom."

They were alarmed, and not unreasonably, at the position of independence and the dictatorial tone which the Church was gradually assuming. Its influence in the nation, always most formidable, had been in some respects increased by that change of polity which had subjected it to the civil power ; for to the great body of the people, the electors of the ruling chamber, its pulpits were in many districts almost the sole vehicle of instruction, and its preachers practically directed the political consciences of those rural classes with whom in the last resort the supreme power lay. Wielding an authority thus extensive and unquestioned, it was now propagating opinions which, whether reasonable or not under the old regime, were incompatible with the very existence of the constitution now virtually established, arrogating to itself privileges sprung from Divine decree, and in their nature, therefore, superior to the most solemn enactments of the State. There was hardly a Sunday morning, in truth, at this time, on which attacks upon the ministers nominated by Parliament, and incitements to defy the law as laid down by Parliament, did not form the staple of the day's discourse in half the parish pulpits from Berwick to St. Ives,

This aim at substituting for the rule of Parliament that of an irresponsible, self-elected confederacy, exercising a dominion as destructive to all free government as the Catholic Association in our fathers' time, or the Irish Land League in our own, had been implicitly avowed by one of its most conspicuous champions on a recent occasion and in a presence which made the offence peculiarly indecent. Henry Sacheverell was a Fellow of Magdalene College at Oxford. In early days he had been the friend and companion of the gentle and accomplished Addison, whose college chambers he had shared. But their paths had widely diverged. By the influence of Somers, Addison had been drawn from his favourite haunts under the elm trees by the sluggish Cherwell, and had taken service with the Whig party. He had become their standing literary counsel. He was now chief secretary to the Lord Lieutenant; and his graceful facile pen, and the charm of his personal character were destined to raise him higher still, to be Secretary of State, and, so far as a silent minister can be, leader of the House of Commons.* Sacheverell had remained at Oxford, and had imbibed the political opinions commonly attached to the peculiar phase of religious belief which chiefly prevailed there. He had at length been chosen chaplain to the church of St. Saviour's in Southwark, and had become distinguished amongst the High Church clergy for zealously preaching in season and out of season their characteristic doctrines.

In the summer of 1709, Sacheverell had been invited by a Tory kinsman, then High Sheriff of Derbyshire, to preach the assize sermon before the judges; and with his accustomed intrepidity he had made it the occasion for

---

* From the elevation of Stanhope to the peerage to his own retirement in March, 1718, Addison was the only minister of cabinet rank in the House of Commons. But the chief burden of debate rested on Craggs.

a violent invective against the Government which those judges represented, and which the orator was pleased to denounce from the pulpit as a "band of associated malignants intent on persecuting the Church and betraying the constitution." The attack was allowed to pass over without notice. But on the 5th of November following, at St. Paul's Cathedral, in presence of the Lord Mayor, aldermen, and common council of the city assembled in formal state at a thanksgiving-day service in commemoration of the landing of King William and of the final deliverance of the nation from arbitrary power and passive obedience, Sacheverell had gone further, not merely repeating in more startling language the invective of the preceding summer, but making his whole address a panegyric on the old polity, and a glorification both of passive obedience and arbitrary power. The sermons had then been published and had an immense sale. Both were scurrilous to an extent which in our time would have deprived them of all their sting. But that was an age of rude license ; and this nauseous compound of truculent language with feeble thought was unhappily only a fair sample of the sort of discourse to which an Englishman was condemned to listen whenever, on a Sunday morning, he ventured into his parish church. Sacheverell, moreover, though not himself a man of mark, having the vanity and pomposity of a college don without much substratum of parts or learning, was, it must be remembered, the representative of a great party, a party whose influence in the nation was immense, and the most conspicuous exponent of doctrines of sacerdotal supremacy and independence which in the infancy of parliamentary government shook the very foundations of the State. Even in its vigorous manhood, exhibited in the theatrical mummeries of a little knot of enthusiasts contemptible alike in numbers and in character, we have ourselves seen these same pretensions move Parliament from its serenity and bring scandal after scandal on the administration of justice. To the Government it seemed that the offence of enunciating such a claim—inconsistent with the authority of Parliament, and just explicitly prohibited by the Crown at the instance of Parliament—on an occasion so solemn and in the presence of magistrates and high dignitaries of the realm, could not be passed over. With much reluctance and many misgivings they determined to assert the authority of the State over the Church once for all, and bring this clerical O'Connell, this insolent and lawless propagator of its seditious teachings, to the bar of judgment.

It was said at the time, and has been often since repeated, that ministers were moved to this course by resentment at an offensive nickname which Sacheverell had fastened on their leader. He had not indeed specifically mentioned Godolphin ; but he had cautioned his hearers against " the wily volpones in high places, whose atheistical double-dealing was propagating all sorts of heresies and schisms ; " and this concise and graphic description of the Lord Treasurer was, it was said, " in the opinion of his friends," tantamount to naming him outright. The story went the round of the coffee-houses. But there is no doubt that the Government, in deciding to prosecute Sacheverell, and in choosing the cumbrous and uncertain but conspicuous method of procedure, a prosecution by parliamentary impeachment, were influenced by no feeling of petty vindictiveness. Their course in that case would have been much more simple. Their object was, as one of the managers of the impeachment asserted during the trial, not to " demand justice on a criminal," but to " establish their own foundations." They desired to put on record in the most authentic manner the principles on which the

Revolution had been effected and the new polity established. They held that the position of independence and supremacy which the Church assumed, and the political doctrines which, in consequence, it taught the nation, had been implicitly condemned by the change of polity, transferring supreme power as it did from the sovereign head of the Church to a mixed assembly equally representing all sects and classes; and they desired to have, from the highest Court of Judicature known to the constitution, an authoritative confirmation of this belief after a solemn trial.

Their relation towards the Episcopalian body resembled, in short, that of the French Republicans in our time to the Jesuit orders and clericalism in general. They were impressed with a strong and just sense of the perils which attended the new settlement at the hands of men who, ostensibly accepting that settlement by entering into its service, cherished opinions radically opposed to its fundamental principles, who openly propagated those opinions on every occasion, and who were in fact stealthily undermining the very Government they were sworn to defend. They wished either to exclude these men from official station altogether, or else to require from them an honest discharge of their duties. The mistake they made was in overrating their own strength in the nation, and the extent to which the nation, in acquiescing in the results of their policy, concurred in and accepted their own interpretation of its meaning. By a premature and high-handed attempt to enforce the authority of Parliament over the Church—an essential principle, no doubt, of the Revolution polity—they turned the country against them at a most critical moment, and put the success of the Revolution in extreme peril. In 1784 the Whig leaders fell into a precisely similar error. Then, also, by a premature and ill-judged attempt to enforce the authority of Parliament over

the Crown—another essential principle of the new polity—
they turned the nation against them, condemned their
party to twenty years' exile from power, and, what was of
far more moment, postponed the general recognition of that
principle for more than two generations.

Nor was their procedure well chosen for the purpose
of striking the imagination of the people. The personal
insignificance of the victim selected for public sacrifice,
when contrasted with the tremendous machinery employed
to crush him, and with the august and venerable ceremonies
of which he formed the absurd central figure, turned the
whole trial into a species of burlesque. Friends of the
established hierarchy, whatever their individual leanings,
were pained at seeing a simple parish clergyman arraigned
before Parliament for preaching doctrines which he believed,
in common with the vast majority of his brethren, to be
enjoined upon him by the solemn homilies of his Church ;
whilst plain men, men not steadily Whig or Tory, men
who accepted the Revolution as an accomplished fact but
considered it no matter of triumph or congratulation, were
unable to follow the subtle distinctions of the managers
of the prosecution between the general unlawfulness of all
resistance to authority and the particular necessity of that
one great act of resistance which they had themselves
engaged in. All these feelings the opponents of the
Government skilfully fomented ; and they spared no pains
to excite the mob, always in England on the side of
orthodox religion. The result was a great explosion of
party and sectarian fanaticism. Theological and political
zealotry joined hands with lawless rapine. Sacheverell
was daily attended from his lodgings to Westminster Hall,
by enthusiastic and obstreperous crowds, who testified to
the purity of their faith and the soundness of their opinions
by burning down conventicles and " rabbling " Whig

statesmen. He was convicted ; but his condemnation by a bare majority, procured by the votes of the libelled ministers themselves, and the light sentence inflicted on him by an assembly notoriously in their interest, were hailed by his friends as a virtual acquittal and a valuable testimony to the success of the tactics they had employed. A rich country living was at once procured for him ; and the journey of the inhibited priest to take possession of his new preferment, the duties of which he was by the recent decision incapacitated from performing, was made to resemble the triumphant progress of some great public benefactor. The enthusiasm then evoked long survived the event which called it forth. The cry of " Sacheverell and the Church " altogether determined the result of the elections held six months afterwards, in October, 1710. The cry of " Sacheverell and the Church " largely influenced the elections held more than three years afterwards, in August, 1713. And two years later still, when the political feeling of the constituencies had turned, when the Revolution was accomplished, when a Whig Government was in power and a Whig dynasty in possession, on mere rumour of an intention to pull down the statue erected at Bristol to the apostle of Passive Obedience, at the cry of " Sacheverell and the Church," the entire population of the western counties rose as one man in its defence.

VIII.

The progress of this trial had been watched by Harley with mingled feelings. Its result showed him that to overturn the existing Government would be a far easier task than to transform it by gradual changes into the ideal administration which he desired to see in power.

It behoved him to feel his way with scrupulous caution, lest, in the process of rebuilding, the foundations of the fragile edifice should sink, its walls give way, and its roof fall in. The trial ended in the third week in March. Early in April Parliament was prorogued ; and it was not until her ministers were dispersed, enjoying at their country seats the first moments of liberty, that the Queen ventured to make, on the recommendation of her secret councillor, the first of the series of changes which were intended to emancipate her from the dominion of one party without throwing her exclusively into the power of the other.

Since the retirement of the High Tories in the spring of 1704, the Chamberlain of the royal household had been Henry Grey, twelfth Earl of Kent, the descendant of a Lord Treasurer of the Plantagenets and the ancestor of a Prime Minister of George IV.'s, a man whose illustrious birth had not preserved him from certain physical disadvantages, of which the satirists of the age took good care to remind him, but one of that inner circle of privileged magnates who, when they condescend to trouble themselves with politics, have an hereditary claim to the highest offices of the State. Lord Kent was now desired by the Queen to resign his staff and key. The step was taken without the knowledge of Godolphin, who was then at Newmarket ; but no effort was spared to disarm the resentment of his Whig colleagues. The honour of a dukedom was conferred on the retiring noble ; and it was intimated that his successor would be Shrewsbury, who was personally more acceptable to the Queen, and who, though he had voted Sacheverell "not guilty," still called himself and was generally known as a Whig.

Two months after Lord Kent's removal, the attack was renewed, this time against a more conspicuous minister. Sunderland was the youngest and, perhaps, the ablest of the Whig junto. He had earned the Queen's dislike when a member of the House of Commons, by moderating the lavishness of Parliament towards her foreign consort; he had confirmed it by being the first of the Whig statesmen to storm the closet after the constituent bodies had pronounced decisively in their favour; and since his forcible entry into office, his strenuous partisanship, his unceremonious manners, his firm will and perfect independence had turned this dislike into positive hatred. Of the younger Whigs none had been more gifted by nature; none had improved his vigorous parts with more assiduous care; none had set before himself more honourable aims in life, and none was more unscrupulous in the means he employed for reaching them. For the Whiggism of Sunderland resembled the passion of a Jesuit for his order and his Church rather than the languid attachment of a politician for his party. Ardent public spirit and inflexible integrity were the chief characteristics of a statesman who more than once brought his country to the brink of ruin, and who ended his days under the grave suspicion of pecuniary fraud. But in 1710 Sunderland was a young man of little more than thirty, and though high in office and foremost in debate, chiefly known to the public as Marlborough's son-in-law. His arrogance and self-confidence had offended his older colleagues. They were made consenting parties to his removal. Lord Anglesea, a Tory peer of whom little is known, and who died a few weeks later, had been designated by Harley as his successor. But the Whigs objected, and his name was at once withdrawn. Nottingham was suggested, an administrator of tried capacity but personally obnoxious to the Queen. Lord Dartmouth, who had married Nottingham's daughter, was ultimately

chosen as the man with whom Somers and Cowper could
"live most easily," a moderate Tory, with much of his
father-in-law's stern and ungracious honesty.

As the summer advanced other minor changes were
made, each elaborately explained and apologized for. At
length, early in August, the great blow was struck, and
the crisis brought on. The Lord High Treasurer, who
had submitted to become a cypher in his own Government,
to see his friends removed, his wishes neglected, places
in his gift filled up without his knowledge, and all substantial power in the State, of which he was still the
virtual head, pass into the hands of a defeated rival,
received a laconic note from the Queen—left at his door
according to one account by a footman—directing him
to break his staff. He lived two years longer, partly
at Newmarket, partly in the house of Lady Marlborough
at St. Alban's ; but he never again took part in public
business. His fall removed from the stage of political
life its most familiar figure. For there had been scarcely
a quarter-day since the Restoration on which Godolphin,
the type and model of a successful man in revolutionary
times, had not drawn salary, stepping from post to post
as sovereign succeeded sovereign and minister supplanted
minister, faithfully serving every predominant party,
honestly conforming to every established religion, inspir-
ing such confidence by his perfect freedom from fixed
opinions or inconvenient prejudices that the humble groom
of the chambers, taciturn and attentive, " never in the way
and never out of the way," gradually rose, by the inherent
levity of his character as much as by his parts and knowledge, to be the indispensable chief of the most famous of
modern administrations. The great place which Godolphin
left vacant was not filled up. Still intent on uniting the
two parties on terms ostensibly equal, Harley contented

himself at first with a subordinate seat at the treasury board. But the removal of the consummate financier who had for more than thirty years directed all its business, and to whose administrative skill had been due no small part of the credit of Marlborough's uninterrupted successes, evoked ominous signs of discontent. The stocks rapidly fell as the moneyed men drew in their loans. The ambassadors of the Great Powers ventured on a combined remonstrance with the Queen. The press began to teem with pamphlets against a bedchamber ministry. And the country squires and rectors, on their side, fully alive to the opportunity presented to them, retaliated with loyal addresses, congratulating their royal mistress, as the Duke of Beaufort put it, on her "late accession to her Crown and dignities."

Thus the issue was joined ; and it became necessary for the Whigs to consider how far they could, with any regard for their personal honour and for the great public objects they had at heart, remain part of an administration so formed and so supported, an administration in which it was abundantly clear that, whatever their numbers, they could not have, and were not expected to have, any preponderating influence. Two great meetings of the party were held. There was at first much wavering ; but at length the honest and manly counsels of Wharton prevailed. It was unanimously resolved to reject all compromise, and assert in opposition the essential principles of the new polity.

After this decision, nothing remained for Harley but to dissolve Parliament and fill up his Government with the strainings of the Cavalier party. The veteran Rochester became, for the third time, Lord President. Another venerable relic of the past, John Sheffield, Duke of Buckinghamshire, a man with parts as brilliant as St. John's and principles as lax, was made Lord Steward. The supine and listless Ormond succeeded Wharton as Lord Lieutenant, an office in which, five and twenty years before, his grandfather had earned the love and esteem of all men. On Cowper's persistent refusal any longer to hold the Great Seal, Harcourt was made Lord Keeper. Newcastle, indeed, whose family was on terms of close intimacy with Harley's, was prevailed upon to retain his place till his death in the following spring, when, to Swift's proud delight, a great cabinet office was conferred, for the last time in our history, on a member of that privileged hierarchy on the support of whose adherents the Government was now to rest. St. John became Secretary of State in place of Boyle. The last few months he had spent in retirement at Bucklersbury, amusing himself with books, and nursing his political interest in the county where his wife's property lay. At the election in October he was returned for Berkshire; and his energy, his chastened and passionate eloquence, his unwearied diligence in mastering every detail of his official duties, above all, perhaps, the perfect knowledge of French which he had acquired in Parisian *salons* and boudoirs, and which in the negotiations about to be reopened he was now to display on the wider field of diplomacy, soon transformed a subordinate into a leading office. Thenceforth, above the group of effete statesmen gathered together by Harley, his figure stands pre-eminent.

CHAPTER II.

I.

THE untoward decision of the Whig chiefs, 'and the disastrous rout of their party in the elections that followed produced a change, not indeed in Harley's wishes, but in the course he was constrained to follow. The palace intrigue of which his Government was the offspring, had been intended at first as a means of extricating the Queen from the thraldom of party, and of vindicating the constitutional principle that her council should be formed on a broader basis. That principle had now to be abandoned. The new Government was just as much a "cabal," the creature and product of faction, as Godolphin's. Of those Whig statesmen who had borne so large an influence in framing it, some, like Somerset, as soon as its party character and objects were revealed, relapsed into opposition ; whilst others, like Shrewsbury, remained reluctantly acquiescing in measures which they condemned, and finally interposing to frustrate and defeat them. The elections, indeed, which took place in October, conferred on the Government one signal service. They purged away the taint of its adulterous origin, and gave it a legal status and a responsible position. But in sending its High Church supporters to Westminster in such formidable numbers, they necessarily brought about this result—that the policy of the State must be administered in the interest of the

High Church body ; and it was not at all the intention of these politicians to put down schism, either political or religious, by a wide scheme of comprehension. "The principal spring of *our* actions," wrote Bolingbroke after-wards, "was to have the Government in our hands ; and our principal views were the conservation of this power— great employments for ourselves, great means of securing those who had helped to raise us, and of injuring those who stood in opposition to us." *   Even the " considerations of public and national interest," which were, as he justly says, "intermingled " with these private and personal aims, had the same sinister motive of fortifying the rule of two great classes in the State under the plea of secur-ing its general welfare. The administration was made " national " by the device of treating the nation and the Church party as synonymous terms ; and the whole object of the leading ministers, from the day on which Godolphin broke his staff down to the memorable 1st of August which consigned them to exile or the Tower, was to restore what Swift calls " old principles in Church and State," the system of sacerdotal and caste privilege which had existed under Charles II., and which the Revolution had overthrown.

The measures of Harley's Government must be judged as a whole, and as a whole must be approved or condemned. The settlement of Europe, negotiated, so to speak, behind the backs of the Powers of Europe in secret correspondence and furtive interviews between the ministers of France and England, a settlement perfectly defensible in itself, though laid down on lines essentially different from those which the Confederates had contemplated, constantly delayed by their hostility, and still at the Queen's death left unexe-cuted through their reluctance to take up the various parts

---

* Works, i. 8 (Letter to Sir William Wyndham).

assigned to them, was the great achievement of the new ministry, displaying on a most conspicuous stage its intellectual merits and its moral defects. But this settlement was merely a part, and indeed a subordinate part of a general scheme of politics, the object of which was to restore to the Church and the landed interest their old predominance in the English Government. The Revolution had established a parliamentary system based on the principles of civil and religious freedom. The Declaration of Right, turned into legal form by the Bill of Rights, and the Act of Settlement, confirming and completing its provisions, had made the heads of the Executive Government the nominees of Parliament, and had imposed on them the obligation of governing according to the laws of Parliament ; and the effect of these statutes had been, as by direct enactment, to subordinate the Crown to an assembly claiming to represent all classes and orders in the State, and by necessary implication to impose on the sovereign the duty of conducting the government in conformity with its expressed opinions. In like manner the Toleration Act, the great charter of religious, as the Bill of Rights and the Act of Settlement are of civil liberty, by taking away from all loyal Protestants any obligation to attend the services of the Anglican Church, and by legalizing with carefully framed theological restrictions the public worship of the principal Nonconforming bodies, had destroyed, as by express enactment, the claim of the Episcopalians to the exclusive possession of divine truth, and led by necessary implication to the political and social equality of all religious sects before the law.

Such was the free republican constitution in Church and State which the recent change of polity had established. But this constitution, though it contained the germs of all the fundamental doctrines of our complex representative

system, was then in its infancy, environed on every side
with perils. Its fate depended on the opinions, the
character, the political integrity of the public men by
whom, in the critical stages of its development, the new
system should be administered. Left free to expand, and
shape itself to the new wants and circumstances of the
time, under the fostering care of men who had some
sympathy with the cause of progress, some sense of the
inevitable transitoriness of all human institutions, the
political organism to which the Revolution had given
birth would gradually disclose, as it has disclosed, its
large inherent capacities for freedom and self-government.
Stunted in its natural growth, its liberal tendencies
repressed, pruned down, and distorted by the hostile arts
of men, all whose feelings and traditions bound them to
the system which it replaced, of men inaccessible to fresh
ideas and unapt to discern how the world was moving, the
new republic, fashioned as it was in the image of the old
monarchy, would degenerate and dwindle into a mere
reproduction of it. It presented in all its parts the marks
of that habit of compromise and dread of unnecessary
innovation which are the peculiar characteristics of
English law-making. A new meaning and spirit had
been insinuated into the body politic with the least possible
change to its shape and physical construction. The
subordination of the executive power to the supreme
legislature ; the subordination of the legislature as a whole
to the prevailing party in the representative chamber ; the
subordination of the representative chamber to the combined will of the entire nation—these are the three
cardinal principles on which our parliamentary system
works. But they were altogether latent in the new polity
which bore, as it still bears, the outward form and linea-
ments of a feudal monarchy. The parliamentary sovereign

had succeeded in theory to all the undoubted prerogatives of the legitimate sovereign. The ministers of State were still his servants at will. The enactments of the State still ran in his name. The insignia of the State still bore his image and superscription. The supreme power in the State still "advised and consented" to his laws. The ruling chambers were still, in theory, as in the old Plantagenet times, a convention of estates and orders of the subject people, summoned and dismissed at the bidding of the Crown, meeting for consultation not for active government, and claiming all their privileges as grants renewable or not at the royal pleasure.*

In ecclesiastical affairs, again, liberty of conscience, freedom of public worship, the right to form and express independent religious opinions, the social and political equality of all theological creeds, though most of them practically guaranteed and all implicitly admitted, were still, in theory, discountenanced by the State. The entire nation was still solemnly commanded to attend the services of the privileged Church; and, in certain cases, where the culprit who neglected this admonition refused to testify to his loyalty and his Protestantism, the emancipating clauses of the great Act of Indulgence passed him by; and the ancient penalties might, down almost to our own time, be still inflicted. No doctrine inconsistent with her articles and homilies, no vestment or ceremony prohibited by her rubrics, no prayer or thanksgiving not contained in her liturgies, were anywhere ostensibly permitted; and the dissenting clergy who proposed, with the sanction of Parliament, to violate the standing law, could only relieve themselves from the pressure of the old stringent penal code by making

---

* See the speech of the Speaker at the commencement of each new Parliament.

individual confessions of faith in forms cunningly devised
by Parliament, as combining the widest latitude of thought
and opinion with the smallest apparent deviation from
her precepts and her ordinances. For the performance of
municipal duties, for the enjoyment of municipal privileges,
for all civil and military employments in the gift of the
State, a submission to Episcopalian observances had still to
be made, though this submission had ceased to be regarded
as involving any expression of belief in the efficacy or
lawfulness of the Episcopalian system.* The peculiar
form of Catholic truth known as Anglicanism was still, it
seemed, in the south of our island the orthodox religion,
the prevailing religion, the religion especially favoured and,
in the general view of the law, exclusively countenanced by
the State.

In politics, no doubt, the case was somewhat different.
The peculiar form of national opinion known as Toryism

---

* By the Corporation Act (13 Car. II. st. 2, c. 1) passed by the hotheaded
Cavalier Parliament of 1661, no person could be elected to office in any corporate
town who had not within the year taken the Sacrament of the Lord's Supper,
according to the rites of the Episcopalian Church ; and by the Test Act (25
. Car. II. c. 2), passed by the same Parliament twelve years later, when its
theological animosities had been revived by the first Declaration of Indulgence,
the holders of all civil and military offices, with a few trifling exceptions, were
required to undergo the same ordeal. These statutes remained in force down
to George IV.'s time. They never, however, affected the general body of
Protestant Nonconformists. The Presbyterians, as a rule, submitted to the
proposed requirement, not as acquiescing in the superiority of prelatical forms
of Church government, but as consenting to Episcopacy in so far as it bore on
the performance of their municipal or other public functions. They continued,
of course, to frequent their usual places of religious worship. This practice,
which was called Occasional Conformity, and in which the most eminent
Dissenters—Baxter, for instance, Howe, Bates, and Philip Henry—saw nothing
to condemn, grievously outraged the more refined sensibilities of Parson Trulli-
ber. The Test Act, indeed, as its preamble shows, had been levelled exclusively
at the Roman Catholics. But the High Churchmen of Queen Anne's time,
anxious to take advantage of so ready a weapon for the purpose of lowering
the political influence of their party rivals, maintained that no one could,
without gross impropriety, attend even a Presbyterian meeting-house after
discharging any public duty in an Episcopalian State ; and they proposed in
the Occasional Conformity Bill to visit the practice with stringent penalties.

was not an " established " belief.   But it was undoubtedly
the opinion to which on ordinary occasions the majority
of the nation leaned, as after the great religious schism
men still clung to the old observances, even when disliking
and prohibiting the abuses with which they were inseparably bound up.   And its leading doctrines—government by
hereditary descent, the concentration of political power in
the land-owning class, the exclusion from civil rights of
all who refused to conform to the theological requirements
of the State—however repugnant to the spirit of the new
polity, might still be traced in its system, as after the
great religious schism you might trace in the prayers
and thanksgivings of the reformed Church doctrines of
Romanism implicitly condemned in her articles of belief.

It was on these considerations that the new ministers
founded and justified their policy.   Their mission was,
as Bolingbroke afterwards defined it, the " establishment
and fortification of Toryism." *   Just as in more modern
times that great party in the Anglican Church which still
draws its inspiration from Rome has been apt to give
undue prominence to those parts of her complex system
which she derived from the ancient breviaries, has shut
its eyes to the confessions of faith in which the Calvinistic
tenets of her founders are expressed, has always insisted
on her continued fellowship with the Holy Catholic Church,
and has been forward to mark her separation from all other
Protestant communities, so in the reign of Queen Anne
the leaders of the High Church party in politics, in their
dislike to the vital changes which had transformed a feudal
monarchy with strong sacerdotal leanings into a progressive, free-thinking republic, persisted in keeping before
them the monarchical, ecclesiastical, and territorial elements
in the new polity which were a " survival " from the old ;

* i. 23 (Letter to Sir William Wyndham).

held that the supremacy of the Church and the landed gentry was an essential part of the new system as it had been of the old ; and in the interest of the Revolution itself sought to confine political power exclusively to the friends of the unreformed constitution. The measures which they had in view for this purpose were necessary, as Bolingbroke frankly admits, for their " party interest." But, as he also reminds us, they were in this sense neither unreasonable nor unjust that they " enacted nothing new." They were merely an " enforcement of ancient laws ;" of laws judged necessary for the security of Church and State when the memory of the ruin of both was fresh, and when the party charged with the defence of both was last supreme ; of laws, too, which still remained on the statute book, however much their meaning and scope had been transformed and modified by subsequent legislation. Nor was the plan which they favoured for enforcing these laws in itself a new one. It had already been worked out in all its details by Danby, in view of a temporary alliance in his time between the court and the enemies of the Church and landed gentry, for securing power to these two great bodies under all vicissitudes. It consisted mainly in a system of " tests " at the polling booth, and " qualifications " for office and Parliament so contrived as to shut out from public life all those new sects and classes which were their possible rivals, which were now fast rising in public importance, and which the Revolution, as interpreted by the Whigs, had been designed to free and enfranchise. And if the measures framed for these objects had the anticipated effect, it would not be necessary to tamper in any way with the Act of Settlement. The parliamentary sovereign, whatever his individual leanings, would be powerless in the hands of the High Church leaders ; and the old system would revive under the new dynasty.

Into this policy of party consolidation, veiled under the plea of vindicating old constitutional principles, the new Government entered with many advantages. The recent attempt of the State to make good its ascendency over the Church had roused among the parochial clergy, and the powerful class of rural magnates, whose opinions they directed, a dangerous ferment, under cover of which almost any measures of retaliation might have been safely ventured on. The members of the new House of Commons had come up to Westminster animated by a zeal at once religious and political ; and they felt for their Whig opponents, not the languid antipathy natural and proper to party rivals, but an intense and vindictive loathing, such as a disinherited nation is apt to feel for an alien race of conquerors. Like the old Celtic and Norman inhabitants of Ireland, from whom their Tory nickname was derived, they considered themselves despoiled of their just rights and held down, not by numbers, but by superior organization and a completer mastery of the arts of government. The sentiment which then prevailed—far more akin to race or colour hatred than to mere party spirit, yet natural enough when the circumstances are considered and the relative strength of the two parties measured—is curiously exhibited even by a man so free from prejudices and illusions as Bolingbroke, whenever in his letters, or in the graver works in which he afterwards treated of these events, he comes to speak of what he calls the "faction." His tone is that of a descendant of the O'Neils towards some band of Cromwellian settlers cultivating their fields under the protection of Ormond's guards. "We supposed the Whigs," he writes,* "to be the remains of a party formed against the ill-designs of the court under King Charles II., nursed up into strength and applied to contrary uses by King

---

* i. 10 (Letter to Sir William Wyndham).

William III., and yet still so weak as to lean for support on the Presbyterians and the other sectaries, on the bank and the other corporations, and on the Dutch and the other allies." "We supposed the Tories to be the bulk of the territorial interest, with no contrary influence blended into its composition." It was time by a vigorous effort to shake off this usurped ascendency. It was time to reverse the relative position of the ruling and the subject castes, and restore to the old proprietors of the soil the dominion which of right belonged to them ; to "break," as he expresses it, "the body of the Whigs, render their supports useless to them, and fill all the employments of the kingdom down to the meanest with Tories." "We supposed that such measures joined to the natural effect of our numbers and our property would secure us against all attempts during the Queen's reign, and that we should soon become too considerable not to make our terms in any events that might happen afterwards." * It was the old gambling policy of Tyrconnel and his Rapparees, but played for a larger stake and by men more skilled in seizing the turns and chances of the game ; and it ended in the same collapse—four years of feverish triumph expiated by half a century of subjection and humiliation.

In setting about their task of saving and regenerating society, the High Church leaders of Queen Anne's time anticipated in fact the familiar policy of a modern Buona-partist or Legitimist in our own day, when some unexpected turn of fortune lands him in the ministry of the Interior. They established a *gouvernement de combat* against the "principles of '89." Foremost among the "supports of Whiggism," the new *couches sociales,* whom the Revolutionary statesmen had raised up and brought within the pale of the reformed constitution, were the "Presbyterians and

* i. 10 (Letter to Sir William Wyndham).

the other sectaries." In the furtherance of an enterprise which aimed at restoring to the adherents of the Church Establishment their old exclusive supremacy in the State, it was necessary to fix a new ban on these disturbing influences ; and it is interesting to notice how skilfully St. John, as at once a Tory in politics and a free-thinker in religion, distinguishes between oppression for a political object and mere persecution. The persecution of Dissenters, he assures us, " entered into no man's head." [*] An indulgence to tender consciences which prejudice, perhaps, or evil habits had rendered scrupulous, was agreeable to all the rules of sound policy. But no Government was bound to connive at the propagation of these prejudices, or at the forming of these evil habits. The *effect* was without remedy, and therefore deserved indulgence ; but the *cause* was to be prevented, and could be entitled to none. And to strip these men of all civil and political rights; to threaten with stringent penalties those who should, after discharging any public duty, worship God according to the simple forms which their consciences prescribed ; to root out with a heavy hand the schools and colleges they were setting up for the free instruction of their children so jealously excluded from the national seats of learning ;—this was not persecution. It was to deprive them of their powers of mischief, to " take away their sting," to hinder them from gaining strength and spirit enough under the colour of moderation to " provoke " the Church party, and to show them that the being tolerated by Act of Parliament did not amount to a legal establishment or put them on as " good a foot " as the Church itself.

And so, again, with reference to the second " support of Whiggism," the Bank of England, the East India Company, the commercial and industrial interests of the kingdom

* i. 10.

generally, in order to restore its old authority to the class possessed of land, it was necessary to plunder and proscribe the classes possessed of money. But nothing was further from the thought of the new ministers, Bolingbroke assures us, than the "entire subvertion of their property." [*] Here, again, the argument is somewhat nice and requires careful following. The proprietor of land, the merchant who brought home riches by the returns of foreign trade, bore, we are told, the whole immense load of the national expenses. But the same proprietor of land, if by chance, his income exceeding his wants, he became a "lender of money," specially interested therefore in the stability of the State; the same merchant, if, instead of squandering the riches that he brought home, he husbanded them and invested them in some new public enterprise, or advanced them under the authority of Parliament to the Crown for the extraordinary services of the State, these men and their fellows "throve by the public calamity, and contributed not a mite to the public charges." Their influence on the legislature and in matters of State must be "restrained;" they must be made to "contribute more" to the support and ease of a Government under which they "enjoyed such privileges:" while, in the interest of Conservatism and moral order itself, the country gentlemen, four-fifths of whom were disaffected to the State,—the country gentlemen who formed the bulk of the Tory party, with no contrary influence blended into its composition,—the country gentlemen, so often "vexed" and "baffled" at their elections,—must be protected by stringent laws excluding all but landowners from sitting in Parliament.

Last among the "supports of Whiggism" came the Dutch and the other Confederate Powers, who had guaranteed the Act of Settlement and remonstrated with the

---

[*] i. 11.

Queen on her change of counsellors. With respect to the Allies St. John found, as was perhaps natural, "no differences of opinion at all among any of those who came into power at that time." "Peace was judged to be the only solid foundation on which we could erect a Tory system." *

II.

In the following pages both the methods and the results of the famous pacification of Europe, which was the great achievement of St. John and Harley, will be treated at length and criticized with some freedom. For their peculiar management of the negotiations, besides setting the characters of the two statesmen into effective relief, affords the real explanation of the difficulties amidst which, four years later, their Government foundered, and of the state of weakness and isolation in which England, notwithstanding the specious advantages won for her, was left at their downfall.

But in justice to St. John, especially, it is necessary to bear in mind his peculiar position. It is necessary to remember with what different eyes a minister bent on restoring, either under the old dynasty or the new, the old political and ecclesiastical system of England would regard the questions of policy involved in the Revolutionary struggle against France ; how differently he would estimate the importance to England of maintaining, in peace as well as in war, a union of great Powers against France, and the relative value to her of the concessions which she had made and was making for this purpose; what different means, too, he and his friends possessed of conducting the contest with vigour on the old extended

* i. 19.

footing, or of concluding it on the old stringent conditions. To make peace on terms consistent with the engagements of England and the pretensions of the Allied Powers was indeed scarcely possible to a Government situated like Harley's ; for the terms demanded were such as King Lewis, long accustomed to domineer and give the law to Europe, could not accept, even from a united confederacy, without humiliation, without confessing in fact that the whole policy of his life had broken down.

His ambition, almost from the very beginning of his reign, had been so to extend his frontiers at the expense of the great inheritance of Charles V., as to become, to an extent which Charles V. had never been, the undisputed master of Europe. On the other hand, the object of the associated Powers, adopted more than twenty years before, and always under all vicissitudes retained as the ultimate goal of their efforts, was to drive back the frontiers of France to their ancient limits, the limits assigned to her in 1648, when the last great pacification of Europe took place. In the treaties of 1701, which form the basis of what is commonly called the second Grand Alliance against France, this object, no doubt, had been for the moment abandoned. Those treaties were the last and, in some respects, the greatest effort of King William's statesmanship. They were concluded at a time when all Europe was disheartened by failure. England in particular, burdened by an ever-increasing load of debt, and smarting from commercial losses which, beginning with bad harvests, had gradually reached and palsied all her trading interests, was resolutely bent on peace. Under King William's guidance she had fought many hard campaigns, in which her success was by no means proportioned to her efforts and her sacrifices. The treaties of Ryswick were far from answering the ends proposed or, indeed, the engagements taken by the authors of the war. The "exorbitant power of France" had been reduced both in extent of dominion and strength of barrier, but not to anything like the point originally contemplated. The dangerous pretensions of France to the "succession of Spain"—which was to have been "secured" for the House of Austria—were not reduced at all. And yet so general was the feeling in England of the uselessness of further effort, so cruel had been the trials through which her various industries had lately passed, that at the first whisper of a renewal of war the ministers most devoted to King William and most impressed with the wisdom of his policy shrank back: the overburdened nation murmured and protested: the disaffected Parliament openly rebelled. It was necessary to temporize, to cover his large designs with an air of studious moderation.

It was just at this moment that the King of Spain died, and the great question which had filled the minds of statesmen and taxed the resources of statesmanship for two generations came on for settlement. Lewis, encouraged by the languor of Europe, and seduced, it is said, from the path of honour by feminine importunities, accepted, in spite of his oaths and treaty engagements, the whole immense inheritance of Charles II., bequeathed to his grandson partly as the result of Jesuit wiles, partly in the honest belief that of the two competitors the Bourbon would prove the least unlikely to hold its scattered territories together; and England and Holland, turning back on the policy of forty years, recognized the Bourbon king—both, no doubt, to some extent under duress; William at the instance of what a great writer has called the "tottering imbecility" of his divided counsels; the United Provinces in order to obtain the release of the Dutch troops garrisoning their barrier towns, which the

King of France, on taking possession of the Spanish
monarchy, had, in ostentatious defiance of law, surrounded
and made prisoners. When, a few months later, the war
broke out, both Powers were fettered by this enforced
composition with their great opponent, as well as by the
mingled supineness and unskilfulness of their ally, the
Austrian Court. Under the stress of untoward events
they had been compelled to accept the union of France
and Spain as an accomplished fact. The ostensible pretext
of the new war, the technical *casus belli* seized upon by
William, had no reference to the Spanish succession at
all. It was France's insolent recognition of the Stuart
Pretender, on his father's death, as King of Great Britain.
In like manner the ostensible object which the Confederated
Powers now set before themselves and pledged themselves
to attain was not to wrest the Spanish crown from Philip.
In the preceding war, with Spain on their side, and acting
therefore on the defensive, they had barely held their own.
Now they would be the assailants, with the strong places
of Flanders and Belgium already in the enemy's hands,
and with the wealth of the Indies in addition swelling his
already too formidable resources. In that period of
weakness and depression all that they felt strong enough
to try and accomplish, all at any rate that they bound
themselves to accomplish, was to procure for the Emperor
and for the general balance of power "a just and reasonable
satisfaction" for the great inheritance he had lost. The
plan of compounding with France by "parcelling out the
Spanish monarchy in lots"—which had so wounded the
Castilian pride, which had directly provoked the testament
of Charles II., and driven Spain into the arms of France,
into which King William had been in a manner forced by
the short-sighted and expensive parsimony of the country
gentlemen, for their early subordinate share in which the

Whig ministers—Somers, Halifax, Portland—had been impeached by Henry St. John at the bar of the House of Lords, and which Bolingbroke was himself to consummate in the treaties of peace, and to spend his old age in justifying by elaborate sophistries—still infected, and to all appearance governed, the diplomacy of Europe.

But the Grand Alliance of 1701 was not a new confederacy. It was the revival and development of an old one, of that league of 1685 in which the princes of Germany first banded themselves together against their perjured and ambitious neighbour, which was known to be the handiwork of William of Orange, and to which, three years later, England and Holland formally acceded. Its object, as embodied in the great treaty of May, 1689, between England and the United Provinces, which forms the root of all the subsequent combinations against the House of Bourbon, was to restore all things by war to the terms of the Westphalian and Pyrenean treaties, and to preserve them in that state after the peace by a defensive alliance against France ; and the meaning of the engagement then taken would, as Bolingbroke most justly says, have been plain enough without that separate article in which England and Holland obliged themselves to assist " the House of Austria in taking and keeping possession of the Spanish monarchy at the death of King Charles II. without lawful heirs." This was the aim and purpose of the Grand Alliance. The various plans and suggestions put forth during the five years of truce—the five years which divided the two parts of the great war—for partitioning the disputed inheritance, were plans of compromise offered on the part of the Allied Powers without " prejudicing," as a lawyer would say, their original claims, claims which they still believed to be just in themselves, and, if only they could be made good, advantageous to the general welfare.

And with the first sound of the cannon the period of compromise passed away. In the treaties of 1701–2 power had been explicitly reserved to the contracting States, by the foresight of the English King, to fall back on their old demands in case the fortune of war should declare itself signally in their favour. So early as the second year of the long conflict, in the treaty by which Portugal was drawn into the alliance, the Austrian claimant was again recognized by England as the successor of the Catholic King. And in 1707, when the disastrous battle of Almanza had reduced to the lowest point the authority of the Allies in Spain itself, but when on the side of Flanders, of Germany, of Savoy, their victorious legions were closing in round France, Parliament unanimously resolved with a Roman spirit that no peace could be just or honourable which left Spain or any part of the Spanish monarchy in possession of the Bourbons.* Thus the policy of 1689, which aimed at raising up in the House of Austria a great maritime State with an hereditary enmity to France and to the full as powerful as France, emerged again after so many vicissitudes in all its pristine integrity. It may be called the European basis of peace To reduce the boundaries of France within the limits assigned to them in 1648, and to settle the succession of Spain on the principles laid down in 1659, was the policy of Heinsius, the wisest statesman, and of Marlborough, the greatest soldier in Europe, as twenty years

* " It generally happens," writes the late Prince Consort (November 19, 1854) " that the ostensible cause of war does not embrace the whole or even the strongest motives which impel States to resort to that last extremity. A peace to be satisfactory and durable should satisfy *all the objects* for which the war has been undertaken ; and it becomes necessary on the approach of peace fully and honestly to consider what these were."

before it had been the policy of King William ; and in May, 1709, twenty years almost to a day after the Prince had first instituted it, this policy was again formulated by the eight Confederated Powers in the famous preliminaries of the Hague, which followed with a curious minuteness the terms of the original Grand Alliance.*

On this basis Lewis had twice consented to treat. So early as 1706, indeed, after the heavy blow of Ramillies, he had sued for peace, but for peace on the old exploded basis of the Partition Treaties, and on a basis moreover cunningly devised by himself as likely to breed dissension between Austria and the two maritime powers. His proposal, which was in fact open to all the objections so speciously and in many respects so justly urged against the abortive measures of 1698 and 1700, which would have "dismembered the Spanish monarchy," which would have "transferred large sections of the Spanish monarchy to France," which would have imposed the will of England, France, and Holland on the disappointed Austrian or the reluctant Spaniard, forcing the Emperor to relinquish rights which he claimed as just, or placing on the throne of Madrid a Prince whom the people of Castile at any rate disliked and repudiated—this insidious compromise, which Bolingbroke as a historian maintained to have been wise and honourable, though St. John as a politician had denounced it and even impeached and tried to ruin the ministers whom he falsely held responsible for it, was rejected mainly at the instance of Godolphin's Government, of which both St. John and Harley were then distinguished members.

Three years later, however, in 1709, when, after the

* It is instructive to compare the two. The preliminaries may be read in De Torcy's Memoirs (i. 304), with his comments upon each. He represented France at the Conference. The treaty of the Grand Alliance is in Dumont *Corps diplomatique du droit des gens*, vol. vii. part ii. p. 229.

battle of Oudenarde, Marlborough had penetrated the frontiers of France and taken Lille, when the terrible winter of 1708 had dried up the sources of her revenue, and a blight had smitten all her various industries, the olives of Languedoc, the vineyards of the Rhone, the jessamines and orange-gardens of Toulon and Hières, Lewis, awed into meekness by the gaunt spectre of Famine, with Pestilence at its heels, traversing and devastating his unhappy country, had offered under the compulsion of his empty treasury to treat on the conditions imposed by the Allies. He had offered, so far as rested with himself as head of the house of Bourbon, to withdraw all the pretensions of that house to any part of the Spanish monarchy. He had offered to cede to the Dutch a barrier of strong towns, and to sign in their favour a treaty of commerce. He had offered to banish the Pretender, to demolish Dunkirk, to restore Newfoundland, and to give up Lille and Tournay, Strasbourg and Luxembourg, provided Naples and Sicily, or even Sicily and Sardinia, were bestowed on Philip, not as a matter of right but as a gift, an inducement to him to relinquish Spain itself. In the following spring at Gertruydenburg he had repeated these offers. But he made them, as he was careful to say, *for himself alone.* He had withdrawn his troops from Spain. He had no further authority or influence over the Spanish Government. He could not undertake to execute that part of the proposed treaty which related to Spanish affairs ; nor could he consent to postpone the execution of the entire engagement till his grandson had yielded up that part of the disputed inheritance which was still in his possession.

Such and so guarded were the promises made by Lewis. As to the exact nature of the guarantee which might be safely taken as an earnest of the due performance of them, the Allies in some degree differed ; and this difference, as usual, he dexterously turned to his own advantage. Some amongst them, England, for example, and Holland, were not unwilling to purchase the complete submission of the Bourbons by a substantial "equivalent," such as the gift of Naples or Sicily ; but then they insisted on making the withdrawal of the whole clan from Spain a preliminary condition of the peace, without which no part of the engagement should stand. Others, again, amongst whom was Austria herself, were not unwilling to conclude with France at once, accepting the cautionary towns which Lewis offered them as a sufficient guarantee for the fulfilment of whatever, either on his own part or his grandson's, he might undertake ; but then, they persisted in requiring the whole Spanish monarchy.

And the result was that the confederacy as a body formulated *two* conditions unpalatable to Lewis. For all Europe agreed that Spain must be given up in some effectual way. The war in Spain had been marked by strange vicissitudes, and had not on the whole been favourable to the Allies. But outside the Peninsula their arms had been everywhere successful. Germany had been saved by the great victory of Blenheim. Italy had been conquered mainly by the exertions of the Austrians themselves. By the genius of Marlborough, and the valour of the Dutch and English troops which he commanded, all the various strongholds of the Low Countries had been successively reduced. The armies of the confederacy were now encamped on French soil, prepared, unless indeed diplomacy could stay their advance, to march on Paris and dictate their terms to Lewis in his palace at Versailles. To make peace with France on the basis of the evacuation of Spain with no guarantee, and indeed no expectation that Spain would be relinquished, was simply to abandon the attack at the place where the breach was made, to throw away the preparation for a campaign which could hardly fail to be decisive, and to transfer the war to a new scene where, as the British general justly said, "armies might march about till doomsday" without getting any effectual hold on the country, leaving the disturber of Europe, in the meanwhile, to recover his strength and meditate some new outrage against his neighbours.

It was for these reasons that the representatives of the Allied Powers insisted on the famous thirty-seventh article of their preliminaries. It provided in effect that the King of France should make good his own engagements ; that he should undertake within the space of two months to procure the evacuation of Spain, and that if he failed in or neglected this enterprise the war should continue. In that case the Allies would retain the cautionary towns which, as a test of his sincerity, Lewis offered to place in their hands. In this ultimatum, whatever we may now think of its wisdom, and however much they may have themselves differed as to its necessity, all the Confederated Powers unanimously concurred ; and it was a fundamental condition of the treaty engagements which bound them together, that no one Power had the right without the general consent to withdraw from it.*

* See especially the eighth article of the treaty concluded between King William and the Emperor Leopold (September, 1701), and the ninth and tenth articles in the treaty of March, 1677–8, incorporated in the engagement which bound England to the States-General (November, 1701).

Bolingbroke, in the elaborate justification of his own conduct as minister which he inserted in the last of his Letters on History, objects to this thirty-seventh article as having an "air of inhumanity." To do him justice, he was too familiar with the events of those times and too much of a statesman to bring this charge in the unqualified terms which modern historians are fond of using. He makes it apologetically and with diffidence. Louis XIV. had, he justly says, "treated mankind with too much inhumanity in his prosperous days to have any reason to complain." But the expedient had, he thinks, an "air" of inhumanity, as obliging an aged grandfather, if persuasion failed and unless he preferred to lose the benefit of the treaty as regarded himself and his own

III.

Such was the state of affairs when the new Government took office. It must in candour be acknowledged that their position was a difficult one. A complete change of administration "down even to the meanest" at the very crisis of a great war is a perilous undertaking. As the shrewd American President said, no one cares to swop horses in mid-stream, even when the new horse is a stronger and sounder animal than the old. But here the reverse was the case. The Whigs had many advantages in the conducting of public business which their successors altogether wanted. They were trained and practised administrators. They had in Godolphin the most experienced, and in Halifax the most inventive of living financiers ; and as the creators of that system of public credit which gave profitable employment to the surplus earnings of commerce, they had the confidence of the rising middle-class of merchants and tradesmen, whom they had bound to the new settlement by close ties of interest, and who alone could provide the means for carrying on an expensive war. They were the party which King William had especially trusted, which inherited his traditions, and concurred in his policy. As such they had the confidence of the leading statesmen of Germany and Holland. They were at one with those statesmen as to the scope and objects of the war. They believed that on the preserving of the European concert against France depended the very existence of a free government in England. They believed that the Austrian succession to the Spanish Crown and

subjects, to make war on a beloved grandson. Later on Bolingbroke admits what every statesman then knew, "that Philip must have evacuated Spain if his grandfather had insisted and *been in earnest to require him*" (ii. 464). Of course there was never any question of an appeal to arms.

the Hanoverian succession to the English Crown would stand or fall together; and they knew that the great confederacy which was now sustaining both these European demands would fall in pieces unless England, the leader and mover of that confederacy, was prepared to take upon herself a far larger share in the common burden than ten years before, in the distracted state of her politics and the disordered condition of her finances, had been laid upon her.

The Whigs had thus a distinct political and party interest in maintaining the Grand Alliance. William of Orange, a man naturally as arbitrary in temper and as fond of personal rule as Charles I. or James II., had made himself the chief agent in establishing what was in fact a Republican polity in England, in the hope of seeing England resume under a free government her old influence in Europe, and of fixing with her help the yoke of united Europe on France; and in like manner the Whig statesmen, men naturally, as Walpole afterwards showed, as averse from extravagance at home and disturbance abroad as the younger Pitt, expended the resources of England with a hand as lavish almost as Pitt's, mainly in the hope of making that European supremacy over France, which King William had valued in the general interest of Europe, a safeguard and protection to themselves in the hard task of consolidating her parliamentary institutions. The recognition of the Jacobite Pretender in September, 1701, was to Somers and the Whig junto what the declaration of the Jacobin convention in November, 1792, afterwards was to Pitt—an intimation of the secret designs of France, of what might be confidently looked for unless France was steadfastly withstood, and a reason for making England a principal in the struggle against her.

But when we turn to their successors in the Government,

we shall see how differently these same considerations operated. They had no political interest in maintaining the Grand Alliance, because they had no attachment to the political system which the success of France would imperil. So far from wishing to see a number of foreign guarantees in force all tending to preserve the parliamentary settlement, great armies in the field pledged to maintain the rights of the parliamentary heir, and a powerful and rising class of Englishmen bound by interested motives to support the parliamentary system, they desired to have England perfectly unfettered when the Queen's death should occur, and had as a party " no very settled resolution," * as their leader candidly confessed, what course it would then become them to take.

With the leading statesmen of Europe, again, their relations were those of hostility thinly disguised under the forms of diplomatic respect. Their accession to power had been felt as a blow to the cause of the Alliance. They were regarded with distrust and their intentions with misgiving; and most of the Allied Powers had, through their representatives at St. James's, remonstrated with the Queen on her change of counsellors. For differing from the Whigs, as the new ministers did, with respect to the nature of England's interest in the contest, they naturally differed as to its scope and objects, as to the extent to which England should participate in it, and the manner in which her contribution to the general fund should be expended.

The High Churchmen had inherited from the Cavaliers a rooted dislike to the military service. They distrusted any scheme of politics, whatever might be its merits in other respects, which led to the employment of force on a large scale. The notion that the external interests of

* Works, i. 10 (Letter to Sir W. Wyndham).

England ought to be defended solely by her fleet, and that
this consideration ought to regulate and fix the limits
of her foreign policy, governed the action of the Tory
party for almost exactly a hundred years. It began to
take definite shape shortly after the Revolution of 1688,
when England, under the impulse of King William's statesmanship, became the moving power in a great European
struggle against the French monarchy, and it died out after
the Revolution of 1789, when England, under the impulse
of Burke's genius, became the moving power in another and
a still more costly struggle against the French Republic.
On questions of foreign policy, Harley and St. John were
not, perhaps, strictly speaking, Tories; but they had been
brought by a different road to the same principles of
government.   Both men of open and receptive minds, they
were much under the influence of a leading Commissioner
of Trade and Plantations, a man of acute and vigorous
understanding, under whose guidance they had anticipated
most of the economical and political doctrines of our modern
Manchester school. They were opposed on economical
grounds to the barbarism of a standing army. They
regarded Austria as a power hopelessly bankrupt and
decrepit, overtaxed by her own internal troubles, incapable
of sustaining the weight which Europe was thrusting on
her. They were anxious in any new European settlement
to shift the probable scene of future wars to a distant
part of the world, a part where England could be no
longer tempted to, what St. John calls, "the extravagant
ruinous plan of maintaining armies on the continent." *
Caring little about the public objects for which the war
was waged, believing such expressions as the "balance
of power," "the liberties of Europe" to be, as Bolingbroke
called them, imposing forms of words "designed to mask

* St. John to Peterborough, July 18, 1712.

the private aims and selfish ambition of princes," they had come to estimate the value of the struggle to England almost entirely by its effects on her material interests, as we have seen the value of India estimated by the proportion of our export trade for which she finds a market as set against the cost of maintaining the British ascendency there. They held, what was perfectly true, that under the plea of readjusting the balance of power, both the House of Austria and the States-General were obtaining large additions of revenue and new openings for their commerce, which would to some extent "recoup" them for their sacrifices in the war; and that England alone of the three, though she had by her fondness to engage in every article of expense, by her private assurances, and by her public parliamentary declarations that no peace should be made without the entire restitution of the Spanish monarchy, made herself in the opinion of all the confederates just as much a principal in the contest, had no "immediate benefits" either in possession or in expectancy as a reward for bearing the burden and heat of the day. Yet the military and naval enterprises she was engaged in, while their cost was altogether out of proportion to any political advantage she was likely to gain from them, were not directed to the points where her material interests lay.*

All these considerations tended to separate England under her new rulers from the rest of Europe, both as regards the objects she aimed at in the war and the results she hoped to derive from it. And besides these considerations of foreign policy severing the new Government from the cause of the Grand Alliance, were the considerations of domestic interest, which made peace on almost any terms a necessity to them. As a political party, they were intent

* St. John to Lord Raby, May 6, 1711.

on a work of internal politics, which could hardly be begun
so long as their energies were absorbed in the management
of a great war and their freedom of action fettered by the
engagements incidental to it.   That was a time when the
most momentous constitutional issues depended on which
of the two rival factions should hold office at the Queen's
death, when to secure Toryism against hostile attacks, and
to enable it to "make its terms" amidst all dynastic
changes, by vesting in loyal supporters of the old polity
all legislative and executive power, seemed to zealous
Conservatives a paramount duty; and already the slackness
of ministers in this great work—a slackness imposed upon
them by the necessity of keeping the wheels of government
in motion—was rousing a formidable mutiny in the ranks
of the extreme High Churchmen.   Yet if every experienced
servant of the Crown who owed his position to Godolphin
or Marlborough was to be dismissed and his place taken
by some new and untried man, if all those moneyed classes,
by whose exertions and at whose cost the war was being
conducted, were to be estranged by a policy of plunder
and proscription, it was inevitable that the conduct of
affairs must suffer.

Already there were ominous signs of a turn in the tide
of prosperity.   By the change of ministers the credit of
the State had been rudely shaken, and Harley as finance
minister put to the greatest difficulties in finding means
for the year's expenses.   The capitalists and men of
business, the chief creditors of the Government, and the
only class in a position to help it in an emergency, had
been frightened at the threat of special taxes designed
to make them "contribute more" to its necessities, and
so far from voluntarily opening their purse strings were
realizing their old loans as fast as possible. Since the
removal of Godolphin, the funds had gone down thirty per

cent., and they were still falling.* The State, though its countenance bore the outward hues of health, had, in the opinion of St. John, " corruption eating into its very vitals." It was idle to expect them to continue the war on the old extended footing ; and, in fact, before they had been in power six months a series of misfortunes befel the British arms, misfortunes for which it would be unjust perhaps to hold the new ministers directly responsible, but which were undoubtedly the direct result of the peculiar incidents attending their accession to office.

True to their favourite policy of expending a large share of England's contribution to the common cause in operations which would benefit her directly by some profitable acquisition, they had, at the instance of St. John, withdrawn a considerable body of troops from the army which Marlborough commanded, and which was then meditating the final invasion of France, to take part in a projected attack upon Quebec. This expedition proved a failure. Entrusted to incompetent hands, insufficiently furnished with stores as well as ill-commanded, and delayed by rough weather in the St. Lawrence, and by disputes amongst its officers till its scanty supplies were exhausted, it put back to Portsmouth at last after a six months' absence without accomplishing or even attempting the object for which it was sent out ; whilst the army of Flanders in the meanwhile had been so depleted that Marlborough, though he brought all the resources of his fine intellect to his help and penetrated the French lines by a masterpiece of strategy, found himself—as he had warned the Government he should be—

---

* The stocks fell thirty-four per cent. after the change of Government. Swift, in writing to Stella (October 28 and January 12), attributed the financial difficulties of his new friends at a terrible loss, as he says, for money to the natural perversity of the Whigs, " who will only lend amongst themselves while all others deal with them indifferently."

too weak for his main purpose of striking at the heart of
France and forcing peace on Lewis before the walls of
Paris ; and this, too, just at the moment when a complete
and overwhelming success in the region where Spain was
being conquered was made all the more essential to the
allied cause by the fact that their arms had encountered
a damaging reverse in Spain itself, a reverse distinctly
traceable in its turn to the confusion prevailing in the
domestic counsels of England.

The minister charged with the management of the war
in Spain had been Sunderland, a bitter partisan and a man
of violent temper, but a skilful and energetic administrator.
On Sunderland's removal in June, 1710, it had been
Harley's intention that Lord Nottingham should succeed
him, and the choice was in many respects judicious;
for Nottingham had served a long apprenticeship to office
under the keen eye of King William, and had as much
experience in business as any of the Whig junto. But
Nottingham, in spite of his high character and sound
churchmanship, was personally disliked by Queen Anne;
and in deference to her feminine humours his son-in-law
Lord Dartmouth was preferred to him. Lord Dartmouth
deserves to be mentioned with respect by the historian of
those times, for he was one of the very few High Church
statesmen who never wavered in his attachment to the
legal settlement of the Crown, or stooped to traffic with St.
Germains. Unluckily, he was a man of slender capacity :
he was quite unused to office ; and before he had made
himself familiar even with the routine work of his department, the Prime Minister, Godolphin, whose knowledge
and vast experience might have been of the utmost use to
his new colleague, was dismissed from the treasury. At
this time the allied forces operating in Spain were
adequate to the work before them ; for Lewis, pending

the issue of the conferences at Gertruydenburg, had with-drawn his troops from the Peninsula and left his grandson for the moment to his own resources. The allied cause was everywhere triumphant. On the 9th of August, the very day after Godolphin's removal, a great victory, the last fruit of his statesmanship, was won at Saragosa; and in September, Madrid was occupied once more by the Austrian King.

But now the strife of factions in England, co-operating with the fatal error which the diplomatists of Gertruyden-burg had committed in forcing on France a humiliating and, as it proved, an unnecessary condition of peace, was to destroy the work of so many laborious months. Lewis, exasperated at the rejection of his overtures, and encouraged by the prolonged ministerial crisis which was paralyzing the English Government, again crossed the frontier in force, resumed his old position as the Protector of the Spanish monarchy, and sent Vendôme, one of his ablest generals, to command the Spanish arms. Harley could do little or nothing; his hands were full with bed-chamber intrigues. He was just then putting the final touches to the elaborate Stockmarian process by which his ministry was being constructed, and was preparing for the elections that were to legitimate his power. Always dilatory and procrastinating, except when his personal feelings were strongly moved, he appears to have made, so far as can be seen, no effort at all to meet and counteract the immense exertions of Lewis. Vendôme, a man of genius capable of rising to the level of a great emergency, seized the chance presented to him with happy audacity, separated the Austrian from the English army by a bold and dexterous move, compelled the first to retreat and the second to surrender, and before the close of the same year, just as the new ministers were beginning to feel firm in their saddles and were announcing their intention "to prosecute the war in all its parts, but particularly in Spain, with the utmost vigour," he had reduced the Austrian cause to much the same condition in which it stood three years before, when the Whigs were first rising to power, and when Parliament made its memorable declaration that no peace could be accepted which left Spain to the House of Bourbon.*

It is not surprising, therefore, that after some little wavering the Government should have decided to make peace at once and on terms widely different from those which the Grand Alliance was demanding. Indeed, to straightway ask from France in the flush of her recent triumph the old conditions which she had rejected in her hour of supreme necessity was plainly impossible. Another vigorous and successful campaign—perhaps a second and a third—would be required to replace the belligerent Powers in their old position. But it might perhaps be possible to obtain new conditions, conditions less onerous to France and less favourable therefore to Europe generally, but containing such large individual concessions to England herself as might, in the eyes of patriotic Englishmen, compensate the nation for sacrificing the public objects of the war. It might perhaps be possible to complete a settlement of Europe, the principle of which should be to balance the gains left to France by corresponding gains secured to England, by extending her territories beyond the Atlantic, by giving her a strong foothold in the Mediterranean, by opening out new avenues for her commerce, and by uniting her people in profitable

* The new Parliament met November 25th. The Queen's speech, from which the above words are taken, was delivered on November 27th. On December 8th, Stanhope was surrounded at Brihuega ; and on the following day the Austrian General Staremburg, after fighting a drawn battle against great odds, was compelled to retreat into Catalonia.

intercourse with those of France and Spain. And it might be possible, too, by skilful management, to conceal the real nature of this proceeding (which could hardly recommend itself to the rest of the Confederated States) till the right time for objecting to it had gone by ; to keep the particular concerns of England entirely under her own control, without formally withdrawing them from the cognizance of the confederacy ; and to re-open the conferences on such a basis as should admit of the large modifications which would become necessary in the general concessions to be made by France to Europe, without at first disclosing that any such modifications were intended, leaving each as it seemed to arise naturally as the result of discussion in the congress, and leading the Continental Powers on to their own discomfiture step by step.

It was an ingenious and, in some of its aspects no doubt, a statesmanlike scheme, thoroughly characteristic of Harley's peculiar manner ; and it was worked out with all that misplaced and over-calculated adroitness of which he was master, which brought so many of his schemes to the verge of complete success only at the final moment to mar them. He had no desire to throw over the interests of the Dutch and of the German princes more than was absolutely needful. Just as in establishing his own power as minister he had disclaimed, and sincerely disclaimed, all intention of changing the policy of the men whom he displaced, and had even invited the chief adherents of that policy to retain office under him for the purpose of helping to carry out their common objects, so now he was anxious to promote, so far as he consistently could, the general demands, public and private, of the confederacy, subject to this condition, that when France could not be induced to grant all the Alliance wanted, they, the Continental Powers, must bear the loss ; and it was only when this part of his scheme broke down, when the instruments on which he had relied in both cases failed him—the Whig leaders spurning his humiliating offers, the Allied States refusing to play their walking parts in the tragi-comedy—that he was compelled, much against his will, to fall back upon the enemy, and to huddle up by the help of men whom he distrusted an insecure and make-shift arrangement, the dangers of which no one understood better than himself. The first condition of success was to establish by the most secret means a complete understanding with France ; and here again his course was characteristic. He had established his own power as minister in a back-stairs correspondence with Queen Anne, through the agency of a favourite waiting woman—at once an instrument adequate to his purpose and one not readily suspected by the common run of politicians. And so now, under cover of the warlike professions with which he had just met Parliament, of the engagements in which England stood pledged as a member of the confederacy, and of the formal assurances which just at this very time through his two Secretaries of State he was giving the chief Confederated Powers, that in his judgment " no peace could be safe or honourable unless the first overture came from France," he opened the same sort of clandestine intercourse with the French court.

There was at this time residing in London a man named Gaultier. He was a priest of the Romish Church, who had come over to England in 1698, in the suite of Marshal Tallard. When the embassy left, Gaultier remained behind as an unaccredited agent of the French Government, charged with delicate and peculiar functions, which were not very consistent, perhaps, with a sacred profession, but which his gown, by disarming suspicion, enabled him to perform with all the more success. Ostensibly he filled the position of chaplain to one or other of the great Catholic families. He had even contrived, such an adept was he in his calling, to obtain a confidential post in the household of Count Gallas, the imperial envoy at St. James's, so that he may be said to have served at one and the same moment both the rival kings of Spain. Gaultier was now introduced to the Government by one of his former masters, Lord Jersey, a diplomatist whose rapid advancement in the preceding reign had been due to events which have left a stain on King William's memory; for he owed his peerage and his position in the State to the frailties of his sister, as he owed the chief part of his income and the means of sustaining his new dignities to his own illicit commerce with France. Lord Jersey, a Jacobite, a pensioner of King Lewis, a near kinsman of St. John's, and an embryo cabinet minister, acquainted at once with the *corps* of French spies, then plying their trade in London, and with the desires of the Government, which he shortly afterwards joined, recommended Gaultier as a man well suited for their purpose, enjoying the confidence of the French court, a practised intriguer, able to manage a negotiation, however complicated and delicate, and, above all, "sufficiently obscure"—it was his own expression—to slip backwards and forwards across the Channel without exciting invidious remark. It was in January, 1711, hardly a month after Parliament had been opened with a speech from the throne, breathing the very spirit of the Whig foreign policy, that Gaultier, carrying the proposal of the Government to reopen on a "new footing" the negotiation of the past summer, presented himself at Versailles, and thus addressed the Chief Minister De Torcy. " Sir, do you wish for peace? If so, I bring you the means of procuring it."* It was in this same month of January that Secretary St. John, representing

* De Torcy's Memoirs, ii. 18.

this same Government, wrote these words to the Pensionary of Amsterdam: "As to peace, it seems to me that to obtain a good one we ought to observe inviolably this maxim, *never to make the first advances.*" *

The "new footing" on which the treaty was to be opened was defined and justified by St. John in letters to such of his official subordinates as it was necessary from time to time to admit into their secret.† In the preceding negotiations the allies had first settled and grouped together the various demands of the alliance, both with regard to the common interests of Europe and the special claims of individual powers, and had then pressed these preliminary terms against France with the joint weight of the whole confederacy. This plan was now to be changed. Each ally for the future was to "advance and manage his own pretensions." England, "as a recompense for bearing the burden and heat of the day," was to adjust in the first place her own particular concerns, not openly in a public congress, but by a private and secret bargain with France, through the curious agent whom Lord Jersey had selected for her; and then, but not till then, conferences were to be opened, in which, under her "mediation," the claims of the alliance generally were to be considered, and, so far as they appeared just, were to be satisfied.

It is to be observed that the "engagement under several heads" which England, as the result of nine months' clandestine diplomacy, now "exacted from France,"‡ had no reference to the real objects of the war. It related exclusively to certain private demands put forth by Great Britain for herself. It transferred to

---

* St. John to the Pensionary of Amsterdam, January, 1711 (Corr. i. 41).

† Compare St. John to Orrery, October 9 and 15, 1711; St. John to Strafford, October 12 and 19, 1711; St. John to Argyle, October 18, 1711; St. John to Peterborough, January 8, 1712.

‡ St. John to Peterborough, January 8, 1712.

Great Britain in advance territorial acquisitions and commercial privileges, which in an open treaty she would have had to share with others of the Confederated Powers; it presupposed the abandonment of the public claims, which in the face of Europe she was still maintaining; and it was based on the principle of making England in herself so strong that she could individually afford this surrender and neglect its consequences.

That she was in any manner pledged to maintain these common claims her ministers denied. They drew a distinction, necessary no doubt to the position which England was now assuming, between the engagements taken by her and the rest of the Allied Powers at the outset of the war and the subsequent modifications and developments of them, though made by the same authority and ratified with the same formalities. They held that it was not morally competent for any belligerent power during or at the close of a war to advance on the terms of peace which she had professed herself willing to accept at its commencement.* "Let me give your lordship a hint," wrote St. John some months later to one of the Queen's ambassadors abroad, puzzled to reconcile the new policy which on her part he was now required to maintain with the obligations previously contracted in her name; "let me give your lordship a hint. The eighth article of the Grand Alliance of 1701 is an engagement on the Queen. The preliminaries of 1709 are none."† In like manner they drew a distinction, equally arbitrary and equally necessary to their position, between the public rights of Europe against France before and after the overtures made by Lewis in the autumn of 1706. They

---

* Mr. Bright also laid down this doctrine, which is apparently a principle of the Manchester School, during the war with Russia in 1854.

† St. John to the Earl of Orrery, October 15, 1711.

denied that there was any longer a "common cause" binding the confederacy together. Before 1706 there had been one, no doubt. Then the reduction of the exorbitant power of France was a necessity, in which all Europe had an equal interest, and which gave the Powers of Europe a moral right to combine against her. But when in that year France abandoned her claim to the entire Spanish monarchy, when she confessed that the enterprise she was engaged in was beyond her strength, when she consented to make peace on the footing of an equal partition of her gains, from that moment the contest ceased to be just or honourable, because it ceased to be any longer necessary to maintain that balance amongst the Great Powers on which their common prosperity depended, and became instead a war of avarice, of passion, of individual ambitions, and selfish interests. In the adjusting of these it was no part of England's duty to intermeddle. "France, you may be sure, would willingly have treated with her by way of preliminary concerning the interests of the several allies." But England refused. "She will make no peace without their reasonable satisfaction ; but she contents herself with obliging France to sign such general principles as may include whatever the confederates have to demand." *

Such, as explained and defended in confidential despatches by one of the two chief negotiators, was the "new footing" on which the treaty was to be conducted. To the French court the mere suggestion of peace came as De Torcy said, "like the offer of health to a sick man ;" and they soon learnt to appreciate the merits of a plan of negotiating which left them face to face with each ally in turn, under the "mediation" of a great Power whose own demands they had privately covenanted to settle in full, but who was not to enter on the enjoyment of her pro-

---

* St. John to Orrery, October 9, 1711.

mised gains till all her confederates had had the offer of "reasonable satisfaction."

But before a complete understanding between England and France was arrived at some critical weeks were to elapse. It was only by slow degrees that the real nature of the projected arrangement was disclosed to the French court. To the first overture, therefore, knowing that time was on her side, France held back and affected an air of coyness. His most Christian majesty was in a very different position now to that of six months ago. It could not be doubted that he was well able to continue the war with honour. It was therefore no mark of weakness on his part to give further proof of his "constant desire for the repose of Europe;" and undoubtedly, after his late experience of the "persons governing the Republic of Holland" and their sentiments towards France, he should prefer to offer through England any propositions he "thought fit to make." As to matters of detail, he would see that in any treaty of peace England had a real security for the trade of her people ; he would consent to form such a barrier for Holland in the Low Countries as the Queen should approve of; he would think of all reasonable methods for giving satisfaction to the other allies ; and with respect to the Spanish monarchy itself, in which the affairs of his grandson were now in so good a condition, he would "endeavour to surmount" the difficulties that had been raised about it.

With this reply Gaultier was sent back towards the end of April. It was not very explicit. It contained, however, what the Government wanted—an offer to treat. It was, too, technically, a "first overture" from France. Nor was there in its terms anything absolutely inconsistent with perfect confidence towards the rest of the Allied Powers. It was therefore transmitted to the British

ambassador at the Hague, for the information of the Grand
Pensionary. "The Queen," wrote Secretary St. John, "resolved in making peace as in waging war to act in perfect
concert with the States, lost not a moment in transmitting
to them a paper of such importance." In its expression
it was, perhaps, "rather general;" and there was throughout an "air of complacency" towards England which St.
John regretted, but which could, he thought, "have no
ill-consequences among Powers who understood each other
so well and who acted towards each other with so little
reserve." At the same time, in a private and confidential
despatch, the British minister was warned to be carefully
on the watch "lest the States, alarmed at the whole frame
of this paper, should be put on trying underhand for themselves." *

By the middle of the summer, however, the danger of
being thus forestalled was passed. Gaultier, furnished with
new and more explicit instructions, had convinced the
French court on a point on which at first, knowing the
part she had hitherto taken, they were incredulous—that
England herself, the foremost Power of the confederacy,
the Power who had set during so many arduous years the
high example of self-sacrifice and disinterested exertions
in furtherance of their common cause, was now in the
market, and might be bought at a price not too exorbitant.
In the words of De Torcy, they now recognized the disposition of England "to facilitate a general peace to the satisfaction of all parties concerned in the war, without excepting any
one." They saw clearly that they "ran no risk in engaging
themselves in the manner proposed." Instead of demanding "more assurances on the Queen's part," instead of
threatening as at first to take advantage of "favourable
appearances in another quarter," they became desirous, nay

* Secretary St. John to Lord Raby, April 27, 1711.

"very sincerely desirous," to do all they could for the re-establishment of peace "through a Princess whose sentiments could be no longer doubted by them."[*]   And before the autumn was over, the exact sum which that Princess was to receive from Lewis in return for her services was settled, though not without some chaffering and travelling to and fro by Gaultier. On the 27th of September, nine months nearly after the first clandestine overture was made, eight preliminary articles, enumerating the terms on which England undertook to abandon the confederacy and " mediate," as her ministers put it, between France and Europe, were signed in London, on behalf of the two Bourbon Princes, by Mesnager, a deputy of the Paris Chamber of Commerce, who had been previously employed by France in the negotiations, and on the Queen's part by her two Secretaries of State.

The scene in the Privy Council when this engagement was being contracted, the trepidation exhibited by some of the less conspicuous ministers, their efforts to find a pretext for putting off the irrevocable moment, and the anxiety of the two Secretaries of State to have the Queen's authority in black and white before setting their names on her behalf to this compromising paper, made a deep impression on the French envoy. My Lord Dartmouth, as the highest in rank and a peer of the realm, signed first. In these transactions he played the part of Lepidus to St. John's Marc Anthony. One can fancy the pleasant smile and graceful air of deference with which his younger colleague would hand him the pen.

> " For though we cast these honours on this man
>   To ease ourselves of divers slanderous loads,
>   He doth but bear them as the ass bears gold ;
>   And having brought our treasure where we will,
>   Then take we down his load, and turn him off
>   To shake his ears and graze on commons."

---

[*] Memorial from France, brought back by Gaultier, August, 1711.

At the same time another set of preliminaries, intended for communication to the Powers of Europe and to " serve as an inducement to the allies to enter a congress," was signed by Mesnager alone. It was drawn up in the most general terms, ostensibly as containing " all that ever was or that ever could be demanded," really as concealing under vague generalities the surrender which England meditated ; and it made no mention of the private arrangement which she had just concluded for herself. St. John called it "the paper for Holland." *

It is right to remember that Shrewsbury, who preserved in all his wanderings some regard for his own dignity and some self-respect, took no part in these negotiations, and when the arrangement made with France was first explained to him protested against it. He did not indeed, as he confesses, thoroughly understand its principle ; but he saw enough to show him that the two leading ministers, in their eagerness to obtain peace in the readiest way, and on the most favourable conditions, were really playing France's game, were putting in the hands of France a two-edged weapon, which, if the general negotiation should take a turn unfavourable to her, might be used against England herself with fatal effect. In a remarkable letter addressed to St. John in the August of this year, when the clandestine engagement binding together the two nations was still in draft, he expressed his grave doubts as to the trustworthiness of France; he reminded his young colleague how difficult it was to keep an affair of this sort long concealed ; and he warned him how extremely ill the transacton would look if published to the world at large, as if the Queen, so little notice having been taken of the interests of the allies, had no consideration but of what

* De Torcy's Memoirs, ii. 157 ; St. John to Queen Anne, September 27, 1711 ; St. John to Lord Peterborough, January 8, 1712.

concerned Great Britain, and having settled that with France "would leave her friends to shift for themselves at a general treaty, in which her partiality might be liable to suspicion, since she had beforehand stipulated so many things for herself."* And in a second letter, written some days later, he added that "looking over the paper again" only confirmed his previous impression that, if it should ever be the interest of France (as it would always be in her power) to disclose it to the allies, it would "create great jealousy and just complaint." But Shrewsbury had not the courage of his opinions ; and neither his private remonstrances nor the nervous agitation which, courtier and diplomatist as he was, he was quite unable to hide when Mesnager, with the secret preliminaries in his hand, was introduced before the council, had power to arrest his two colleagues in the course they meditated. They were "not to be frightened, vexed, or diverted from their measures by any suspicions which might be entertained of them or by any clamour which might be raised against them." †

IV.

But in order to carry through the ministerial project, something more was necessary than a secret understanding with France. "When I undertook," wrote Bolingbroke afterwards, characteristically arrogating to himself the sole merit of the achievement—"when I undertook, in opposition to all the confederates, in opposition to a powerful turbulent faction at home, in opposition even to those habits of thinking which mankind had contracted by the same wrong principle of government pursued for twenty

* Shrewsbury to St. John, August 27, 1711.
† St. John to Drummond, September 4, 1711.

years, to make a peace, the utmost vigour and resolution became necessary." * That *confiance reciproque* on which, in this same month of September, De Torcy congratulated the English minister, was a confidence confined to the two courts in which as yet the respective nations had no share. Not the least of the many difficulties which at this time surrounded the Government, and which called forth its vigour and resolution, arose from the general belief that the war, whatever might be its burdens, was a just and necessary war ; that the objects sought to be obtained by it were essential to the prosperity and greatness of England; and that those objects might be best secured by earnest co-operation and mutual forbearance amongst the States engaged in it ;—that it was in fact, just what the Government denied, a war *pro aris et foci*, where no expense or endeavour could be too great, because all the nation valued was at stake upon it ; where the shortcomings of other Powers, if such there were, ought to be met, not by similar and proportional defalcations on England's part, but by redoubled exertions.

And if this was the general feeling about the war, the notion of importing into it the principle of limited liability, of confining the share of England in its operations, whether military or diplomatic, to such efforts as should best recoup her by lucrative acquisitions for the expenses she was incurring, was not likely to recommend itself to the nation. No sustained spirit of enthusiasm was ever kindled, as Burke justly says, in favour of a war of calculation. In 1705 the two rival policies, the insular and the cosmopolitan, had been submitted to the constituent bodies, and they had answered in clear and resolute terms. In the present Parliament the Tories once more outnumbered the Whigs ; but the elections had turned almost exclusively

* St. John to Lord Strafford, April 8, 1712.

on the question of the Church and its ancient privileges. The uneasy doubt how far their plan of making peace at the cost of Germany instead of France would be accepted even by their own supporters was always present with the two leading ministers. It was this doubt more, perhaps, than any natural propensity to crooked ways which led them into the mazes of dissimulation, trickery, intrigue, and falsehood, in which they enveloped and tried to conceal all their diplomatic proceedings. It was this doubt which led them, in their parliamentary declarations, to disclaim all intention of separating England from the rest of the allies, with whom they were at that very moment, they would say, * concerting the means of pressing on the war with vigour; and it was this doubt which led them, in the public instructions afterwards addressed to the British plenipotentiaries at Utrecht, to lay down as a principle of the negotiation that England, in common with the whole confederacy, could sanction no settlement which left Spain or the Spanish West Indies in possession of the Bourbons, though the elaborate engagement which they had just secretly contracted with France was all based on the assumption that Spain and the West Indies should be retained by a Bourbon prince.

But what he calls "vigour" and "resolution," though sometimes wanting to St. John himself, was seldom long absent from the policy of his great leader. It has been said of Walpole by an eminent modern statesman, that he consolidated the throne of the House of Hanover by means of the rotten boroughs. In like manner it may be said of Harley, that he dissolved the confederacy of the Grand Alliance and re-established the ascendency of

* "I think," writes St. John to Lord Strafford, then representing the Queen at the Hague—"I think your excellency ought to *affect to press* the Dutch, the Imperialists, and all the other enemies of peace, to exert themselves and prepare for the next campaign."

the Bourbons in Western Europe by means of a venal press. To Harley belongs the credit of inventing the newspaper editor as an instrument of party government. In an age when public meetings were unknown, when the platform orator was yet unborn, and when no report of what took place in Parliament was ever suffered to pass the walls, the country could be enlightened on public questions only by means of pamphlets, broadsheets, and periodical leader-writing. In such an age, a ready and skilful penman was, as Harley saw, at least as useful a servant of party as a trained debater ; for it was by such a man alone that a political party could address the masters of that body which the Revolution had elevated into the chief authority in the State. In the latter part of the same century, when the proceedings of the House of Commons had been opened to the public gaze, and when the system of nomination boroughs was in its fullest vigour, public speaking became the art in which a young adventurer, ambitious of public distinction, sought to excel; and the age was, as might naturally be expected, pre-eminently fertile in parliamentary talents. The time of Queen Anne, on the other hand, was the golden age of essayists and pamphleteers. The writing of political tracts paid for by private subscription, issued at a nominal charge, and industriously dispersed about the streets and coffee-houses, rose to the dignity of a profession. Men who attained to skill in their calling were assured of a considerable livelihood; and the masters of the craft associated on equal terms with the leaders of party. Every great minister of State, every rising opposition leader, sought to surround himself with a body-guard of literary parasites, men who derived their nourishment and subsistence from clinging round him, and whose protecting arms were necessary to his comfort and satisfaction. The owner of a telling style, in fact, was courted by both the rival factions. He had a cover daily at some great man's table. When his patron came to power, a place was found for him in the customs or the stamp office, or a pension charged upon the public revenues. Sometimes he was made a lord of treasury, or an under-secretary of state; but whatever might be the nature of his ostensible employment, he earned his quarterly stipend, not by the routine work of his office desk, which he commonly neglected, but by pleading the cause of his patrons before the country, generally from instructions which they furnished and in works which they revised.

Foremost among the public writers connected with Government by these strictly business ties was Swift. Swift, like Prior, like Rowe, like Parnell, like most of the pressmen enlisted in Harley's service, had hitherto passed for a Whig. All his early associations bound him to the Whig party. His first livings had been procured for him by a Whig lord lieutenant. His first political tract he had written for the purpose of recommending himself to the impeached Whig lords. His first satire, " The cause of all my woes," he had dedicated to the chief of those statesmen in terms of adulation. He had been admitted into the Whig society, which met at the Lord President's table in Lincoln's Inn Fields, and at Halifax's country villa at Hampton Court; and his well-known figure with its shabby cassock and pudding sleeves was as familiar at the St. James's coffee-house as the tye-wig of Addison. But the Whigs were to Swift what the Tories were to Harley—instruments to be used for his own purposes, not friends and companions with whose objects he was in sympathy. He was before all things a Churchman and a politician only so far as politics affected the Church and his own position in the Church. The ecclesiastical policy of the Whig chiefs, their plan of raising up other Protestant sects into equality with the Anglican communion, was bitterly distasteful to him. He held, like the orthodox country rector, that they were "enemies" of the Church ; nor is it any disparagement to the sincerity of this belief that it grew up side by side with the conviction that whilst the Whigs remained in power he had personally little chance of preferment in it.

And Swift certainly desired preferment. We are told that the Arabian traveller, as he toils through the burning sand, is haunted by the sight of shady woods and pleasant murmuring streams ; and even so had Swift in his Irish exile, reading the services of an alien Church to half a score parishioners, always before his eyes the vision of some trim cathedral close and the coveted mitre, which always receded, alas, and vanished at his approach. "Pray, my lord," he writes to Halifax—"pray, my lord, desire Dr. South to die about the fall of the leaf; for he has a prebend of Westminster which will make me your neighbour and a sinecure in the country, both in the Queen's gift, which my friends have often told me would fit me extremely well." And some months later, in a letter to the same dispenser of patronage, after a characteristic lament over this "gentle winter," which did not "carry off Dr. South," he beseeches his correspondent "to use his credit with my Lord Somers, that as he thought of me last year for the Bishopric of Waterford, so he may now think of me for that of Cork, *if the incumbent dies of the spotted fever he is now under.*" * The Whigs had made some attempts to serve him ; though Halifax, in answer

---

* Swift to Halifax, June 13th and November 13, 1709. "Dr. South's prebend and sinecure" reappear in several of Swift's letters, and seem to have been much in his thoughts. It was a strange irony of fate which kept the venerable prebendary and sinecurist (then upwards of eighty) alive till 1716, when all chance of preferment for poor Swift was gone for ever.

to Swift's reiterated appeals, politely confesses himself " ashamed to see you left in a place so incapable of tasting you." But they were in power barely two years. They knew that Swift was not, as he himself expressed it, " thorough in their designs." They were not disposed to put to hazard their scanty credit at court for the purpose of advancing a divine who had rendered them no particular service, whom the Queen and her favourite archbishop heartily disliked, and who was on the chief domestic question of the day a strong political opponent. Swift seems to have confined his hopes at last almost entirely to the Irish establishment, that refuge for damaged reputations of more than one kind. His name was sent in for promotion to the lord lieutenant; but Wharton, amongst whose numerous faults religious bigotry had no place, and who was bent on obtaining for the Irish Presbyterians that perfect toleration which the Irish bishops were equally bent on denying them, pretended to be scrupulous. He knew that Swift was the secret adviser of his most formidable assailants, and refused to make such a man his chaplain, giving as his reason, doubtless with a laugh and a curse, that he had " not character enough himself" to bear the odium of such an appointment. Swift never forgot that remark. Of all the Whig leaders none suffered more at his hands than the " universal villain " Wharton.

In the autumn of 1710, when every morning was bringing news of the fall of some great minister, Swift, with anger in his heart against the Whigs, came up to London as part of a deputation from the Irish bishops. He was introduced to the new Prime Minister as a man " discontented with his position." In his correspondence he has left us an amusingly *naïve* and graphic account of this famous interview: his delight at finding that Harley had not forgotten his Christian name; the bowing and complimenting which took place when he was presented to St. John and Harcourt; the readiness with which his new friends at once procured for him the wished-for donative to the Irish Church, with an intimation to the two bishops who were his colleagues that the favour had been granted "on a memorial from Dr. Swift;" and finally, when Swift "knew not what to make" of all this overwhelming courtesy, Harley's confession of the difficulty in which his Government stood—"the want of some good pen" to explain their objects and justify their policy—and his offer to "establish Swift in England" if he would join them. In an evil hour for his fortunes, though not perhaps for his fame, Swift consented. He became a sort of standing counsel to the two leading ministers.* To give him his due, he was not consulted about their most questionable proceedings. He knew nothing definite about the peace negotiations till the secret preliminaries were on the eve of being signed. He was never made privy at all, so far as can be seen, to their intrigues with St. Germains. He was treated, indeed, when the first freshness of their intercourse had worn off, with little consideration, though always with the outward show of deference which it pleased him to exact and amused them to render. His function was to communicate between ministers and the public, to dress up into the best literary form such facts and arguments as they could give him, and when he had no case to abuse the plaintiff's attorney. Swift's sudden conversion caused, as might be expected, some talk in the coffee-houses. But to accuse him of ratting is to misconceive altogether the

---

* Mr. Forster calls him a "minister without a portfolio." But this is altogether an inflated idea of Swift's position. He had no more influence in *framing* the Government policy than Mr. Delane had over Lord Palmerston's; and his biographers have done Swift's moral character no service by the attempt unduly to exalt his political authority. Would Harley have offered a banknote to a minister without a portfolio?

nature of his connection both with the Whigs whom he left and with the Tories whom he joined. His offence, if an offence at all, resembled a breach of professional etiquette rather than of public morals. As well might young George Canning have been accused of ratting because, when fresh from Eton, after coquetting with the Whig borough managers, he "turned his jacket," as the wit said, at the offer of a seat from Pitt. To men like Canning and Lyndhurst, the adventurers of a different age, who looked to the close borough system for their introduction to public life, and who regarded the possession of office as the test of success in public life, politics was a profession, a means of livelihood and advancement; and such men choose their side in politics for professional reasons, as a lawyer chooses his circuit or a doctor the district he shall practise in, frankly confessing their mistake when fees don't come. It was the same in their generation with Prior and Swift.*

Swift was now called upon to perform the greatest service ever rendered to an English Government by a man

---

* In the pleasant days of our ancestors a strict attention to the duties by which a Church dignitary earned his income was not rigorously exacted. Bishop Watson of Llandaff, for instance, one of the most estimable of men, spent his long episcopate at Windermere in agricultural pursuits. But this privilege of choosing your own occupations and place of residence was not, it would seem, extended willingly to a mere parish clergyman ; and Swift's long absence from the scene of his parochial functions caused, as we know, much murmuring. From August, 1710, to June, 1713, he never set foot in Ireland, and then only for a week or two to take possession of a new prefer- ment, a visit immediately followed by another twelve months' absence. He kept, it is true, a curate ; and the number of his parishioners did not exceed, as he tells us, "half a score." But he drew from the revenues of the Irish Church, his duties in which he thus systematically neglected, an income which was equivalent at the lowest estimate to some £700 a-year of our money, and which Scott puts at nearer £1200. He might well turn up his nose at Harley's offer of £50. In his journal there is an amusing story of Swift's embarrassment one day at court when a young Irish gentleman interrupted his conversation with some great minister by the malicious inquiry, "Pray, doctor, when shall we see you again in the county of Meath?"

I

of letters. In November, 1711, six weeks after the secret preliminaries had been signed, whilst the States of the confederacy were still doubtful as to the propriety of entering a congress on the base proposed, and whilst the public was still, as he complains, "half bewitched" against a peace,—at the end of November, the meeting of Parliament being three times postponed to allow the utmost care to be bestowed on the work, and its statements with the conclusions founded on them to sink deeply into the public mind, appeared Swift's political masterpiece, "The Conduct of the Allies."

In the preparation of this work, which was designed, in the words of Bolingbroke, to "inflame the nation with a desire of peace by showing in the most public and solemn manner how unequally it was burthened and unfairly treated" in the war,[*] Swift had, indeed, all the assistance which his new patrons could give him.   Lord Dartmouth's office and secretaries were placed at his disposal.   St. John, though overwhelmed with business, gave up many days and nights to arranging with him the best way of marshalling its train of arguments.   The Prime Minister himself revised each sheet as it progressed, made many "small additions and alterations," and suggested one of the bitter mottoes which adorned the title-page.   When the book was finished, it was again sent round in manuscript amongst the three or four leading ministers, "in order to be quite sure it contained no errors" in the complicated matters of fact.

Nor is the little tract unworthy of the care bestowed on it, and of the great and various talents brought to bear on its production.   In spite of Johnson's adverse criticism, it is the best example of Swift's serious style, and the most plausible extant statement of their case as presented by

---

[*] ii. 481.

ministers. Taking up the line of argument which St. John had already laid down for him in a short and trenchant letter to the *Examiner*, Swift begins by assuming that the war was, on the part of all the Powers engaged in it, what Burke calls a war of calculation; that it had its origin in a family quarrel between the rival houses of Hapsburg and Bourbon about a disputed property; and that the chief continental Powers had joined in it, not from any interest in the matter itself, but as a cover for predatory schemes of their own: Prussia, for example, to annex Guelderland and to obtain the recognition of her royal title; Holland to absorb the trade of the Spanish Netherlands; Portugal in return for commercial advantages promised to her by England; most of the rest "purely for subsidies," in exchange for which they gave as little help as possible. Such being the origin and such the purpose of the war, each Power thus entering into it for a different and personal motive and hoping to get from it a different and personal result, it followed, according to Swift, that no State ought to have taken upon itself a larger burden than its own objects and its own hopes would justify; and conversely, that if one Power had from an imprudent and romantic generosity contributed with the knowledge of its neighbours more than its proper share to the victory, it had a perfect right to claim, as against its neighbours, more than its proper share of the spoil. Yet in the terms of peace demanded by the allies at the Hague and at Gertruydenburg, this principle had been neglected; nay, it had been expressly reversed. The Powers which had done least to bring about the victorious result absorbed the whole of the advantages won by it; whilst the Power on whom the burden of the day had fallen, the Power whose lot it had been to supply the deficient quotas of all the allies in turn, found, after bribing her confederates round

to fight out their quarrels, that she had expended this
labour and submitted to these sacrifices with no reward
whatever. What was England to gain by giving Spain
to the Austrians and Flanders to the Dutch? England's
personal motive in first fanning the disturbance had been
to wreak her vengeance on the King of France for recognizing a pretender as her king; and her personal object in
declaring war, the only British interest at all involved, was
the prospect of making conquests in the Spanish West
Indies—a prospect on which the allies of England, with
the connivance of the ministers of England, when they set
up an Austrian claimant for the entire Spanish monarchy,
deliberately shut the door. " Surely no nation was ever so
much abused by the folly, corruption, and ambition of its
domestic enemies, or treated with so much insolence,
injustice, and ingratitude by its foreign friends." "Against
all manner of prudence or common reason we engage in
this war as principals when we ought to have acted only as
auxiliaries. We spend all our vigour in pursuing that part
of the war which could least answer the end we proposed
by beginning it, and make no effort at all where we could
have most weakened the common enemy and at the same
time most enriched ourselves. And we suffer each of our
allies to break every article in those treaty engagements
by which they were bound, and lay the burden upon us."

It is impossible to exaggerate the effect produced and
the service rendered by the publication of this tract.
Written with simple eloquence, presenting throughout its
course an unbroken chain of argument in which—granting
the author's premiss—no flaw could be detected, and
enlivened here and there with a touch of his peculiar
humour, it had the merit of bringing an abstruse political
question down to the level of the plainest understanding.
It was disseminated with the utmost industry by the

agents of Government. The first edition was all exhausted in a couple of days; the second in five hours; the third and fourth within the week. By the end of the year, a month after its first appearance, it was computed that eleven thousand copies had passed into some reader's hand; and its author relates in his correspondence with pardonable complacency how nothing of the kind had ever made so many converts; how, in the debates that followed, all the Government orators drew their arguments from it; how "every one agreed it was my book" which spirited up the court to its severe resolutions against the allies; and how, on the return of peace, the first ambassador accredited to St. James's by the Bourbon King of Spain, on reaching London, "asked to be presented to Dr. Swift," as the man to whom "in all Europe" his royal master and the most Christian King were most indebted.* For it was not in elaborate leaders and pamphlets only, but in the most ludicrous squibs and lampoons, both prose and verse, in ribald ballads, in Grub Street parodies, in virulent anonymous libels which, if coming from the stall of an opposition printer, would have caused that unlucky wretch to exhibit himself in the pillory with his back flayed and his ears shorn off, that this successor of the apostles, by way of earning the mitre that he coveted, furthered the scheme of his new patrons, reiterated the charges brought against his old patrons of corruption and embezzlement, insinuated that their whole policy, foreign and domestic, had been prompted by sordid necessities and family ambitions; appealing even in his gravest arguments to the lowest passions of his readers—their envy of superior greatness, their distrust of personal disinterestedness, their narrow patriotism and insular jealousy of foreign Powers—

* Swift to Esther Johnson, October 18, 1712. "I took it very well of him," is Swift's comment.

with an entire freedom from scruples of conscience or
honesty, but with a profound knowledge of their temper,
and a command of literary gifts which make his tracts,
even when the interest of their subject matter has died
out, amongst the pleasantest reading in the world.

V.

To return to the state of the negotiations at the time
when the secret preliminaries were signed, and when the
assistance of Swift was invoked for the purpose of preparing the mind of the nation for peace on new conditions.

England, still a member of the Grand Alliance, pledged
by its terms to enter into no engagements with France
except "jointly and in concert" with her allies, pledged
also to co-operate with her allies for certain common
objects not to be changed without the general consent of
the whole confederacy, had, as we have seen, established,
without the knowledge of her confederates, a secret understanding with the French court through the agency of
a Catholic priest employed by France as a spy; and by
this engagement she had contracted, in consideration of
certain "particular advantages" to be secured to her by
France, to "mediate," as her ministers phrased it, between
France and the alliance, to press upon the alliance the
policy of consenting to general terms of peace "inferior
to those formerly demanded," to leave in the hands of
France, that is to say, as much as possible of the spoils
which her own somewhat unscrupulous diplomacy had
won for her, and out of which the chief part of these
"particular advantages" were to come. It was much as
though the principal partner in some great commercial
firm, with a doubtful debt upon its books, should privately
covenant with the defaulting customer that, on being

secretly paid his own share of the debt in full with a substantial bonus, he would undertake to use his influence with the firm and prevail on his fellow-partners to remit a considerable percentage of their joint claim.

It is to be remarked that the clandestine intercourse between England and France which resulted in this understanding did not come to an end when the secret preliminaries, which formed the conditions of peace as regarded England, were signed, and when the public conferences for the general settlement of Europe were sitting. On the contrary, down to the final conclusion of the definitive treaties eighteen months later, there were always two distinct negotiations on foot: a *sham* negotiation, conducted in the face of Europe by recognized diplomatists, and having for its object the restoration of peace to Europe on conditions satisfactory to the victorious alliance—a negotiation in which England appeared ostensibly as a part of the great European confederacy against France; and a *real* negotiation, studiously hidden from the eyes of Europe, conducted through subterranean channels by men travelling under disguises and bearing assumed names,* having for its object to impose on Europe conditions of peace satisfactory to France and England alone—a negotiation in which England had contracted in fact a close alliance with France, through which she informed France from time to time of the demands to be made upon her, concerted with France the best means of evading them, made France privy to every communication that passed between her own and the allied ambassadors, and in one case sent France a copy of instructions privately furnished to her own commanders at a critical point of the campaign.

* Gaultier was not very well known to the public, but to make assurance doubly sure he passed in these transactions as M. Delorme.

So skilfully, however, and with such judgment had the affair been managed, that before the opening of the conferences, and indeed for some time afterwards, the Dutch and the German princes, though full of indignation against England, had not begun to suspect her good faith. That England of her own motion was concerting general preliminaries of peace with France; that she was extremely anxious to force her allies into the acceptance of pre-liminary conditions approved of by herself alone; and that the method of negotiating which she favoured, on a basis drawn up as loosely as possible so as to leave each State free to manage its own pretensions in the con-ference, would inevitably result in a diplomatic triumph for France and Spain, influenced as they were by one counsel and moved by one will, and in a diplomatic failure for the confederacy, with its diverse and in some cases conflicting interests;—all this was clear to them. But they appear to have attributed her actions not to deliberate treachery, but rather to the ignorance of parliamentary ministers as to the best mode of conducting a foreign negotiation, and to the anxiety of party politicians to strike out something new, something that should dis-tinguish their policy from that of their domestic rivals. Of the real object of the clandestine intercourse between Great Britain and France, of the real nature of the illicit understanding formed between them, of the fact that England had already secured for herself by sinister arts all that she now cared to get from the war, and would enter the open conferences in which the rights of the alliance were to be determined with the bribe of France and Spain in her pockets, anxious only to huddle up an agreement of some sort and be free to turn their promissory engagements into cash,—of these things the Great Powers were ignorant.

It is true that in the preceding summer an incident had happened which might have shown them that something more than vague general preliminaries was being negotiated. The blood money, in return for which England was to deliver over the confederacy to Lewis, consisted in part of large commercial privileges to be granted to her by the two Bourbon Princes in the event of Spain and the West Indies being allotted to them in the treaties of peace; and in settling the details of these, Gaultier, single-handed, would have been no match for the French negotiators. It was necessary to associate an Englishman with him; and for this duty was selected one of the few great English writers who have combined with literary pre-eminence a practical familiarity with affairs and a distinguished place in the world of business and diplomacy.

Matthew Prior, the greatest master of what a brother poet has called the "familiar style" in English verse, furnishes perhaps the most striking instance, even in an age so fertile in such instances, of the power of a keen wit and lively pen to raise their possessor, in spite of every natural disadvantage, to the highest worldly honours. An adventurer of mean birth and sordid life, a Bohemian in all his habits and his tastes, a man whose favourite haunt was a tavern parlour, his favourite companion a common soldier's wife, he won by virtue of his delightful gift of song-writing a post for which the princely Hamilton stooped to intrigue, and which the fastidious Shrewsbury deigned to covet—the blue riband of English diplomacy, the embassy to the court of the most Christian King. Prior, however, was excellently qualified to supply Gaultier's deficiencies. He was perfectly master of the whole history of the negotiations. More than twenty years before, when fresh from college, he had accompanied King William to the Hague at the time when

the original Grand Alliance was constructed. He had
been secretary to the British Plenipotentiaries at Ryswick
in the congress which closed the first half of the great
war. He had formed part of Portland's retinue when in the
following year he visited Paris as ambassador, had penned
the momentous despatch which opened the long negotiations
touching the partition of the Spanish monarchy, and had
been secretary to the British legation when the treaties
of 1698 and 1700 were finally signed. Since the outbreak
of the war he had been a Commissioner of Trade and
Plantations. As such he had become practically familiar
with those commercial interests of Great Britain which
were made the chief object of the negotiators in arranging
terms of peace. "Of all your Majesty's subjects who have
been trusted with this secret," wrote St. John to Queen
Anne, "Mr. Prior is the best versed in all matters of trade."
Unluckily, the cloak and the dark lanthorn part of the
business was not in Prior's line. In the art of eluding
the vigilance of curious eyes he was less successful than
the supple French priest his colleague. Perhaps his lank
figure did not lend itself easily to the disguises he was
forced to wear. Be this as it may, in one of his journeys
across the Channel, eager to fulfil all the instructions of
his employers, but too much occupied perhaps with high
questions of commerce and diplomacy for that minute
and careful study of histrionic detail which is necessary to
subdue rough art into the semblance of artless nature,
Prior concealed himself from observation with such melo-
dramatic completeness as to arouse the suspicion of the
coastguard-men, who thought, from his air of elaborate
mystery, that he must be engaged in some nefarious project.
He was seized and interrogated, forgot in his confusion the
"alias" he was travelling under, and made replies which
the papers found upon him contradicted. He was lodged

in gaol on charge of being a smuggler. As fast as post horses could travel, the order for his release came down from Whitehall, not without a sharp reprimand doubtless for the too zealous officers of revenue. Happily, newspaper correspondents and "special telegrams" were in that age unknown, and without much difficulty, by the help of a lively *jeu d'esprit* from Swift, suspicion was turned aside till the matter was forgotten.

It was in July that this mishap befel Prior. In October the general preliminaries were formally communicated to the Allied Powers. They were formally summoned to a public conference; and they were distinctly told that England would make no arrangements for a new campaign unless they consented to treat for peace on the conditions proposed. Then followed three months of anxious suspense, three months occupied by Government in endeavouring to soothe the exasperated confederates, in endeavouring to prepare for the storm certain to burst upon them when Parliament met, and in endeavouring to convince the French court how much the Queen's difficulties would be lessened if she were taken fully into their confidence and "empowered separately to offer to the allies what might be reasonable for each to accept." * All the Great Powers formally protested against the course which England was taking. The Austrian minister denounced her proceedings as an "enigma." † The Hanoverian minister delivered a "strong memorial" against them on the part of the parliamentary heir. The minister of the Duke of Savoy expressed more gently his master's "discontent and dissatisfaction." The States-General, dimly conscious that they were betrayed, but not yet fathoming in its lowest

---

* St. John to De Torcy, October, 1711.

† "With the natural impertinence of a German," writes St. John, "improved by conversation with a saucy English faction."

deep the turpitude of their old ally, sent a special embassy
to London under the Pensionary of Amsterdam to convey
their remonstrances to the Queen in person, and to represent to her advisers that this plan of opening a congress,
with nothing settled beforehand as to the demands to be
made upon the common enemy, and of letting loose all the
divergent interests of the belligerents to be wrangled about
in public, with the common enemy looking on ready to
take advantage of every symptom of disagreement, was
fatal to all hope of a safe and durable peace. "At any
rate, let the capital point of all, the destination of Spain
and the Indies, be made the subject of some previous
consultation."

Meanwhile a copy of the general preliminaries offered
by France had found its way into the columns of a London
journal; and the public, ignorant of the double game
ministers were playing, unaware that the interests of
England had been fully considered in a separate and secret
paper, was left to compare these seven articles, drawn up
in terms intentionally vague and misleading, with the
elaborate conditions in which, before the congress of the
Hague, in order to avert the risk of embarrassing public
discussions amongst them, the demands of the allies had
been formulated with the utmost clearness and precision.
Nor were the opposition leaders behindhand in turning
to their own advantage the discontent thus roused, in
inflaming it by every artifice of factious ingenuity, and
in directing it against the weak parts of the ministerial
position. Amongst the friends of Government symptoms
of panic began to show themselves. Shrewsbury had
been chosen by his colleagues to represent them at the
conference; but, till the negotiations were more advanced
he refused to take part in them. Lord Dartmouth, we
are told, "altogether despaired," and was for at once

resigning.* His under-secretary, Erasmus Lewis, a man high in the confidence of his chiefs, made all the preparations for retiring to his seat in Carmarthenshire. It was currently reported that Nottingham, irritated at his exclusion from office, had gone over to the Whigs; that Somerset was actively caballing with them; and that these two great peers, with the Queen's full approval, had laid the foundations of a new ministry, of which Somers was to be the chief, and which was to be based on the principle of maintaining the old obligations of England. Prior, even, a very shrewd observer, thought the game was up; and Swift, in the greatest distress of mind, implored that he might be "sent abroad somewhere as Queen's secretary" till the storm blew over, and he could steal back to his Irish living secure from the vengeance of the men he had traduced.

But at this turning point of its fortunes, Government was rescued from what to its strongest supporters seemed imminent destruction by the most conspicuous instance of that mingled audacity and adroitness which Harley, when driven to bay, hardly ever failed to exhibit. Amidst all these quaking counsels the minister remained firm. He laughed at Swift's terrors, assured him that "all would still be well," advised him not to spend so much of his time with Lewis, a fellow with the "heart of a chicken and soul of a mite." And before many days had passed, the colleagues most jealous of his ascendency and most prone to decry his high qualities were forced to confess that they had underrated their leader's energy and resource. "An entire turn was made," wrote St. John to Lord Strafford,† "in favour of those who had obeyed the Queen and to render her servants safe in the execution of her

* Swift to Esther Johnson, December 19, 1711.
† St. John to Strafford, December 12, 1711.

commands." The Whig pamphleteers had commented
on their proceedings with characteristic plainness of speech.
They were attacked with prosecutions for libel; and in
a single morning fourteen Whig printers and booksellers
were sent to prison on St. John's warrant alone. The
offence of publishing the general preliminaries had been
traced to the Austrian minister. He was forbidden the
court, and a peremptory demand for his recall was forwarded
to Vienna. Somerset, in spite of the Queen's reluctance,
was removed from his place in the Royal Household.
The Batavian envoy was roughly told "what a vain thing
it was to imagine" that his representations could alter the
Queen's resolutions. Parliament had been three times
prorogued to allow Swift's attack on the German princes
to produce its effect on the mind of members. When
at length the two Houses met, the House of Lords, then
a small, highly considered assembly in which parties were
very evenly balanced, and which bore much the same
relation to the House of Commons as the American Senate
of our time bears to the Representative Chamber, passed,
on the motion of Nottingham, and with the support of
Somerset and Marlborough, a resolution censuring in
advance the change of policy on which Government had
privately determined. But the minister was equal to the
occasion. It was "swamped" by the creation of twelve
new peers, chosen out of his personal following, and so
unanimous in support of his measures that Wharton
suggested they should "speak through their foreman."
In the House of Commons the minister had already a
majority. It was there that he "made his dispositions for
attacking." A Parliamentary Representation, purporting
to confirm, as after an impartial investigation, the facts on
which their change of policy had been founded, but really
based on Swift's *ex parte* statement, and drawn up partly

by himself and partly by St. John, was carried on the motion of a private member ; and the answer put forth by the Dutch Government was suppressed, its printer sent to gaol, its sale prohibited under stringent penalties.

These were "strong remedies." "Pray God," wrote Swift anxiously, "the patient is able to bear them."* And a stronger was behind, one on which Harley, bold as he was, could not have ventured unless he had determined to make peace on his own terms and at the earliest moment. The past year's campaign had been distinguished by perhaps the most brilliant of all Marlborough's exploits, the passing of the famous lines joining the Scheld to the Scarpe and Ugy, which the French commanders had fortified with all their technical skill and pronounced impregnable. Adequately and cordially supported by the home Government, there is little doubt that he would have then concluded the war by forcing on Lewis at Versailles the stringent conditions which the royal envoys had rejected at Gertruydenburg. Even as it was, libelled daily in the ministerial press, sneered at in public despatches, harassed in his domestic relations, his army fatally weakened by the withdrawal of troops for objects which he disapproved and which signally failed, he had out-generalled, without losing a man, by the mere force of superior strategy, the ablest of Lewis's marshals, and turned the vaunted *non plus ultra* of Villars into a base of operations for an assault on his master's capital. But Marlborough had both spoken and voted in favour of Nottingham's motion ; and ministers were determined to show that "no riches, no grandeur, no merit could save any one who set himself up in resistance to their designs."† He was cashiered. A charge of peculation was brought against him, was pushed on

* Swift to Stella, December 31, 1711.
† St. John to Strafford, January 27, 1712.

till their object was gained, and then quietly dropped ; and in the meantime, "in order that the matter might receive an impartial investigation," * he was dismissed from all his places.

These bold strokes, which if repeated on the eve of the Queen's death might have restored the ancient line and saved the Tory party, beat off their domestic assailants for a while, and left ministers free to deal with the refractory States of Europe. The conferences were opened at Utrecht. The Bishop of Bristol and the Earl of Strafford were commissioned to represent Great Britain. But still the same system of deception was carried on ; and in . truth the position of Government, though improved by the vigour of its domestic policy, was even yet extremely critical. The Whig writers " would not be quiet." " They had a genius," says Swift,† "levelled to the generality of their readers ; " and—the Chief Justice being unfortunately a Whig—they " get out on bail. We take them up again, and then they get fresh bail and write on, and so the game goes round." The House of Lords, too, in spite of all efforts to swamp it, continued restive and unmanageable. The House of Commons, though so largely composed of the friends of Government, was not perfectly sound on the question of a " peace without Spain ; " whilst the general feeling of the country, what St. John calls its " reviving love of war," was unmistakably displayed when, after the formal opening of the congress, the specific proposals made by France to the alliance were at length disclosed. When, therefore, on the motion of Halifax, a formal address to the Queen was proposed on behalf

---

* *London Gazette,* December 31, 1711. Even Swift doubted whether in this case the surgeon's knife was not cutting too deep. " I cannot approve," he writes (December 31), " of this step, and do not love to see personal resentment mix with public áffairs."

† Works, v. 301.

of the Whig peers, expressing "their utmost resentment at the terms of peace offered to her and her allies by France," * the minister, not venturing to divide against it, affected to share their surprise and indignation ; and in the public instructions addressed to the two British envoys at Utrecht, they were directed to "insist" that the "real security expected by Europe and promised by France could not be obtained if Spain or the Spanish West Indies were allotted to any branch of the House of Bourbon."

The evident reluctance of Parliament to abandon, without further struggle, the great public objects of the war, had the effect, however, of inducing the Government to reconsider the scheme of their projected treaty. The main question at issue, the succession to Spain and its American colonies, had been complicated by two events : the accession of the Austrian claimant to the Imperial throne, and the successive deaths, within a few months of each other, of three French Dauphins, leaving the Bourbon claimant heir-presumptive, after his grandfather and his nephew, to the Crown of France.

It now occurred to the chief minister that it might be possible, perhaps, without sacrificing the "particular advantages" won for England by his diplomacy out of the spoils of Spain, to settle this main question on a new principle—a principle contrary, no doubt, to the strict letter of her public engagements, but fairly in keeping with their general spirit, and free from the great objection of handing over Spain itself to a Bourbon prince. Accordingly in the month of May, Gaultier, on behalf of the English ministers, laid before France a new proposal, widely celebrated in those days as the alternative. Their plan was that, as in the first Partition Treaty, both the Austrian and the Bourbon claim to Spain should be set aside ; that

* Lords' Journals, February, 1712.

Victor Amadeus of Savoy should be transferred to Madrid as King, on the understanding that he should take over and confirm the secret obligations contracted by the House of Bourbon towards Great Britain ; that Philip of Anjou should be transferred to Turin as King of Savoy, on the understanding that he should take with him as an immediate addition to its territories the Spanish province of Sicily, and retain with all their seductive possibilities his prospective rights on France. If, contrary to their expectations, Philip should decline this offer, he was to have the other "alternative" of being recognized as King of Spain, but only on condition of renouncing, for himself and his whole posterity, the more splendid inheritance.

Modern historians, even though belonging to the political party of which Bolingbroke was an ornament, have expressed doubts as to the morality of this transmigratory scheme, which, they object, "dealt round dominions too much like a pack of cards, with no regard to the goodwill or repugnance of the nations most concerned."[*] But statesmen have seldom troubled themselves about such minor considerations ; and though in after years Bolingbroke was accustomed to speak of this expedient with contempt as an abortive device of Harley's "who had his correspondences apart, and a private thread of the negotiation always in his hands,"[†] it is certain that he plumed himself on it at the time as a considerable feat of statesmanship. "You see," he explains to one of his correspondents—"you see that whatever expedient be accepted, the point of preventing the union of the two monarchies is provided for."[‡] He "made little doubt"

---

[*] Lord Stanhope's "Reign of Queen Anne," 521.
[†] Bolingbroke's Works, ii. 490.
[‡] Bolingbroke to Edward Harley, May 17, 1712.

that the House of Bourbon would perceive its "true interest in evacuating Spain." He received with much complacency the acknowledgments of the Duke of Savoy's minister, who would gladly on behalf of his grateful master have confirmed and extended the secret preliminaries. But Philip (in his palace at Madrid) disappointed his English friends. He had fresh in his remembrance the recent history of his royal house with all its momentous lessons. He could recall the life-long efforts of his grand- father to rough-hew the ends which Providence had shaped so wonderfully : with what solemn and repeated formalities Lewis had "renounced" for himself and his whole posterity the Crown of Spain ; how often he had plighted his royal word to hold the renunciation sacred; how in the fervour of his devotion he had invoked the august ceremonies of the Catholic Church, the Holy Gospels, the Cross of Christ, the Canon of the Mass, to strengthen and accomplish his resolves; how the blessing and sanction of the Supreme Pontiff had been implored and given to the arrangement ; how constantly (for valuable consideration paid to France) it had been made an article in the treaty engagements of France with foreign Powers; and yet how futile had been all these efforts of blind and feeble mortals to fore- cast the decrees of Omnipotent wisdom ! Such events could hardly fail to make a deep impression on a mind so susceptible to religious influences as Philip's. He chose the second of the two alternatives.

In the meantime, however, the snows of winter had disappeared, and the season once more come round for military operations. The decision of Philip had not yet been received. The proposals of Lewis for satisfying the allies still remained as when first given in at the opening of the congress. By the United Provinces, the Emperor, and the German Princes, these proposals—less favourable to Europe even than the compromise of 1706—had been rejected. The conferences at Utrecht were at a standstill; and the Confederated Powers had made great efforts to place a formidable army in the field. Their troops were, it is true, no longer commanded by Marlborough. But they had in Prince Eugene a general not inferior in military skill to the French marshal opposed to them. Their forces altogether considerably outnumbered those of Villars; and before long an opportunity offered of compelling him either to fight them at a disadvantage or else to retreat behind the Somme.

But a military success on the French frontier, though it would have strengthened the position of the alliance at a critical moment, and justified the Continental Powers in the course they were taking, would for precisely the same reason have been embarrassing to Great Britain, whose own conditions of peace, though secured, were not yet reduced into possession, who was eager to extricate herself from a war which no longer concerned her, and who now saw her way to making a peremptory declaration in favour of proposals which—supposing Philip to accept her alternative—she held adequate to the existing relation of the belligerent Powers, though in the event of any further advantages won by the alliance they would cease to be so.*

Early in May, therefore, a memorable despatch was addressed by the Secretary of State on behalf of the Queen to the Duke of Ormond, now commanding her forces in Flanders, a despatch which brought matters to a crisis by prematurely forcing the hand of Government. In after years, when the excitement of these events had passed

---

* Bolingbroke puts this more tersely. "Our ill-success in the field would have rendered the French less tractable in the congress; our good success would have rendered the allies so" (ii. 491, "Letters on History").

away and only their ignominy survived, Bolingbroke was anxious to disclaim all direct responsibility for this measure. It was forced upon him, he tells us, by the Queen and the Lord Treasurer. For himself he was "surprised and hurt" at their determination. "If an opportunity had offered of speaking in private to the Queen, I should have advised her, I think, in the first heat against it." But he was her secretary, bound to obey her injunctions, however unpalatable; and within an hour of first receiving the order he had transmitted it to her general "in the very words in which it was advised and given." It laid her "positive commands" on Ormond to "avoid engaging in any siege or hazarding a battle." But he was directed to "disguise the receipt of this order" from the allies, and to "invent pretences" for answering the proposed end without owning that which might at the present time have "an ill effect." This famous despatch closed with a famous postscript; and the whole transaction sets in the clearest light the relation which England had assumed towards the two sides in the struggle: "I had almost forgot to tell your grace that communication is given of this order to the court of France." * Ormond had many faults; but he was a soldier with the instincts of a great profession to guide him, and a gentleman proud of a name sullied by no breath of dishonour. He could not bring himself to execute these instructions. The scandal leaked out. The breach between England and her allies was complete. At Ormond's request an ungracious apology was tendered. He undertook and was permitted to cover the siege of Le Quesnoy. But the concession was made, not to outraged public opinion, "the affected alarm and clamour raised with so much industry both here and abroad, which gave the Queen," says her

* Secretary St. John to Ormond, May 17, 1712.

secretary, "no uneasiness whatever," but to her general's own expostulations; and St. John gently admonished his over-scrupulous colleague that "true glory results from obeying the prince one serves punctually, and promoting the interests of one's country steadily, in preference to all other considerations of private honour or advantage." * Nor could any apology have restored, after such a disclosure, the old relations so wantonly broken. A month later all attempt to preserve them was abandoned. The mask was thrown aside. A suspension of arms was declared between England and France. In the midst of the campaign the British regiments were withdrawn from the allied army. Eugene was left to sustain single-handed the attack of the French. The Imperialist forces were defeated at Denain, and were saved from the destruction which threatened them, and which the ministers of England had anticipated, only by a timely "mutiny" on the part of the German mercenaries in the Queen's pay, who, basely preferring their private honour, refused at her bidding to desert their comrades.†

---

* St. John to Ormond, May 27, 1712.

† Their conduct made St. John very angry. "A beggarly German general," he writes, "commands the troops, which have been so many years paid by Her Majesty, and which are actually so at this time, to *desert* from the Queen, and to leave her subject forces, for aught they know, exposed to be *attacked by the enemy;* this is, I confess, *surprising,* and what very few instances can be produced to parallel" (St. John to E. Harley, July 12, 1712). The italics are St. John's. That so accomplished a writer should be betrayed into such a literary solecism shows the agitation of mind under which he laboured. In a few days, however, he was sufficiently himself to remember that the desertion of these "beggarly Germans" would simplify ways and means, and make the next session of Parliament "short and easy" (St. John to the Bishop of Bristol, July 23, 1712).

VI.

With the restraining orders, the armistice, and the withdrawal of the British forces, came to an end in an abrupt *finale* the second act of the eventful drama of which the first was closed by the signing of the secret preliminaries. It was what St. John called it, a "passing of the Rubicon,"* an enforced confession of the fact hitherto concealed and denied that England had already concluded her own conditions of peace—that at the moment when in her public declarations she was "protesting" that she "regarded the interests of her allies as inseparable from her own," she had in fact separated her interests from those of her allies; that when through the mouth of her public envoys she was "insisting" that neither Spain nor the Spanish colonies should be allotted to a Bourbon prince, she had secretly consented, for valuable consideration to herself, that both Spain and the Spanish colonies should be retained by Philip. The excitement in Parliament was very great; and in order to allay it, the Queen came down to the House of Lords early in June, and publicly announced from the throne what the price was to be of this great concession. She divided her speech into two parts. The first related to the special interests of Great Britain, "the particular advantages which I have demanded and obtained for my own kingdoms." These the Queen set forth at full length; and she expressed the hope that they would be found on examination to make her subjects "some amends" for the "great and unequal burden" hitherto cast upon them. With regard to the second part, "the proposals of France for satisfying my allies," these, she confessed, were still in the raw state. "I have not taken upon me to determine the

* St. John to the Earl of Strafford, July 5, 1712.

interests of my confederates. These must be adjusted in the congress at Utrecht." But her "best endeavours" should not be wanting to procure for them "justice" and a "reasonable satisfaction." *

A few weeks later when, in consequence of the withdrawal of Ormond and his battalions, the fortune of the campaign had gone against the allies, and they were no longer in a "state of giving or France of receiving the law," ministers greatly regretted the precipitancy of the disclosure thus prematurely forced upon them : "for now," said Swift, "we are in a manner pinned down and cannot go back an inch with any good grace ; " and he feelingly deplored "this very new thing amongst us of every subject interposing his sentiments upon the management of foreign negotiations," "this giving a detail of particulars which in the variety of events cannot, during the course of a treaty, be ascertained," as "too great a strain on the prerogative." †

For now the Government found itself face to face with the very contingency which, twelve months before, Shrewsbury had pointed out as not unlikely to happen. When the German powers, exasperated at this treatment, refused any longer to concert with England either in peace or war, and ministers proposed to France to carry out the secret preliminaries at once into a separate treaty, France declined. "No ; not till the general pacification is made complete under your *mediation*—that is to say, on terms favourable to us. It was on this understanding and in this expectation alone that we granted you, without demur, all your extended demands." In truth, just as the fundamental error of their foreign policy in considering the war as on the part of all the Powers engaged in it, England included, a war of plunder simply, and in subordinating its great

* "Parliamentary History," vi. 1143.
† Swift to Archbishop King, September 30, 1712.

public object, the reduction of the exorbitant French power, to petty schemes of individual aggrandizement, had the effect of leaving France at its close actually stronger, as regarded Europe, than she had been when the Grand Alliance was first constructed, so the fundamental error of their diplomacy in trying to separate the interests of England from those of the alliance, in disclaiming for England all responsibility for the pretensions of the alliance, had the effect of throwing upon England the sole responsibility of determining these pretensions. The conferences at Utrecht collapsed. The public treaty was turned into a private arrangement hastily concerted between St. James's and Versailles. Europe, speaking no longer through a united and victorious confederacy but in the person of a single discredited Power, with no army in the field to sustain her demands, uncertain how far the terms she was making on their behalf would be accepted by her different allies, yet unable to secure her own conditions of peace till some general agreement was concluded, stood matched against France, no longer borne down and vanquished in an unequal struggle, but well able to hold her own both in arms and in diplomacy. The result could not be doubtful. France began to "assume a superiority and to prescribe in the negotiations."* She saw in fact that she had bid too high for the support of England in the congress, that the influence of England over the allies was not what she had imagined ; and these considerations acting on the mind of a sovereign never remarkable for a strict adherence to his engagements, caused him, as the isolation of England and the weakness, the utter disorganization of the confederacy, became daily more apparent, to hang back, to withdraw concessions which the Queen in her speech from the throne had announced as

---

* Bolingbroke to Strafford, September 30, 1712.

already granted, to put his own interpretation on others—to practise all those " arts of negotiation " of which in past years he had himself so bitterly complained.

He refused to give up Dunkirk. He demanded back Tournay. At the very time when (says St. John indignantly) we were knitting the bonds of friendship between the two nations with all possible industry, the French fleet suddenly attacked the Leeward Islands, a most untoward event which he contrasts, reasonably enough, with the restrictive orders privately sent to Ormond and his own official notification of them to the French generals. " I will not *say* that this order saved their army from being beat ; but in my conscience I think it did." * That order —he might have added, and the suspension of arms that followed—not only saved France from being beat. It contributed directly to her success at Denain, to the raising of the siege of Landrecies, to the recapture of Douai, Le Quesnoy, and Bouchain ; it freed the soil of France from the armies of the confederacy ; it roused against England the bitter resentment of every independent state in Europe ; and the return of France for these services, rendered her at such a cost and at such a moment, was to haggle with England about the price covenanted to be paid for them, and to harry with fire and sword her undefended colonies.

It was to try and allay what he calls " this sneaking chicane of De Torcy," as well as to procure certain advantages for the Duke of Savoy with a view of binding his interests to those of Great Britain, and thus helping to secure for her that " stronger foothold in the Mediterranean," which was one of the most far-sighted and statesmanlike, though, as it turned out, one of the least enduring provisions of the Treaty of Peace, that St. John—now created Viscount Bolingbroke—undertook in the course

* Bolingbroke to Prior, September 19, 1712.

of this summer a short mission to Paris, where honours which brought the blood to his cheek were paid to the saviour of France.* Later in the same year the Duke of Shrewsbury was sent there to settle, with Prior's help, the disputed points in the treaty of commerce, and to fix the exact terms on which Newfoundland and Nova Scotia were to be ceded. Neither statesman was altogether successful in his mission. Bolingbroke indeed was betrayed by his gallantries into a serious breach of official decorum, which threatened gravely to compromise his Government, and which emboldened the Prime Minister, always on the watch for an opportunity of depressing his aspiring colleague, to take from him for a time, and restore to the more prudent and submissive Dartmouth, their correspondence with the French court.

But this eclipse of his diplomatic activity was short-lived. Nothing but the vigour and energy of the younger Secretary of State, the comprehensive mastery which he soon acquired over the various interests involved, his industry in grappling with every detail in each nation's demands, and his unfailing readiness of resource in dealing with them, could cope with the mass of labour which now overwhelmed the ministry, or hope to evolve out of so many conflicting claims a settlement which might be pressed on Europe with any chance of acceptance.

And as autumn passed into winter and winter into spring, with nothing finally determined ; with the whole negotiation virtually resting on himself—the allies holding stubbornly aloof, the Emperor still in arms, the German Princes sulking, Portugal and Savoy discontented, and the

---

* "They fatigued him," he writes to Lord Dartmouth, "quite as much as the toils of his journey." It is amusing to notice one of the most recent of Bolingbroke's apologists, Mr. John Skelton, advocate, calmly ascribe these honours to the "estimation in which Bolingbroke was held as a European statesman "—an alarming draft on the ignorance of the Scottish reading public.

Dutch alone cowed into a dull submission ; with France
playing false about what he describes as the "most
essential article of our whole engagement," and endeavouring to elude promises "made, repeated and confirmed ;"
with the French ministers at Utrecht declaring against the
very proposals which Lord Strafford had opened, under
his instructions, as certain to be made by France ; with
the meeting of Parliament put off from day to day, and
week to week, and month to month, till the session which
had been first fixed for November had not begun even in
March ;—at length Bolingbroke's energies were overtaxed,
and his buoyant spirits began to flag. "We stand indeed,"
he writes to Prior in a characteristic letter—"we stand
indeed on the brink of a precipice ; but the French stand
there too. Pray tell M. De Torcy from me that he may
get Robin and Harry hanged, but affairs will soon run
back into so much confusion that he will wish us alive
again. To speak seriously, unless the Queen can talk of
her interest as determined with France, and unless your
court will keep our allies in the wrong, as they are
sufficiently at this time, I foresee inextricable difficulties.
My scheme, then, is this. Let France satisfy the Queen ;
let the Queen declare both in Parliament and in the
congress that she is ready to sign ; at the same time let
the French plenipotentiaries show a disposition to conclude
with all the allies ; offer to the Dutch what they have
already offered ; offer to Prussia and the German princes,
whose interests admit of little dispute, complete satisfaction ; yield to Savoy the small contested article which
they must confess is necessary to give him the real security
so frequently promised ; consent to our proposition on
behalf of Portugal ; content themselves for Bavaria with
what my Lord Strafford opened ; and even offer to treat
with the Emperor if expedients may be found to soften

him on this and other heads. If such overtures are not instantly accepted, our separate peace would, sitting the Parliament, be addressed for, made, and approved; and the cause of France for once become popular. If they were accepted, let M. De Torcy sit down and consider *what a bargain would be made for France.* Let him remember his journey to the Hague, and compare the plans of 1709 and 1712." *

At length, in February, 1713, more than two years after the first clandestine overture through Gaultier had been tendered, an ultimatum embodying the terms thus roughly sketched was addressed by Bolingbroke to Shrewsbury, and by him formally presented to the French court. It dealt in the first place with the disputes that had arisen touching the "particular advantages" contracted to be paid to Great Britain herself. On these a compromise was offered, a compromise of which we have felt the evil effects even in our time, whilst its advantages were thrown away by the blear-eyed conservatism of Parliament. On the chief points that remained undetermined in the general plan of peace, the French ministers were reminded by Bolingbroke that her Majesty had done everything in her power to moderate the expectations of her allies; that it was "impossible to constrain them to submit" to anything lower than the terms which she now proposed, and on which she felt bound to take her stand; that the general plan so modified came very near the original scheme which Lewis, at the opening of the treaty, had "thought fit to offer;" they were informed that if the French King should be willing to conclude on these terms and with the additions and alterations then proposed, her Majesty would herself be answerable for their execution; and that her plenipotentiaries at Utrecht should be

---

* Bolingbroke to Prior, January 19, 1713.

instructed, whether the allies accepted or not, and without
waiting for their formal decisions, to sign at once on her
behalf, power being reserved for each ally to come in on
the scheme so settled within a time to be fixed by the
French and English ministers. These, however, were the
Queen's final resolutions. On the answer given by the
French King it depended whether she should announce
to her Parliament, now about to assemble, that peace was
made, or demand from it subsidies for a new campaign.

This timely exhibition of firmness brought matters to
an issue. On reflection their "bargain," as Bolingbroke
called it, appeared to the French court as favourable to
them as he had judged it, and far too valuable to be
sacrificed. The additions and alterations, stated by
Bolingbroke with masterly clearness, were all agreed to
by Lewis; and finally, with some grumbling, the conditions so settled were accepted by a majority of the Allied
Powers. For what else in truth could they do? And
so at last, on the afternoon of the 11th of April, according to the style then in vogue on the continent, after
twenty-seven months of negotiation, the treaties of Utrecht
were signed by the ministers of England and France, by
Savoy, Portugal, and Prussia in the evening, and by the
Dutch at midnight. The Emperor, encouraged by a
subscription got up for him by the great Whig magnates,
determined to try another campaign. Of himself, said
Bolingbroke contemptuously, he had neither money nor
troops, neither arms nor magazines. He was altogether
overmatched in the struggle, even in the region within
which he confined it, and in the following spring at
Rastadt made his peace with France. But he refused to
acknowledge, as did King Philip on his side and the States-
General on theirs, the scheme of partitioning Spain which
the treaty of Utrecht had contemplated ; and the provisions

framed by Bolingbroke remained, therefore, in respect to the great public object of the war, mere preliminaries, mere suggestions having no binding force, repudiated in fact by the three Powers chiefly interested, until in the following reign—by the conventions of November, 1715, and December, 1718, assuring to the Emperor his sovereignty in the Spanish Low Countries; by the convention of May, 1716, confirming his possession of the Italian provinces of Spain; by the Triple Alliance of the January following, which placed the Orleans claim to France under the protection of a European guarantee; and, lastly, by the great Quadruple Treaty of August, 1718, in which the House of Austria, for valuable consideration, finally relinquished its nebulous pretensions to Spain itself—the arrangements of Utrecht, modified in some ways, but substantially unchanged, were made the subject of a new Grand Alliance, and took their place amongst the recognized public law of Europe.

VII.

Many years afterwards Bolingbroke acknowledged with honourable candour how far these arrangements fell short of what the circumstances required, and how much the equilibrium of Europe was afterwards due, not to the measures then taken for ensuring it, but to what he calls want of enterprise on the part of France—to the ambitious hopes excited in the Regent's mind by the Triple Alliance of 1717, giving as it did an adventitious security to those renunciations the legality of which France denied, and causing her ruler to neglect in his own selfish interest her traditional policy. "I shall not be surprised," he wrote in one of the letters addressed in 1735 to his friend

Lord Cornbury—"I shall not be surprised if you think the peace of Utrecht was not answerable to the success of the war, nor to the efforts made in it. I think so myself, and have always owned even when it was making and made that I thought so. . . . We ought to have reaped more advantage from it than we did. We ought to have reduced the power of France more than we did, and to have strengthened her neighbours more than we did; to have still further disarmed her frontiers by the cession and demolition of many more places than she yielded up at Utrecht, and so have reduced her power of injury, not for the moment only, but for generations to come." * And though he attributes this preservation of the French power as a standing peril to her neighbours— this failure to obtain the conditions which in his sober opinion he knew to be essential to the repose of Europe, if ever again the ambition of France should equal her power of injury, to any cause but the true one, to the action of the Continental States in persistently differing with England as to the real aim of the war instead of to the conduct of England herself in persistently separating her own interests from theirs, in striving to overreach them by secret bargains, and in thus forcing them to combine against her in defence of their common rights: still, this is merely the plea of the prisoner in arrest of judgment, and his own confession on the main charge is a sufficient answer at any rate to his modern apologists, who profess to regard the Treaty of Utrecht as an adequate settlement of the questions at issue, and its negotiation as a masterpiece of successful diplomacy. Well, that was not certainly the opinion of its author. He claimed for himself, and justly, the merit of his exertions. But even in the act of throwing the responsibility on others, he

* Works, ii. 474-477.

honestly recognized and openly lamented the deficiencies of his work. "The Queen desired to humble and weaken the power of France; the allies who opposed her desired to crush it. Neither succeeded. Those who meant to ruin the French power preserved it by opposing those who meant to reduce it; and thus the war ended much more favourably to France than the men who put an end to it designed." *

In truth, the concessions made by France fell short, not merely of the extended terms of peace formulated at the Hague in May, 1709, which, though ratified by England, though adopted mainly at the instance of England, were not, according to Bolingbroke, binding upon her. They fell short of what had been contemplated in the compromise of 1701, and very far short of what had been demanded in the public instructions furnished by the Queen's command to her plenipotentiaries at Utrecht, at the close of December, 1711. In the engagements of 1701, the contracting Powers had bound themselves to make war on France until the Italian and Flemish provinces of Spain should be relinquished by her to the Emperor. They were to be his "reasonable satisfaction" for the loss of the great inheritance which he claimed, which Europe had designed for him, and on which France, in defiance of reiterated pledges, had forcibly seized. In the engagements of 1701, the West Indian colonies of Spain had been reserved for the disposal of the maritime Powers; and to the usurping Bourbons had been left only the bare trunk of Spain itself, stripped of the rich dependencies which chiefly made it formidable.

Again, in the instructions given to the representatives of England under Bolingbroke's hand prior to the opening of the congress, they were expressly charged to see that

* Works, ii. 481.

the frontier of Germany should be strengthened against
French aggression by the restoration of Strasbourg with
its ranks and privileges—which Lewis had stolen from the
Empire during one of its struggles with the Turk, and
which in the first draft even of the Treaty of Ryswick he
had promised to give back,—by the surrender of Brisac,
and by the restitution of the whole province of Alsace,
according to the German interpretation of its limits. At
the same time, though the claim of the Emperor himself
to Spain and the Spanish West Indies was no longer
recognized by England, her ministers were directed to
" insist " that neither Spain nor the Spanish West
Indies should be allotted to a prince of the rival
House. *

What were the provisions of the treaty as actually
concluded? The Italian provinces of Spain were divided
between the House of Austria and the House of Savoy.
The sovereignty of the Spanish Netherlands was disjoined
from the possession ; the first only going to the Emperor,
the second to the States-General. Brisac, indeed, and
Kehl were restored to Germany ; and the French Rhine
fortresses were destroyed. But Spain and the Spanish
West Indies were both formally "secured " to the House
of Bourbon. The rebellious Electors who had sided with
France in the war, and whom the allies had dispossessed,
were reinstated in their lost privileges, and with their old
capacities for mischief. Strasbourg, with its surrounding
territory, was permanently added to the French dominions.
Well might Bolingbroke prophesy at an early stage in the

---

* " There are in every negotiation," says Bolingbroke in his Letters on
History, "two kinds of demands : *essential* demands, all in particular that
are really necessary ; and *specific* demands, made either to encumber the
negotiation or to have in reserve, according to the artifice usually employed
on such occasions, certain points from which to depart in the course of it with
advantage " (ii. 480 . This, I suppose, was a specific demand.

negotiations, "This peace will be made at the Emperor's expense." *

Nor were the conditions of the treaty less open to objection from the side of the United Provinces. They obtained, indeed, through what St. John calls "the Queen's condescension to them," the renewal of their old trading privileges with France, and, at the cost of Germany, a "barrier" against France. But it was not at all the sort of barrier which they had been induced to expect, or which England in express engagements had covenanted to provide for them. They obtained no new territory. England kept fast hold of Gibraltar and Port Mahon. But Aire and Bethune, Lille and St. Venant, the strongholds on their frontier which would have bound France to them in heavy penalties, these the Dutch relinquished. England took care to stipulate that Dunkirk, the arsenal which threatened her naval power, should be destroyed; but Holland furnished the "equivalent" for purchasing the consent of Lewis. Rapacious England, her old rival in trading enterprise and maritime supremacy, transferred to herself a lucrative commerce, and annexed a vast colonial empire. But from all these advantages the Dutch, though they had done most in proportion to their means to win them, though they had honourably rejected similar exclusive privileges when tendered to themselves, were jealously shut out. †
To the Dutch the war, after its years of triumph, brought only losses and increase of weakness; and thenceforth the Republic, overburdened by its exhausting struggles,

---

* St. John to Strafford, November 21, 1711.

† In 1707, Mesnager had been employed by Lewis to try and tempt the States into a separate treaty by the offer of trading privileges in Spain; and when in London, in September, 1711, finally settling the secret preliminaries, he did not conceal his opinion that the States were being hardly treated. "He was a little fellow," said St. John, "and a Dutchman in his inclinations."

and deprived of all just share in its compensations, fell back into the second rank of States.

Of the three Powers principally concerned in it there remains Great Britain. Great Britain, as might be anticipated after her nine months' start of her colleagues, came out of the negotiations most laden with spoil. And undoubtedly her gains, though larger perhaps in appearance than in substance, and purchased at the cost of bitter and lasting enmities, were very great.* Spain ceded to her Gibraltar and Minorca, the conquests of Rooke and Stanhope. France made over the sovereignty of an extensive if somewhat sterile region on the shores of the Frozen Sea, Hudson's Bay, Nova Scotia, Newfoundland, reserving however some rights in it, which seriously impaired its value; she renewed the promise made in 1697, and broken four years later, to recognize the Revolution dynasty; she ceded her half-interest in St. Christophers; and she undertook, on receiving back the town of Lille, to demolish Dunkirk. Each of the Bourbon princes in addition opened to the subjects of the English Crown a new and important source of wealth: Philip by transferring to them for a term of years the coveted privilege of the Assiento contract, hitherto enjoyed by France—the exclusive right of kidnapping African negroes and selling them to the Spanish planters; Lewis by recognizing this transfer and by consenting further to sign in their favour a treaty of commerce, which provided for a free interchange of goods between the two countries on the principle of the most favoured nation clause.

This treaty of commerce, the enlightened policy of

---

* This, of course, was the strong plea in the Government defence. "If in the end it appears," wrote Swift to Archbishop King, "that we have made a good bargain for you, we hope that you will take it, *without entering too nicely into the circumstances*" (Swift to Archbishop King, March 28, 1713).

which Pope commemorated in some of his noblest lines, *
anticipated the great measures framed by Pitt in our
grandfathers' time, and by Cobden in our own. It was
the work of a leading Commissioner of Plantations, who
exercised at this time a great influence over Bolingbroke,
and who was to exercise, a few years later, a similar influence
over Walpole; † Arthur Moore, a man who, beginning life
it is said as a footman, had gradually raised himself by
industry and a keen mother wit till he became a chief
authority on all matters of finance, who was versed in the
theory as well as the practice of trade, and who had, like
his two contemporaries, John Locke and Dudley North,
successfully thought out the principles on which the wealth
of a nation depends. It is to the credit of Bolingbroke
that, though profoundly ignorant of such subjects, his clear
intellect at once detected the force of Moore's reasoning ;
whilst his judgment told him how much an open and
extended commerce between the two countries would help
in breaking down the old barriers of patriotic animosity,
and in knitting together those bands of friendship to which,
with a statesmanship far in advance of his age, he looked
as the surest guarantee for the future repose of Europe.
"Nothing," he justly said, "unites like interest."‡ He
explained and justified his favourite scheme in despatches
which are models of perspicuous argument, and defended
it, though unhappily without success, against a most
formidable coalition of friends and enemies. For the
measure was opposed to the insular traditions of the country
party. At the same time it was conceived in a spirit too
liberal for the merchants and traders of those days. It

* See the closing lines in "Windsor Forest," beginning—

    "Thy trees, fair Windsor, now shall leave their woods."

† Bolingbroke to Harcourt, March 22, 1725.

‡ Bolingbroke to Prior, May 31, 1713.

was contrary to the well-established mercantile system.
It would be an unbusinesslike arrangement. It would
drain us of money, and stock us with goods. The city
joined hands with the landed interest in protesting against
it. The Low Church Lords "scanned, strained, and mis-
represented" every article; and the High Church Commons,
on the motion of a Tory country gentleman, threw out
at its final stage the bill which repealed the existing pro-
hibitions.

Its failure, when contrasted with the success of the
companion arrangement made with Spain, sheds a curious
light on the state of public morality and commercial
knowledge in Queen Anne's time. The Assiento contract
made England the greatest slave-trader in the world.
It was purchased, moreover, from Philip in exchange for
a provision in the treaties which practically excluded her
general commerce from all the Spanish colonies. But it
was a direct material injury to France; and therefore,
though morally disgraceful and economically unsound, it
extorted a sulky approval even from the bitterest opponents
of Government. The French commercial treaty would
have augmented the wealth of England at no cost of moral
degradation and with no counter-balancing disadvantage.
But then, it would have been equally profitable to France.
It was therefore repudiated with indignation by a Parliament devoted to the minister who proposed it.

Such were the chief provisions of the treaty regarded
from the side of the three principal allies. It is when,
however, we turn to France; when we examine the gains
and losses of France; when we remember that the great
object of the war, as stated by Bolingbroke himself, was
to reduce the exorbitant power of France, and then
compare the France of 1689, when the Grand Alliance
was first constructed, with the France of 1713, when it was

finally dissolved, that the weakest parts of the engagement appear. In what ways had the exorbitant power of France been reduced? By the material losses inflicted on her whilst the war continued? Bolingbroke has himself exposed the fallacy of this consideration. "Those who took the exhaustion and bankruptcy of France as a sufficient reduction of her power looked," he says, "but a little way before them and reasoned too superficially." * In loss of territory and of military prestige? On the contrary, the territory which she ruled, even under her direct sway, was as strong and as compact after as it was before the war. Her military prestige, destroyed for the moment by Marlborough's victories, had received fresh lustre from the achievements of Villars in the two campaigns which followed Marlborough's removal from the command; whilst her ascendency in Europe, which she owed quite as much to the triumphs of her diplomacy as to her success in arms, had been altogether re-established by the issue of the recent negotiations. In every one of the concessions made by France the wily ministers she employed had succeeded in getting some drawback, in reserving some mischievous right or privilege, which in many cases went far to destroy the value of the concession itself.

She agreed to demolish Dunkirk. But she obtained as an "equivalent" Lille, and very nearly obtained Tournay. Having received her equivalent, she omitted to perform her part in the compact; and when at length compelled to do so, she began to build a new and more formidable Dunkirk a few miles distant along the coast. She "recognized" the King of Prussia, and "acknowledged" his sovereignty of Neuchatel. In return, she obtained his renunciation of the principality of Orange and of King

* Works, ii. 474.

William's estates in Franche Comté. She recognized the title of her enemy, the Elector of Hanover; and she reinstated in their old dignities and lost possessions her two friends, the Electors of Bavaria and of Cologne. She gave back Kehl and Brisac; but she kept Strasbourg, and annexed Landau. She partitioned the Spanish monarchy. She ceded the Flemish and Italian provinces, and she ceded them in such a manner as to relieve herself of an embarrassment, and to entail on their new possessors a heritage of discord. She retained the nucleus of the Spanish kingdom; and she retained it unconditionally, with the sources of its power untouched, with its subject races bound hand and foot at the mercy of their new masters, and this although the word of England had been pledged to preserve their ancient liberties. Beyond the seas she yielded to Great Britain colonies of imposing bulk indeed, but small intrinsic value, reserving to herself the right to share their chief natural product; and she obtained instead, through a cadet of her royal house and with all its trade privileges carefully fenced in against rival enterprise, a new transatlantic empire, larger in extent, more populous, and blessed with a happier climate.

In fact, for every purpose of aggression against her neighbours, France had, on the return of peace, to the full as strong a vantage-ground for attack as before the war; she had her resources augmented by a new fund of wealth; whilst at the same time she was relieved from the old necessity of detaching a large proportion of her strength to watch and safeguard the passes of the Pyrenees.

And this last advantage alone was worth to her all the concessions of the treaty. Before the accession of the Bourbons to the Crown of Spain, the Pyrenees had formed in truth a part of the German frontier. In respect of those rich provinces of his kingdom comprised within the circle of Burgundy, the King of Spain had been a German prince ; and these Flemish provinces formed a part of his territory which lay very open to attack from France, which France was known to covet, and which could only be effectually protected against her by the help of the German confederation. This drew the King of Spain naturally and inevitably into the great league of German powers. Every burglarious scheme matured by France, every attempt of France to push forward her boundaries at the cost of the German people, was opposed to the clear interests of the King of Spain ; and in every one of these France had upon her flank, ready to spring upon her from the Pyrenean passes, an open or a secret enemy.

It is true that the hostility of the Spanish Government was no longer a thing to be greatly dreaded. The Spain of Melgar and Portocarrero was not the Spain of Ximenes. Yet what a fund of reserved power lay concealed in that torpid body, when quickened into life by the energy of a great minister, was shown only five years later under Alberoni's brilliant administration. And even in the days when least formidable to France as a rival, Spain had not yet sunk into her dependent ally. Still the Pyrenees existed. Still the danger to France lurking behind the Pyrenees was a security for peace and for the freedom of nations.

To remove that danger by abolishing the Pyrenees had almost from his earliest years been the crowning ambition of Lewis. For this he had woven the most elaborate meshes of his diplomatic chicanery. For this he had stooped to acts unworthy of a man of honour, had borne false witness, had broken his plighted word, had prostituted the solemn mysteries of his religion to the vilest purposes of statecraft. And now, as he boasted in his triumph to the constable of Castile, the Pyrenees had "ceased to exist." " The French

and Spanish nations are so united that they will henceforth
be only one." His prophecy has been called a vain one,
falsified by the events that followed. * But it will hardly be
thought so by any student of history who sees those events
in their true bearing, who calls to mind and realizes to
himself how completely in those days the policy of nations
was determined by dynastic objects, and who contrasts the
mutual relations of the two Crowns before and after their
union in one royal house. In all the great conflicts which
afterwards divided Europe, in the war of the Pragmatic
Sanction, in the Seven Years' War, in the shameful and
perilous years of the American War, whenever the arms of
England were matched against the arms of France, France
had Spain at her beck and call. The law which governed the
motion of the two countries being now the same, the larger
State, moving in her appointed course, attracted the smaller
into her orbit. To the reciprocal renunciations executed by
Philip and his kinsmen succeeded the Family Compact, that
great charter of Bourbon politics in the eighteenth century.
It was in no sense a national compact, as we are sometimes
asked to believe. Its object, no doubt, was to destroy the
maritime supremacy of Great Britain, the chief guarantee
for European freedom ; but its principle was to connect
together two nations, politically distinct and with interests
naturally antagonistic, by the strong invisible bands of a
palace alliance. The Family Compact gratified the ambition
and furthered the malign purposes of France to the full as

* " Family affection," says Macaulay, " has seldom produced much effect
on the policy of princes." Family affection, perhaps ; but what, I should like
to ask, were the " common interests " and " common enmities " which afterwards, as Macaulay admits, so closely united France and Spain, but the family
interests and family enmities of the House of Bourbon ? What was the cause
of that single quarrel between the two nations on which—though it lasted
barely two years—Macaulay lays such stress, but a family dispute between the
two Bourbon princes who governed them as to their rival claims to be head of
their royal house ?

well as a corporate union would have done ; whilst the renunciations on their side were equally useful to her as setting at rest the irritable pride and disarming the opposition of the Castilian patriot. No misgivings as to his country's vassalage ever crossed his mind. The law which swung her round in the train of France was quite unknown to him. Like the astronomers of old, he believed the earth on which he stood to be the centre of the universe.

CHAPTER III.

I.

To the reader who has followed these negotiations with full knowledge, who is familiar besides with the antecedents and the necessities of the two chief negotiators, it will probably appear that the peculiar system pursued throughout which excited such remark—the secret compact with France and the large concessions promised to England; the device by which the allies were drawn into the congress on a basis which seemed to offer all they wanted; the steps taken at home to bear down resistance and procure a Parliament subservient to the designs of ministers; the double set of instructions under which the representatives of the Queen were required in public to treat the interests of her confederates as "inseparable from her own," while privately concerting with the French agents the means of "getting the better of them;" the process by which information extracted at Utrecht was transmitted to Whitehall, and thence through Gaultier to Versailles with the comments of the St. James's cabinet and their suggestions for evading unpalatable demands; the dubious expedient for separating the two Crowns; the secret orders sent to the commander-in-chief to hinder so far as he could any forward march of the confederates, lest a victory in the field should make them "less tractable" in the congress; and the sudden drawing away of the mask, the "passing of the Rubicon" as St. John called it, the change of front, which placed England openly on the side of France, bent on forcing their joint intentions on Europe, or at least so much of the original scheme as France could be induced to fulfil; —it will probably appear, I think, that these "troublesome invidious steps to peace" may all be sufficiently explained without attributing to ministers anything worse than a characteristic disregard for treaty engagements of which they disapproved, and a characteristic desire to secure at all hazards a settlement which they really believed to be more favourable to England herself, whatever it might be to Europe generally. It was an instance of how men, honest enough in their intentions but perfectly unscrupulous in their methods, may be led astray by following a narrow, exclusive, shortsighted patriotism, by forgetting that the real interests of a great nation can never be promoted by conduct which imperils the security of its neighbours and shakes all confidence in its own integrity.

But their contemporaries put a different and a more sinister interpretation on their proceedings. They accused them of a deliberate intention to set the great Powers of Europe by the ears and so play France's game—break up the ring of States that was holding her down, and set her free to ravage once more with her claws still unpared. They accused them of being influenced not merely by party but by treasonable motives, by the desire to re-establish for their own personal aims the old ignoble relation between the two kingdoms which had existed under the later Stuarts.

"For the last fifty years"—it was thus that the zealous Whig would argue—"for the last fifty years the single ambition of France has been to establish a paramount ascendency in Europe. This ambition was first detected and frustrated, in the interest of English liberty, by the

Whigs of King Charles's reign. The Triple Alliance between England, Holland, and Sweden was their work. It was the foundation of the Whig foreign policy. It gave the first check to the growing power of Lewis. It caused France to loose her hold on the Flemish provinces of Spain, after which she had always hankered, on which she had just then seized under the excuse of a fabricated rule of public law, and which she would have forthwith used in her attack first on Dutch and then on English freedom.

"But the Triple Alliance had been forced on the Stuarts and the court party, and was as much opposed to their interests as to those of France. It was therefore soon got rid of; and the Treaty of Dover was substituted. The principle of the Treaty of Dover was 'non-intervention' in foreign affairs; English connivance at French aggression; French support to a Popish and despotic English dynasty; and this ignominious policy which made the Sovereign of England a pensioner and vassal of France, which played the game of France, which guaranteed the supremacy of France, prevailed, with the support of the Tory party, through the whole of King James's reign.

"Then came the Revolution and the entire change of system. The Revolution was intended to rescue England from an isolated foreign and an exclusive domestic policy. It was brought about, no doubt, by a momentary union of the two great English parties. But it was in its results, as in its principles, altogether a Whig measure. It was shaped by the Whig leaders to their own ends. The Tory plan of a Regency in the interest of the Stuarts was defeated. The Tory system of religious intolerance in the interest of the Episcopalians was overthrown. The Tory scheme of *laissez faire* in foreign politics in the interest of the Bourbons was suspended. Hatred of France was the ruling passion of the new Sovereign; and hostility to

France became the guiding principle of the new Government.

"But the effect of this Whig triumph was that France changed her tactics. The triumph was not yet complete. Foiled in her attempts to replace in England a Government favourable to her projects, France signed the truce of Ryswick and turned her intrigues directly against Spain, still with the same object of furthering her great scheme of universal monarchy, and with the ulterior design of wrecking English liberty when she had succeeded. By a complicated web of mingled cajolery and intimidation, she lured the court of Madrid into her toils. She pandered to the superstitious fears of the Spanish Charles II. as she had before pandered to the lust and greed of the English King; suborned the priests and confessors who surrounded his dying bed as she had bribed the courtiers and mistresses of his pleasure-loving namesake; and by the very same arts which had procured the ignoble compact of Dover extorted his consent to the monstrous instrument which bequeathed the dominions of Charles V. to the hereditary enemy of his royal race. Having gained her point, she threw aside the mask of submission, tore up the treaties just concluded, and once more domineered over Europe. She annexed under the plea of administering Belgium ; she overthrew the Dutch barrier; she recognized the Stuart Pretender as King of Great Britain ; she invaded Germany, and carried her victorious arms to the gates of Vienna. Never since the mighty Armada sailed from Spain had the liberties of Europe been in more deadly peril.

"And how," asked the Whig partisan, "was this danger averted ? Once more by a temporary effacement of Toryism, by a revival of Whig spirit throughout the country, by a renewal on a more extended scale of that Triple Alliance which was the foundation of our Whig foreign policy, and by a reunion of all parties in support of those Revolution principles which we alone really cherish. Slowly and by a series of painful efforts which tried the strength of England, no doubt, but raised her military glory to the highest point, and with it that prestige on which the true strength of nations ultimately depends, the French invasion was driven back ; the countries seized upon by France were taken from her ; the people tyrannized over by France were freed from her yoke ; the chain of iron strongholds forged by France, nominally—poor innocent ! —for her own defence, but really, as every one knew, as robber fastnesses from whence to sally forth and prey upon her hapless neighbours, was broken in pieces. Victory declared itself on the side of Europe ; and the statesmen of England, in conjunction with their European colleagues, bent all their energies towards providing against the possibility of a renewal of those dangers to which twice in their lifetime the liberties of Europe had been exposed. They did not neglect the particular interests of England. On the contrary, the first idea of most of the concessions since *exacted*—that is the phrase used—since exacted from France may be traced to those much maligned instructions given by our own leaders to Marlborough and Townshend, the envoys who represented them at the Hague. But they did not make the particular interests of England the beginning and end of their policy. They were statesmen. They recognized the fact that the interests of England form part of the interests of Europe. They laboured to make the Grand Alliance, formed for the defence of these common interests, a permanent union in peace as well as war. They sought to strengthen that great free commonwealth of nations, on the safety of which all these common interests depend, by crushing once and for ever the power of its most formidable and most perfidious enemy, by drawing round France the old limits within which she was harmless, and still further fortifying the power of Germany against her by securing the Hanoverian claim to the English and the Austrian claim to the Spanish throne.

"Such was the aim of our wise and sagacious leaders. All the different treaties into which under their guidance England has entered, all the subsidies she has expended, all the guarantees she has exacted in exchange for them, have been directed towards this end, towards making these two successions, on which the repose of Europe depends, a part of the public law of Europe. Their object has been to preserve our parliamentary constitution. With the Austrian claimant at Madrid, with the European concert maintained, with France muzzled and chained up, with the full claims of the allies conceded, with the guarantees given by them still in force, that constitution was secured. But now what chance is there of saving it when the patron and protector of the Stuarts has been strengthened by all the resources of the Spanish monarchy, when the European concert has been broken, and when every Power that favoured the existing settlement has been wantonly outraged by England's defection?

" It is true, no doubt, that so far as words go, ministers disclaim all intention of disturbing that settlement. They have required that France shall 'recognize' it in the treaties. They intend to insist, we hear, on her 'expelling' the Stuart Pretender from her territories. They have even gone further. They have brought down their royal mistress to the House of Lords in her state carriage and made her denounce publicly from the throne as the 'height of malice' the assertion that, under the rule of a Tory Government, the Protestant succession in the House of Hanover can be in any danger whatever. But then, is not this a part of the regular ministerial system? Is not organized deception a recognized principle of official Toryism? And is not the poor Queen invariably made an accomplice and participator in the fraud? They decide to reopen the negotiations for peace on a new footing and by clandestine agency. And they forthwith write to the principal allies in the Queen's name, engaging to take no steps towards peace without their knowledge and approval. They throw the public off the scent by putting into her mouth an unusually warlike speech to Parliament. They profess to agree with her allies that the offers made by France furnish an insufficient security to Europe, even when her secret preliminaries of peace, based on these very offers, are on the eve of being signed. And they instruct her plenipotentiaries to announce publicly on her behalf that no peace will be accepted which allots Spain to the Bourbons, at the very time when she has settled with France the conditions on which the Bourbons are to keep Spain.

"The truth is, that in dealing with a Government of ecclesiastics and fine gentlemen you must look solely to their actions, and pay no more heed to their solemn asseverations than to the whistling of the wind. We know that all their interests lie in overthrowing the parliamentary settlement. We know that with the Queen's life, unless they can succeed in doing so, their whole authority is gone. And we see them, while expressing extreme attachment to that settlement, insidiously pursuing a policy which leaves England without an ally in Europe favourable to it; which weakens and alienates every Power that has covenanted to support it; which strengthens and aggrandizes the already too powerful State whose constant aim it has been to subvert it. What are we to think? Are we to suppose that they have no other object than the mere malicious pleasure of upsetting arrangements made by their party rivals ? "

It was by such arguments, urged in speeches, in pamphlets, in letters, in familiar conversations, that, not zealous Whigs alone, but a large proportion of those neutral politicians whose vote determines an election, and a considerable minority even of the recognized supporters of Government, were led to the conclusion that, just as the Whig foreign policy had been a development of the old Triple Alliance, so the ministerial foreign policy had its roots in the rival Treaty of Dover, was intended to renew the old secret understanding between the two courts which dated from it, to further with English connivance the aggressions of France abroad, to restore by French help and maintain by French gold the Catholic line at home.

How far the Whig statesmen shared in this belief which they propagated with such industry and turned to their own advantage with such skill, it is impossible now to say. They were astute party politicians. They saw what an excellent cry it gave them, how well it would serve to withdraw public attention from those parts of their own policy which the public disliked, how easily the party charge of "danger to the succession" might be made to take the place of that equally damaging party charge of "danger to the Church," by which Atterbury and his clerical friends had destroyed Godolphin's majority.* Accordingly, as soon as the provisions of the treaty were made known, they "scanned and scrutinized" every step in the negotiations, and professed to discover in every article of the engagements clear proof of an intention to subvert the Revolution settlement. "They demolished before our eyes," says Bolingbroke plaintively, "the very

---

* This is well and fairly put by Bolingbroke in his " State of Parties at the Accession of George I." (Works, iii. 138).

work which was to have been our strength, and stoned us with the ruins of it." They fixed on the Government, in spite of all its struggles, the stigma of Jacobitism. They succeeded in thoroughly impressing this belief on the Electoral Court of Hanover, and in counteracting the natural prepossession of a German Prince and his surroundings for the party of reaction and prerogative. They succeeded in impressing this belief on almost the whole episcopal bench, and in counteracting the natural desire of Churchmen, like Dawes and Smalridge, to support a sacerdotal policy. They succeeded in impressing the belief on that small though powerful body of Tories who loyally accepted the parliamentary settlement, in completely separating them from their party, and in making a breach in the ministerial ranks which was never afterwards closed. Pressing on their attack, they forced the Government in very self-defence to rely more and more on the Jacobite contingent. They drove back the main body of landed gentlemen nearer and nearer to the brink of treason. Finally they pushed them over the edge, and shattered their political influence in the fall. It was a strange result of that peace of Utrecht, which was to restore and consolidate Toryism, that it threw all the power of the State into Whig hands, gave a new weight and influence to the commercial classes, filled the bench of bishops with latitudinarians and schismatics, established the parliamentary system on sure foundations, and annihilated the old cavalier party.

In the new reign the Low Church leaders, having recovered power, attempted to condense these floating beliefs into fixed articles of impeachment. They brought against both Bolingbroke and Oxford a definite charge of high treason, basing it in part on the terms of the treaty and in part on the method of negotiation pursued in it.

Reciting the various steps which had been taken by England in conjunction with the great Powers of Europe to stop the dangerous growth of France, and especially to prevent her from laying her hands on Spain, they accused their opponents of "conspiring together and getting possession of the Government" solely for the purpose of undoing this work, of joining Spain to France, of abetting France's scheme of universal monarchy, of bringing on Europe the very perils which England in her public declarations of policy was even yet striving to avert. They accused them of "betraying" in the pursuit of this object the "particular interests of their own country" as well as the common welfare of Europe, by making their demands in loose and inadequate terms and by purposely allowing them to remain unsettled till France had become sufficiently powerful to neglect them. They accused them of contributing to this traitorous design during its progress, by systematically weakening the confederate armies and by dissipating their forces in expeditions which had no bearing on the general result. And they accused them, finally, of concealing the design when complete under a pretended expedient for separating the two crowns, which they knew from the admission of their partners in the fraud to be altogether null and invalid.*

Such were the formulated charges, some of them palpably false, others true in substance but twisted and exaggerated out of all semblance to truth, under cover of which the Whig ministers of George I. began to consolidate parliamentary institutions, made a clear sweep of their political rivals, and secured to themselves for two generations a monopoly of power. No anticipated danger to the State, no benefits subsequently conferred on it, will justify

---

* See the articles of impeachment, "Parliamentary History," vii. 74, 114, 129.

such a system of warfare.* But in apportioning blame to the Whig chiefs it is right to remember the provocation given them. In their parliamentary exigencies they had recourse to weapons, the use of which we must condemn. But they had wrested these weapons from their opponents' hands. For four long bitter years they had seen themselves held up daily to public scorn and reprobation, in invectives surpassing in virulence any that party malice has bequeathed to us, as an ignoble self-seeking faction governing by corrupt arts and intent on base personal aims. They had seen their most distinguished leaders, one of them the foremost soldier and statesman in Europe, prosecuted, imprisoned, or driven into exile on charges which their accusers, when the object was gained, frankly admitted to be factitious. They had seen laws passed over their heads which shut out from public life large classes of their supporters, and a policy instituted of which the avowed object was to render permanent the ascendency of their party rivals. When the time came they retaliated, and being men of stronger nerve and more practised statesmanship they retaliated with success. They struck in their turn as hard as they could; and we cannot wonder at their doing so.

But posterity will freely acquit Bolingbroke and Oxford of all these criminal and treasonable accusations. They had no more desire to sacrifice the interests of England to a foreign power, to play the game of a foreign power, to further the aggressions of a foreign power, than Mr. Bright had when he denounced the Crimean expedition

---

* The articles charging high treason as distinguished from misdemeanour in the impeachments of Oxford and Bolingbroke were inserted chiefly (like the counts charging theft and embezzlement in the indictment of the Glasgow Bank directors) for the purpose of depriving the accused of their right to be out on bail. They would have been dropped at the trial. And the legal point in procedure on which the prosecution fell through was suggested to Harcourt by Walpole himself—one of the original promoters of the impeachment.

and the alliance for the defence of Turkey. The real charge against these early pioneers of non-intervention is that they regarded the material interests of England to the exclusion of all wider considerations, and that in their unscrupulous pursuit of an object in itself legitimate or even praiseworthy they endangered and nearly missed the results at which they aimed.

Nor is there anything in the treaties of peace, even if we include the secret arrangements made by Bolingbroke for the convenience of Mary of Modena, more directly favourable to the exiled House than the provisions made by King William at Ryswick sixteen years before. We now know, indeed, what their contemporaries suspected, but could not prove, that Harley from the summer of 1710 and St. John from the following spring maintained a pretty constant communication with the Pretender's agents and with the French ministers acting on his behalf. But the general drift of all the evidence since furnished to us tends to show that they were not Jacobites. Their offence was precisely similar in kind to that of Godolphin. When Godolphin was removed from office, the friends of James, as we now learn, lamented this event as a heavy blow to their cause; and Godolphin himself in his retirement is said to have expressed his "deep regret" that he had not "stayed in long enough" to bring back the "rightful heir." Yet no one now supposes that Godolphin, if he had "stayed in" forty years instead of twenty, would have lifted his little finger to bring back the "rightful heir," or would have looked on his return as anything but a public and private misfortune. Harley and St. John were perhaps a little more sincere than Godolphin. Godolphin, at least in his later years, had no Jacobite followers to conciliate; and his treason, if you can dignify it by such a name, was merely the worldly wisdom of a practical statesman, in an age of disputed titles, seeking to spread his political investments over as many securities as possible. To St. John and Harley the support of the Jacobite wing of the Tory party was indispensable. Without this support their majority in the Commons would have been grievously reduced; whilst in the Lords they would from the first have been hopelessly outnumbered. To secure this support it was necessary to be on friendly terms with St. Germain's. Accordingly attachment to the cause was professed, promises were made, advice was given. In return the Jacobite members of Parliament received express instructions from Berwick, both in 1711 and again three years later, to support the Government.

But when called upon to perform their part in the compact, to frame some definite plan, to take some irrevocable step which should commit them in the face of the country, both St. John and Harley, though now opposed to each other and bidding against each other, invariably drew back. Their autumnal promises always ended in vernal excuses. The time was not favourable. The Queen was difficult to manage and must not be hurried. It would be better to wait until after the peace. After the peace, rather to the surprise of the French court, their friendship seemed to cool. They were for the moment sufficiently strong in both Houses to stand on their own bottom. The new Parliament was now to be the millenary time of Jacobite fruition. In the summer of 1713, Parliament was dissolved; and in the following December— the support of the Jacobite members not having been yet assured to them—the French court was expressly informed by Oxford that at the opening of the new session a "plan" would be at length disclosed. The plan which the Jacobite leaders had formed, and which they pressed on Harley's attention, was for the Queen to present her brother to

Parliament as her destined successor. It was thought by them that the two Houses, being "taken by surprise," would not find courage to protest, and that the British public, being "proverbially very fickle," would be caught at once by the novelty and impudence of the proceeding. But as the time approached for putting this hopeful scheme into execution, difficulties as usual began to show themselves, and pretexts for delay to be invented. The Prince must first abjure the Catholic faith. He must dismiss, besides, all his present advisers, and he must give himself up entirely into the hands of the High Church leaders. To his uncle Berwick, the wisest and most experienced of those advisers, these constant excuses "looked ill." To negotiate for two or three years, and then make at the last "impracticable suggestions" and propose "an impossible thing," seemed to him a "*querelle d'Allemand*." *

The truth is beyond all doubt that a restoration formed no essential part of the Government policy at all. It was a measure to be kept carefully in reserve, like the false king in the sleeve of an ecarté player, not to be brought out until the turning point of the game, or unless the winning trump should be in the adversary's hand. Just as the Whig foreign policy sought to consolidate a parliamentary Government in England by making it for the time a matter of European interest, by linking it to the several objects of other States, and by organizing in its defence a union of Great Powers, so the Tory foreign policy aimed at setting England free at every cost to her

---

* Berwick to James Stuart, August 18, 1713, and March 23, 1714. The direct evidence inculpating Oxford and Bolingbroke was extracted from the French archives by Sir James Mackintosh in 1814. It consists chiefly of letters between the French Government and their agents—Gaultier, D'Aumont, and D'Iberville. A fair summary of it is given in the *Edinburgh Review* for October, 1835. But what seems to the Reviewer "decisive proof that the Tory Government was engaged in a *design* to restore the Pretender," will hardly be accepted as such by the well-informed reader.

neighbours from these continental entanglements, free to
manage her own affairs without foreign help or foreign
hindrance. The ulterior object of the treaty no doubt was
to re-establish Toryism. That was never denied by Bolingbroke. " Peace," he tells us, " was the only solid foundation on which we could erect a Tory system." But Toryism
was not necessarily Jacobitism. A Tory system meant
the old constitution in Church and State, rigid political
and religious tests, government by royal initiative in the
interest of the clergy and landed gentry, the exclusion
from civil rights of the trading and dissenting classes ;
and to this system a legitimate sovereign surrounded by
Jesuits and escorted by French troops might be just
as hostile as a parliamentary sovereign surrounded by
Presbyterians and convoyed by a Dutch fleet. After the
Queen's death, indeed, in the disgust at seeing their hated
rivals monopolizing power and their own weapons and
tactics so successfully turned against them, all thought
of danger to the privileged Church was forgotten ; a
restoration of the old line by any means and on any
conditions became the main object of the whole constitutional party ; Toryism was merged in Jacobitism ; and
Bolingbroke, borne along by the tide, became an active
conspirator and rebel. But even then he was never a
Jacobite. The means he employed differed at different
times. But his object was throughout consistent. It was
to establish the Tory party in power by appealing to the
principle which seemed at the moment to divide them
the least, and by using the instruments which seemed at
the moment most handy. And whilst the Queen still lived,
whilst the opinions and intentions of her successor were
still doubtful, whilst the Tory Government still retained
possession of power, and whilst the laws they had passed
for perpetuating that power seemed not unlikely to work,

there was no "formed design" amongst the ministers, because there was no "general resolution" in the party, to disturb the Act of Settlement.*

II.

It was in the summer of 1713, when the question of peace or war had been finally set at rest, that the subject of the succession again came to the front in the parliamentary struggle between the two parties. The policy of the Whigs was clear and definite, and their course throughout consistent. Their object was to defend by every means in their power the legal settlement of the Crown, and to confirm the common belief that their opponents were bent on subverting it. Public spirit and party interest pointed in their case in the same direction. No differences of opinion impeded their efforts. They were perfectly united; they had sagacious leaders well able to advise them; they had an unrivalled party organization; they pursued their object, as Bolingbroke enviously said, "in good order and in concert." The Tories, on the other hand, though they had on their side the Church, the Parliament, the Crown, and a majority, perhaps, in the nation, were weak precisely where the Whigs were strong. Personal rivalries and private jealousies paralyzed the Government. Conflicting attachments divided and distracted the party. The result was a scene of confusion

* The position of Bolingbroke with respect to Jacobitism in 1714 closely resembled that of Mr. Disraeli with respect to Protection in 1852. In neither case was there any "formed design" to interfere with the settlement made a few years before. In neither case was there any belief in the opposite doctrine, which nevertheless in order to conciliate powerful supporters it was necessary sometimes to profess. In both cases there was a desire to leave things as they were, which desire would in both cases have yielded to a stronger necessity had the bulk of their party pronounced decisively against it.

and vacillation which Bolingbroke has painted in the most sombre tints. "The prospect before us is dark and melancholy, and what will be the end no man can foretell." "I hoped that the whole Church interest would as one man have supported the Queen, exclusive of all other assistance, to vest all power in themselves, and by these means establish themselves for the present age and for futurity." "But the best dispositions are unimproved. The party stands at gaze, expecting the court will regulate them and lead them on ; and the court seems in a lethargy." *

So long as the policy of ministers had been determined for them by the unanimous injunction of their followers, their own private dissensions had interfered but little with their public conduct. The process of party consolidation had been pursued in many vigorous measures. Parliamentary censures had been passed on the "mismanagement" of their predecessors and on their "misappropriations" of the public money. Parliamentary representations had been carried to the throne denouncing their "wild and unwarrantable schemes" of domestic politics. Addresses had been voted praying the Queen to employ in places of public trust only such men as had given testimony of their affection for the Church interest. Treaties of alliance with foreign powers, designed to secure the new settlement against foreign enemies, had been condemned as destructive of British interests, and the negotiators of them branded by the Commons as "enemies of their country." Inquiries had been set on foot under cover of which formidable assailants of the new ministry had been expelled from Parliament. New conditions had been attached to the right of voting in boroughs, intended to

* Bolingbroke to the Lord Chancellor of Ireland, April 13 and May 20, 1714; Bolingbroke to Shewsbury, April 13, 1714.

disfranchise the nonconforming bodies. New qualifications had been imposed on the members elected, intended to confine the representation to the proprietors of the soil. It was hoped that by such measures the opposition would be, to use the expression of Swift, "disabled;" the "sting" of the Dissenters taken away; the "body" of the Whigs broken, and their "supports" rendered useless to them. A Parliament chosen exclusively by Churchmen, and consisting exclusively of country gentlemen, could hardly, it was thought, be hostile to a Tory system of government.*

In the policy which dictated these and kindred measures, Tories of all denominations had heartily concurred. It was when ministers had been rendered tolerably safe, as they hoped, against "attempts during the Queen's reign," and began to turn their eyes to the "events that might happen afterwards," that questions arose which provoked controversy—questions concerning which, says Bolingbroke candidly, "few or none of us, to speak the truth, had any very decided opinions." How was political strength thus gained to be nursed up and employed for the purpose of making their domination permanent? Was the Act of Settlement to be loyally accepted, or openly repealed, or traitorously set aside? How were the conflicting attachments of the country gentlemen—their love of hereditary power, their hatred of Popery—to be reconciled? Were conditions to be imposed on the parliamentary heir in the interest of the privileged party? Or were securities to be exacted from the legitimate King in the interest of the privileged Church?

To these questions several different answers were given. At one extremity of the party was a body of sincere and uncompromising Jacobites, whose zeal for the hereditary

* "Parliamentary History," vi. 1026, 1003, 1092; Swift's Works, v. 403.

line outweighed their dread of Romanism, who were in favour of recalling the legitimate King without conditions, and who treated the Act of Settlement as a nullity. These men looked to the Duke of Ormond as their leader. Ormond was now commander-in-chief and warden of the Cinque Ports. He was engaged, as his enemies alleged, in purging the army of every officer favourable to the Protestant cause, and in securing it for James's interest. His titles to public confidence and respect were few; but his great name, his lavish expenditure, and the winning courtesy of his demeanour, had earned for him no small share of his grandfather's immense and deserved popularity. With Ormond were closely allied Harcourt, the Lord Keeper, and Buckingham, the Lord President. But his most noted parliamentary adherent, and in some respects the most remarkable man of those times, was Francis Atterbury, now Bishop of Rochester, the most turbulent and the most consistent of all High Churchmen, who had asserted the independence of the clergy as regards the civil power; who had asserted the independence of the priesthood as regards the episcopal bench; who had steadfastly maintained that no mere positive law could ever extinguish the rights of the anointed line; who, in pursuit of his high aims, was deterred by no scruples of what worldly men call honour or timid moralists conscience; who afterwards boasted that he had let slip no opportunity of injuring that parliamentary Sovereign at whose coronation he had officiated, or of serving the cause of that Pretender whose title he had solemnly abjured; and who was in his old age by a dramatic retribution stripped of his spiritual functions and banished by a decree of that Power whose laws he had throughout his life systematically and on principle set at nought. It was whispered about, though the rumour was probably false, that the Queen herself was in secret sympathy with these men, and that she had received from Buckingham, and read with strong emotion, a letter in the Prince's hand, making an earnest appeal to her sisterly compassion.

At the other end of the party was a body smaller in numbers but of greater parliamentary weight, which accepted the Hanoverian settlement loyally and without misgivings. Its leader was a country gentleman of great estate, Sir Thomas Hanmer, member for Suffolk, and for a short time Speaker of the House of Commons. Hanmer had been hitherto one of the most zealous supporters of Government. So far as they had been published, he had warmly approved of the peace negotiations, and had consented to father the famous Parliamentary Representation, drawn up by Swift and Bolingbroke, in which, after the opening of the congress, ministers replied to the thrust of the Whig lords touching the insufficiency of the French offers. Hanmer was an intimate friend of Ormond's. After the labours of the session, he witnessed, as the guest of the commander-in-chief, the events of the campaign—the refusal of the English general to march against the French, his retreat from the side of the allies when the French marched against them, his gallant capture of Ghent and Bruges from the Dutch garrisons. There is reason to believe that the member of Parliament was then initiated by Ormond into the Jacobite intrigues now beginning to take shape, and that his journey to Paris in the autumn of the same year was prompted by the desire of becoming personally familiar with the character and surroundings of the legitimate heir to the Crown.

It would have been well, perhaps, if other distinguished Tory gentlemen had followed Hanmer's example; for he returned home a sincere and indeed an ardent Hanoverian. In the following session it was Hanmer's sudden defection

at the most critical point of the debate—he had profited
by his short experience of military affairs—that sealed the
fate of Bolingbroke's commercial treaty with France, and
gave the Government a blow from which it never afterwards rallied. In the same summer Bromley was promoted
from the chair of the House of Commons to be Secretary
of State; and Hanmer was chosen to succeed him, in the
hope, as Oxford took occasion to inform the French court,
of "disarming his opposition," but really, it is more
reasonable to believe, in order to mark the Prime Minister's
secret attachment to the party which proposed to carry out
the existing law. Certainly Hanmer's opposition was not
"disarmed." Throughout the stormy and critical session
which ensued, he exerted the whole of his great influence
as Speaker to further the objects of the Whig leaders, and
supported every motion, however embarrassing to his old
friends, which tended to confirm the chances of the legal
heir.

In the House of Commons Hanmer directed a body of
men counting between forty and fifty members. As parties
then stood, this was hardly sufficient to turn the scale
against Government. In the House of Lords, however,
where numbers were more evenly balanced, and where the
brunt of the contest lay, he had a stronger and more
distinguished following. Here he was supported by two
ministers of the Crown, who had themselves borne a large
share in the peace negotiations—Dartmouth, now advanced
to be Lord Privy Seal, and Bishop Robinson, now preferred to the metropolitan see. He was supported by the
newly elected Archbishop of York, who, in the great debate
on the succession, turned against the Government which
had just appointed him; by all the High Church prelates,
with the single exceptions of Crewe of Durham, who had
sat in James's High Commission, and the audacious

Atterbury, who was ready to proclaim the Popish Pretender in the lawn of an Anglican bishop; by Argyle, chief amongst the Scottish nobles, to whose great influence in the northern kingdom the success there of the Revolution was afterwards due, and who was now intriguing as viciously against Bolingbroke as four years before he had intrigued against Marlborough; and by Anglesea, the leader of the Irish Tories, who, whilst warmly advocating Bolingbroke's domestic measures, denounced his foreign policy as fatal to the Protestant cause.

Filling the space between these two wings, and leaning sometimes to Protestantism and sometimes to right divine, came the bulk of the Tory country gentlemen. Their future as a political party, and his own lasting success as a statesman, depended, as Bolingbroke well knew, on his power of giving what he calls "a regular motion to all the wheels of government," of inventing some common policy which might satisfy both these attachments, or, failing this, might unite his followers by fixing their thoughts on one.

The scheme which Swift suggested for this purpose had the merit of clearness and consistency. Swift had a great contempt for the doctrine of indefeasible hereditary right. He had a great respect for the Established Church as a political institution. Both these feelings impelled him to side with Hanmer. But he differed with Hanmer as to the extent to which the spirit of Jacobitism had infected their party. The nation, according to Swift—and when Swift or Bolingbroke speaks of the nation he always means the landed interest—the nation was pretty nearly unanimous on two points: first, to preserve the Church in all its rights and privileges, all schisms and heresies to be put down, all doctrines in politics which she discountenanced to be prohibited; secondly, to maintain the Protestant succession

N

in the House of Hanover, not out of any partiality for that illustrious House, but as the nearest Protestant heirs, anticipating the next two reigns with some misgivings, and looking forward to that of the "young grandson," whose name Swift could not remember, but who might surely at his tender age, if sent into England at once, be taught something of the language, and even the institutions and interests of the people, before being called upon in the course of Providence to govern them. In a remarkable paper written in the early summer of 1714, he drew up for Bolingbroke's guidance a plan of campaign which would, as he conceived, render ministers secure of retaining power even under a Sovereign predisposed to favour their Whig rivals; and in a remarkable letter written in the week following the Queen's death, he ascribed the discomfiture of his friends and the breaking down of what he calls "their machine of four years' modelling" to the neglect of his advice. "Those wonderful refinements of keeping men in expectation and not letting your friends be too strong might be proper in their season: *sed nunc non erat his locus.*" " I never left off pressing my Lord Oxford with the utmost earnestness that we might be put in such a condition as not to lie at mercy in this great event; and I am your lordship's witness that you have nothing to answer in that matter."*

Swift's plan was to unite together the different elements of the Church party by once more appealing to their common Toryism. He had passed the best years of his life in Ireland, and he doubtless remembered how often the strong political differences which there divided the dominant caste had been forgotten in the still stronger

---

* Swift to Bolingbroke, August 7, 1714. Compare D'Iberville to Lewis XIV. " My Lord Bolingbroke est pénétré de douleur de la perte de la Règne, au point de sa fortune particulière et de la consommation de toutes les affaires qui ont esté faites depuis quatre ans."

antipathy which they all bore as Englishmen to the subject Irish nation. Even so would the dominant party learn to forget its petty divisions if united and animated by an attack on the common enemy of its cherished privileges. Let the parliamentary heir be brought in as the symbol of a Tory triumph, and he would be regarded with complacency, even by Churchmen of Jacobite leanings. And the very same measures which animated and united the Church party would strengthen and consolidate the Tory Government and render it master of the situation. "No prince objects to a quiet reign or fails in the long run to understand his own interest, and with the whole civil and military power in the hands of the present Government, and the strength of the Whig confederacy broken, it would not be in any way for the quiet and interest of the new Sovereign to gratify so small a faction as would then remain."

As to the measures necessary to be taken, well, ministers must have the courage of their opinions. They had shown that they knew how to deal with those who differed from them, but they had seemed half ashamed of this knowledge. In the House of Lords, for instance, after securing a party majority by filling it with their own adherents, they had allowed the power so gained to slip out of their hands. "Nothing has given me greater indignation," says Swift, "than to behold the ministry acting ever on the defensive in the House of Lords, with a majority on their side, and instead of calling others to account, as it was reasonably expected, misspending their time and losing many opportunities of doing good, because a struggling faction kept them continually in play." Even in the House of Commons, where their strength was naturally so great, they had not exerted that strength steadily and vigorously to make all opposition vain. The measures they had taken for extending the Church's influence in politics and for confirming power to its members would take a generation at least to bear fruit; and in the meantime there was this danger, that before the protecting fences set round Toryism could grow up they might all be swept away, if, in the changes of public life, the party opponents of Toryism should regain power. What was wanted was some means of preventing this, some means of protecting the State from men who, whilst they were perfectly willing to take the religious tests which the State imposed, were hostile to the political system which those tests were designed to support. "Do not confine the attack," therefore urged Swift, "to the open enemies of the Church (under which head I include at least Dissenters of all denominations) by not admitting them to the smallest degree of civil and military power. Let her secret adversaries (under the name of Whigs, Low Churchmen, Republicans, moderation men, and the like) receive no mark of favour but what they shall deserve by a sincere repentance." "Were this policy pursued in all its parts and asserted as the avowed resolution of the court, there would soon be an end of faction." Swift passes in review in his pleasant way the various reasons which had been given for not "wholly subduing the discontented party;" and he dismisses them as "too great a sacrifice of the nation's safety to the genius of politics, considering how much was to be done and how little time might probably be allowed" for doing it, considering also "the obnoxious tenets of the Whigs in religion and government." "It is really not safe temporizing in this conjuncture; first, because their principles and practices have been already very dangerous to the constitution in Church and State, but principally because they have prevailed by misrepresentation and artifice to make the successor look upon them as the only persons he can trust;

upon which account (concludes Swift) they cannot be too soon nor too much disabled, neither will England ever be safe from the attempts of this wicked confederacy until their strength and interest shall be so far reduced that for the future it shall not be in the power of the Crown, though in conjunction with any rich or factious body of men, to choose an ill majority of the House of Commons." *

Such was the policy which Swift recommended for animating and uniting the Church interest and consolidating the Tory position. A year later, in the life-long exile to which the failure of their schemes condemned him—with the Whig confederacy in power, Whig majorities in both Houses, and a policy of proscription in the interest of Whiggism beginning to take shape—he laments with unavailing bitterness how wantonly his friends had thrown their chance away, how "one or two acts, which might have passed in ten days, would have put it utterly out of the power of the successor, with very little diminution of the prerogative, to have procured a Parliament of a different stamp." † But he exonerates Bolingbroke from the responsibility of this failure ; and there is no doubt that the young minister, had power been his, would have followed the advice so given. Like Swift, he had no religious prejudice in favour of divine right. He was not indeed bound to the Act of Settlement, as Harley was, by a paternal tie ; but he had attended at its birth, and watched over its cradle. As a matter of speculative liking he would have preferred to serve under a parliamentary King—his quiet succession secured by the adherence of the Church party, his title too weak to let him interfere with their designs, his gratitude and his sympathies alike binding him to the ministers of prerogative. Like Swift, too, Bolingbroke was essentially a statesman, with none of

* Swift's Works, v. 393, 396, 403.   † Ibid., vi. 64.

the military adventurer's contempt for constitutional forms;
and indeed a *coup d'état* in the interest of legitimacy, with
the army divided, with the nation lukewarm, with all the
foremost statesmen on both sides hostile, with the military
arrangements of the legal heir directed by the greatest of
living generals, and his person escorted by the powerful
Dutch armament which the States-General, in a compact
framed by these very ministers, had covenanted to provide
him,—a *coup d'état* was an adventure from which a bolder
man than Bolingbroke might have shrunk. It would be
far safer and pleasanter to play the game out on the
square. To the last he continued to make substantial
bids for the favour of the electoral court. To the last
he continued to put off the Jacobite leaders with vague
promises, and send them away amused with lively anecdotes
about the domestic arrangements in vogue at Herrenhausen.

III.

But in the preliminary process of extirpating the
political and religious factions opposed to Toryism, and
of rendering the Church interest sufficiently powerful to
dictate its own terms, and await the issue with confidence,
Bolingbroke was fatally hampered at once by the passive
resistance of the Lord Treasurer, and by his own want of
influence with the complex party that followed them ; and
these two causes acting together so impeded his efforts,
that when at last the first was removed the propitious
moments had passed by, and the fate of his Government
was already sealed.

The enmity between the two leading ministers was now
of old standing. It had its origin in essential differences
of character and opinion. At the time of the formation of

his Government, Harley, when deprived of the support on which he had calculated in the tried statesmanship of the Whig leaders, had augured ill from the uncompromising ambition of his High Church colleague, and admitted him to a chief share in its councils with misgivings. Every incident of ministerial life tended to widen the breach between them. The honours and rewards so lavishly bestowed on Harley in the spring of 1711, after his escape from the murderous attack of Guiscard, roused the jealous cupidity of the young Secretary of State, and were made all the more galling to him by the slights and humiliations to which he conceived himself exposed. More than once their rivalry threatened to bring the negotiation for peace to a standstill. At length, about the time of the dissolution of Parliament, in July 1713, the hatred of Bolingbroke for his chief broke through the restraints of decency, and showed itself in personal abuse delivered in presence of the clerks and messengers of his office. It was scarcely possible, perhaps, for two men so variously constituted by nature to act cordially together, even had their opinions and their objects agreed. As the shrewdest observer of those days remarked, after four years of close personal intercourse with them, they differed in all their ways—in their studies, in their diversions, in their mode of transacting business, in their choice of company, and in their manner of conversation.* Oxford was essentially a man of the middle class ; and in spite of his earldom, his white staff and his blue riband, he retained to the last the traces of his Puritan origin. His speech was confused and hesitating, his figure was mean, his air constrained and secret, his manner at once diffident and presuming. His intellect, assiduously cultivated with the learning of the schools, was slow and lethargic ; his temper reserved and cautious.

* Swift's Works, vi. 32.

His conversation, generally instructive and sometimes lively, savoured of the circuit mess rather than the London dinner-table. Even his virtues, his warm domestic attachments, his horror of raking and gambling, his uprightness in money matters, were in the highest degree unfashionable.

But it was in politics that the two statesmen most differed, and here their designs and objects were altogether antagonistic. Though the head of the High Church connection, Harley had never believed in High Church principles. It was as an advanced Radical, as we should now call it, an enemy of party combinations, a friend of peace and retrenchment, of frequent and pure elections, of the strict subordination of ministers to an independent House of Commons, that he had organized towards the close of King William's reign his formidable and at length successful opposition to the Whig junto; and his early principles, though somewhat corrupted by his associations, retained a strong hold upon him. Some he was willing to sacrifice to his ambition, but not all; and his annoyance, when the rampant Toryism, of his followers took a form more than usually repulsive to him, showed itself so plainly that the idea of his unsoundness, of what Bolingbroke calls his "insincerity," rapidly spread. In truth, the election of 1710, by returning a Parliament devoted to the High Church interest, made the position of the first minister a false one. The intemperance of political faction was as offensive to Harley as the extravagance of courtly vice; and the solemn airs of mystery which he afterwards affected, the wonderful refinements of which his colleagues complained, had their spring much more in his dislike to the proscriptive policy marked out for him than in the natural indolence of his temper. The sort of Government which he had desired to see in power was not a cabal of party politicians animated by the ferocious spirit of the

October Club, and bent on forcing Church principles on the nation by rack and thumbscrew, but a council of grave statesmen so mingled together as to be free from extreme party bias, deciding every public question on its merits, and recording their various judgments, subject to the criticism and, in extreme cases, to the punishment of a free Parliament, but owing allegiance solely to the Crown, and each accountable only for his own department, for the documents which he signed, and for the advice which he gave his Sovereign. Such a Government, born of compromise and prone to temporizing counsels, exactly suited his peculiar disposition, and gave full scope to the exercise of his peculiar talents. To the last he clung to the idea of a moderate and comprehensive scheme; and from the evil day when the High Churchmen gained the mastery began to clog the wheels of government, and to lean once more to the opposing Whigs and his old nonconforming friends.

He took a leading and vigorous part in putting an end to the Whig war, the lavish expenditure and extended responsibilities of which, he had never cordially liked. But the accessory measures, as Bolingbroke calls them, the measures for establishing and fortifying Toryism, of which peace was to be the preliminary, these, so far from favouring, he did his best to frustrate. The projected attack on the Nonconformists was not carried out till Harley's influence in the Government had waned, and was shorn of its harshest features by his secret hostility. The projected attack on the great mercantile corporations, a favourite scheme with the country gentlemen, received no countenance from the first minister, whose policy was not to destroy but to stimulate commercial industry, and to counteract the weight which the Bank and the East India Company brought to their party opponents by creating

rival bodies bound to the Tory interest as they were to
the Whig. The importunate demand of the extreme High
Churchmen, pressing for a thorough change in employments and a complete remodelling of the civil and military
administration in their party interest, he put off with the
same dilatory pleas, the same promises and the same
excuses with which he met the request of the Jacobite
leaders urging him to frame some "plan," and with the
same inevitable result of breeding suspicion and discontent.
At court he did his utmost now to lessen the sinister
influence of Lady Masham, exercised as it was in the
exclusive interest of the High Church party; he resolutely
put a limit to her pilferings of public money; and his fall
was chiefly due to her intrigues against him. In Parliament he was aghast at the spirit of faction which he had
raised, hindered so far as he decently could the commissions that had been nominated in the first flush of
the Tory triumph for the purpose of bringing to light and
punishing the supposed malversations of the late ministry,
prophesied their certain failure and the party discredit
that would inevitably ensue.

But the minister had by this time earned for himself
such a character for successful dissimulation that no party
in the State would any longer trust him, even in matters
where he had no object and no interest in deceiving them.
That he was at heart unfavourable to the Jacobite claims
was not doubted by his colleagues, and will hardly be
doubted by any one who attentively studies his career.
And yet, whilst the adherents of the Pretender saw through
his hollow professions and rated his pretended sympathy
at its real value, the Whig leaders persisted in treating
him as the chief of a daring Jacobite conspiracy; and
mainly through their efforts the public at large, and the
Hanoverian envoys in particular, held him responsible

for every high-handed act of Government at the very time when its own supporters were justly attributing to him what they called its general feebleness and slackness. It was a grave disadvantage to Harley that his closest personal friends—Ormond, Bromley, and, outside the Government, Trevor—had little in common with him in politics; whilst the more moderate members, the men nearly allied to him in political objects—Dartmouth, for instance, and Shrewsbury—he had offended by his secrecy and reserve, his indifference to their personal wishes, his habit of keeping in his own hands all the power and patronage of the State. During the last few months of his official life he stood utterly alone; his party estranged from him, his popularity gone, his character understood but his objects misinterpreted, fighting the battle of civil and religious freedom against a host of personal and political enemies. In his isolation the tranquil and courageous spirit, the "soul supreme in each hard instance tried," which his illustrious friend ascribes to him, and which he had hitherto preserved in all the failures and successes of his eventful life, for the first and last time forsook him. He became morose and acrimonious, subject to long fits of sullenness, alternating with violent and ungovernable displays of passion. He had always been too fond of wine; and he now indulged his favourite vice at unseasonable hours, and on occasions when the commonest prudence and good breeding should have restrained him. Yet so long as the session lasted, such was his rare skill in parliamentary fence, such the difficulty of fixing on a successor who would unite the discordant party, that he was able to parry and even return the blows aimed at him from so many different sides.*

* Swift's Works, vi. 37; Arbuthnot to Swift, June 26, 1714; Lewis to Swift, July 6, 1714. "The dragon," writes Arbuthnot, "dies hard. He

Bolingbroke led on the attack from the side of the extreme High Churchmen. In after years he adopted Harley's radical principles, united them to the monarchical theories proper to Toryism, and formed out of the union a new and more popular variety. He was now, however, playing the part of an orthodox Tory. He aimed at uniting the Church interest by "vesting all power in themselves," and aspired to head a Church Government based on the true Tory policy of exclusion and proscription.

But in truth his position in the party was hardly less insecure than Harley's. Between himself and the great body of country gentlemen and country clergymen were moral and intellectual differences which hindered all hearty co-operation, and which no efforts on his part could overleap. In Clarendon, antipathy to religious freedom and reverence for the Anglican priesthood were not put on as part of the livery of political service and laid aside in the familiar intercourse of private life. In his own grave and decorous intolerance, in his arrogant contempt for everything unfamiliar to him, in his superstitious respect for privilege and constitutional traditions, he well represented the inbred conservatism of the old historic Cavalier. Rochester, again, to whom after a few years' interval a large part of his father's influence descended, was an excellent type of the Cavalier degenerating into the more modern Tory; shrewd and businesslike, hot-tempered but placable, rough in his manners and impatient of contradiction, convivial in his habits, but a firm believer and

---

is kicking and cuffing about him like the devil; and you know parliamentary management is his forte." "The two ladies," writes Lewis, "seem to have determined the fall of the dragon (Oxford), and to entertain a chimerical notion that there shall be no *monsieur le premier*, but that all power shall reside in one and all profit in the other. The man of mercury (Bolingbroke) soothes them in this notion with great success; for he will be *monsieur le premier* by virtue of the little seals. His character is too bad to carry the great ensign."

sincere Churchman, willing in pursuit of power and money to go a long way in the path of compromise but with fixed opinions, both political and religious, with which no hope of worldly gain would induce him to tamper. Even Danby, corrupt and shameless as he was, had all the English gentleman's respect for Protestantism and narrow jealousy of foreign influence, and earned the confidence of his supporters less by his despotic schemes than by his hearty and unfeigned indignation against the courtiers who would have established arbitrary power in England at the price of her subjection to France and Rome. St. John, with natural gifts far exceeding theirs, never attained to the political authority which these three leaders possessed. His Toryism, so to speak, was never in the grain. More than once during his short career as minister his want of common interests with his followers, his failure to understand them, to fathom the depth of their ignorance or measure the extent to which prejudice had warped their minds, betrayed him into acts which, however beneficial to England or honourable to him as a statesman, had a disastrous effect in disorganizing his party. It was as an orator, a House of Commons' orator, that he exercised dominion over them ; and his empire ceased when the tones of his voice no longer filled their ears.

As a party orator he was without a rival. In the momentous session which preceded the peace, when the failure of the ministerial policy seemed inevitable and the fall of the Government a question of days, when their warmest friends assured them that the game was over, when the preposterous and insulting offers given in by France to their allies had once more inflamed the national indignation against her, when the public conferences on which the success of their plans depended had ceased to meet, when the House of Lords, in spite of the large

additions just made there to their party following, had
passed a unanimous vote condemnatory of their party
schemes, it was St. John's eloquence which saved them by
stirring up that spirit in the House of Commons and by
inciting it to those resolutions which alone, as he most
justly says, rendered the conclusion of the treaties practic-
able. Nor is he to be seriously blamed for the means by
which this influence was from time to time sustained,
legitimate as they have always been considered in the
strife of contending factions, practised as they have been
by both parties in their turn, and well calculated as they
undoubtedly are to govern a body like our House of
Commons. " You know," he used afterwards to say when
recalling those stirring weeks—" you know the nature of that
assembly ? They grow like hounds fond of the man who
shows them game and by whose halloo they are accustomed
to be encouraged." But an ascendency purchased by such
arts as the prosecution of Marlborough and the expulsion
of Walpole, though for the moment complete, is apt to be
shortlived. The country gentlemen, shrewd, honest in the
main, and patriotic, could hardly help, when the pleasure
of pursuit was over and enjoyment had cooled their
passions, feeling resentment against the minister who had
so skilfully turned them to his purpose by pandering for
their public vices. In the case of one of the most eminent,
a man who had borne a leading part under Bolingbroke's
direction in the resolutions of that very session and who
continued to the last to approve his domestic objects ; a
thorough Tory, anxious to perpetuate by all lawful means
the authority of the landed interest ; a zealous Episcopalian, bent on enforcing by the most stringent penalties
the supremacy of the Anglican Church ; but before all
things a Protestant Englishman, who had seen for himself
the effect of the policy which he had supported in alienating

from England the confidence of Protestant Europe, and
the hopes it was exciting amongst the enemies of the
Protestant cause ;—this resentment prompted him to
abandon ministers at the crisis of their fate, and to play
the game of the Whig chiefs with whose main objects his
own were in direct antagonism.

Nor was Bolingbroke's personal character, with all its
striking features, one likely to prove attractive to a party
of English fox-hunters, whether lay or clerical. He was,
it is true, a three-bottle man. He could carry his liquor
discreetly ; and penned many an effective despatch with
towels round his head, still dizzy from the fumes of his
night's debauch. And he sometimes showed himself,
faultlessly appointed, at the covert side. But these were
sacrifices made to the requirements of his position, just as
he would take the consecrated bread and wine as prescribed
by the Test Act, according to the rites of the Anglican
Church ; and he was, in fact, as much a man of cities and
drawing-rooms and as little of a sportsman as Harley.
Whilst Harley, in emancipating himself from the religious
convictions of his family, retained the decorous habits and
grave demeanour of his youth, and was extorting by his
domestic virtues the respect of the very men whose political
confidence he was forfeiting by the moderation and
sobriety of his opinions, St. John, sprung like Harley from
a Puritan household, had developed into an accomplished
roué and man of the world, dissolute and sceptical, an adept
in every courtly vice, a master of Machiavelian statesmanship. His polished manners, his lively wit, his quick
perceptions, his facile speech, his ready invention, the ease
with which he caught and mimicked the intemperate tone
of his rude supporters, his fondness for subterfuge and
artifice, his affectation of philosophical indifference to the
objects for which he was at the moment most eagerly

...g, his vanity, his industry, his simulated idleness, his unfeigned respect for speculative truth, his falseness in all public and personal relations, the vastness and boldness of his political enterprises, the nervous apprehension of physical danger which at the critical moment marred so many of them, the loftiness of his moral conceptions, the looseness and even dirtiness of his private life,—all these things were the marks of a character which in its strange and various traits an Italian of the great age of Florence would have studied with respectful interest, but which repelled the Trullibers and Westerns from its very dissimilarity to their own.

In the statesmanship of such a man there is no doubt a natural propensity to indirect and tortuous ways, to sinister intrigues, to organized deceptions, to statements which, when literally true, are calculated and designed to give a false impression, to concealed engagements and sudden surprises. Bolingbroke has himself explained this necessity in a characteristic passage and under a fine simile. "The ocean which environs us," he writes, "is an emblem of our government; and the pilot and the minister are in similar circumstances. The minister, like the pilot, can seldom steer a direct course, and is forced to arrive in port by means which frequently seem to carry him from it. He is exposed to accidents and hazards; he is compelled to manage men of different characters and different in their interests: he is distracted by measures which have no relation to his purpose, and obliged to bend himself to things which are in some degree contrary to his main design. But as the work advances, the conduct of him who leads it on with real abilities clears up, the appearing inconsistencies are reconciled, and when it is once consummated the whole shows itself so uniform, so plain, and so natural, that every dabbler in politics will be apt to think he could have done the same."

And the result is that when, as in Bolingbroke's own case, the work is never consummated, when the vessel founders in mid-ocean, there is a certain difficulty in reconciling the appearing inconsistencies of the pilot's course ; and much of his conduct, instead of showing itself plain, uniform, and natural, remains what it was at first— a riddle to the world. But he has made no concealment as to the object which he proposed to himself, and, so far as the accidents and hazards of public life permitted, steadily pursued. His "main design," as indicated by himself in countless passages of his correspondence, was to deliver the great body which formed the Tory interest from the vicissitudes to which under a free constitution all political parties are exposed. He sought to do for the High Churchmen what Cromwell had done seventy years before for the Independents—to establish in their ranks the discipline and enthusiasm which distinguished the parliamentary army, and then by their means to put down the conflict of factions by vesting all right to power in themselves. His "purpose" was to make dissent from the privileged Church, and opposition to the privileged party an offence against the law, a criminal attack on the established constitution in Church and State. It was not to be brought about, as he well knew, by any change of dynasty. Even if the rightful heir had consented, by dissembling his religious belief and dismissing his Jesuit counsellors, to bring himself within the letter of the Bill of Rights and the spirit of the Act of Settlement, and so had united the whole Church interest in his favour, this would not have fixed the yoke of that interest more securely on the nation ; and this was the point about which Bolingbroke was anxious. What he calls the "fortifying and establishing of Toryism," the "securing those who had been principal actors in the administration against future events," the "inducing the whole Church interest to join as one man in fixing Government on that foundation not for the present age only but for futurity,"—these were the questions which occupied his mind, and which ought, but for Oxford's resistance, to have determined the ministerial policy. It is to this that Swift alludes when he laments the breaking down of their " scheme of four years' modelling ; " and to this no doubt that Bolingbroke referred a few days after Oxford's fall in his remark to D'Iberville, which that zealous Jacobite transmitted to his court as a proof of Bolingbroke's Jacobitism : " In another six weeks matters would have been put in such a state that come what might I should have had nothing to fear." * The fortifying and establishing of Toryism was to be brought about by measures very different from the recall of a young prince with the antecedents and surroundings of the Pretender. Had not the Pretender's father owed his throne entirely to the exertions of the privileged Church ? And how had he requited those exertions? By making apostasy from her principles the condition of his favour, by depriving her ministers of their freeholds, by imprisoning her foremost dignitaries, by turning her schools and colleges into hotbeds of Popery. What if James III. should follow in the footsteps of James II. ? Bolingbroke regarded a restoration in short as a measure which might indeed be forced upon him, and for which therefore it was necessary to be prepared—forced upon him as a subordinate detail in a great scheme of mingled statesmanship and ambition by the necessity to which all party leaders are subject of postponing in secondary matters their own judgment and their own inclinations to the prevailing desires of their followers. But it is certain that he regarded the step with grave misgivings. He was anxious to put off his final decision as long as possible.

* D'Iberville to De Torcy, August 13, 1714.

With his clearer intellect and wider knowledge of affairs, he augured from it none of the advantages which so many of his supporters and some, perhaps, of his colleagues anticipated. " The Tories," he wrote many years later to the most trusted of those colleagues—" the Tories always looked on a restoration of the Stuarts as sure means to throw the whole power of the Government into their hands. I am confident that they would have found themselves deceived." *

IV.

After the prince's declaration of March, 1714, even the ministers most favourable to his cause were forced to confess that the idea of reconstructing Toryism on the basis of Jacobitism must for the time be abandoned. For many months repeated efforts had been made to impress on James the absolute necessity of at any rate temporizing in matters of religion, and to hold up before him the example of his great-grandfather Henry IV. and his uncle Charles II. In this necessity some of the most eminent Roman Catholic leaders themselves concurred. Towards the close of the preceding year D'Iberville, the new minister accredited from France to St. James's, arrived in London ; and within two months he reported to his court that there was " not one Tory in England foolhardy enough to acknowledge King James, nor perhaps really disposed to favour him, unless he would become a member of the Established Church." † It was, he said, an " indispensable step " to a restoration. He recommended that the prince should at once and publicly conform ; and he afterwards lamented his obstinacy with the irritation natural to a

* Bolingbroke ⬛ r W. Wyndham, July 23, 1739.
† D'Iberville ⬛ De Torcy, February 26, 1714.

man of the world who sees a promising cause sacrificed to a morbid scrupulosity.

Even the Protestant non-jurors, who had sacrificed all their own worldly prospects to a scruple of conscience, felt that at such a conjuncture, in view of the immense public interests at stake, a point might well be stretched. It would be necessary, they urged, to be cautious. Their master must on no account give colour to the charge that he was capable of dissembling his real opinions, as in that case less credit would be given to whatever he might undertake to promise. But he might express himself as not yet quite decided : he might offer to " consider " the arguments which the Anglican divines would lay before him ; and in the meantime, " as a sort of toleration " and a pledge of what his subjects might expect from him when he should mount the throne, he might allow to his own Protestant attendants the privilege of worshipping God after their own fashion. *

On this point James was willing for a time to humour them. Early in the year Charles Leslie, who had testified to the sincerity both of his religious and of his political convictions, was invited to Bar, and was suffered to hold a Church of England service there, in a back room of the ducal palace. But even this act of weakness was soon repented ; † and on all other points James was from the first, as Wyndham said, " impracticable." He would make no concessions. He would not even conceal the fact that he intended to make none. Whilst his friends in England were extolling his freedom from religious bias, were auguring the best results from Leslie's teaching, and were pointing out in elaborate pamphlets the real principle of the Act of Settlement—to entail the Crown, namely, on the

* See the curious memorial drawn up by Leslie (Macpherson, ii. 215).
† Lathbury's " History of the Non-jurors," 367.

nearest Protestant heir, and how in case the legitimate king should turn Protestant and be willing to make the declarations prescribed by the Bill of Rights, that principle would in fact be violated by the accession of the Hanover line—he disconcerted all their plans by suddenly announcing his fixed resolution to remain under every temptation a Catholic, and by pleading this refusal to "apostatize" as evidence to character! It was a heavy blow to the Church interest. "The article of religion," said Bolingbroke, "was so awkwardly handled in that epistle that it produced the same effect on me which it had on all those Tories with whom I communicated at that time. It made us resolve to have nothing more to do with him." *

It would have been well for Bolingbroke if this wise determination had been adhered to in subsequent years. At the time of which he speaks it was probably sincere. It is certain at any rate that during the next three months, with Bolingbroke's help or in spite of Bolingbroke's resistance, all the public acts of Government were conceived in the interest of the parliamentary cause. The great load under which they laboured was the alleged insecurity of the succession, and this they believed that they had taken, as Bolingbroke assured Lord Strafford, an "effectual method" to remove. † Early in the year, Thomas Harley had been sent on a special mission to Hanover. He was instructed to represent to the Electress and her son the interested motives of the Whigs in raising this question, to inquire whether they were themselves dissatisfied with their prospects, and whether they had any additional securities to propose; and he was directed on behalf of Government to assure them that whatever suggestions they

---

* Bolingbroke's Works, i. 90.

† Bolingbroke to Strafford, February 13, 1714.

made consistent with the Queen's comfort and with the existing laws, should have its warmest support.

Harley's mission, unfortunately, failed in its object. The Elector continued to seek his advice in the counsels of their opponents; and later in the year, when Bolingbroke's influence was becoming supreme, a second embassy, on a grander scale and headed this time by one of his own adherents, was organized "to give that court, if possible, a better notion of its own interest," and to explain the various steps which had been taken for securing its success.* At the same time considerable pressure was put on the Duke of Lorraine to induce him, in conformity with the wishes of Parliament, to remove the Pretender from his territories. A proclamation was issued, offering a large reward for the prince's apprehension in case he should land in England. An act was passed making it high treason to be enlisted or to enlist others in his service ; and it was put in force with a vigilance and severity sufficient at any rate to exasperate the Jacobites, sufficient also, as Bolingbroke hoped, "to calm the minds of men by showing them that they were safe under the care and protection of his Government." †

It is true that when the Jacobite members of Parliament, becoming restive under this treatment, threatened to secede in a body and join the Whig chiefs in stopping supplies, Bolingbroke sent for some of their leaders and explained to them that he was not himself responsible for any of these measures. Shrewsbury had proposed some, and Oxford others. For himself, he had consented to them "chiefly to divert suspicion." It was necessary, he reminded them, to proceed with the utmost caution. Before any decisive step could be taken, the army must

---

* Memorial to be delivered by Lord Clarendon, June 19, 1714.

† Bolingbroke to the Lords Justices of Ireland, July 28, 1714.

be carefully purged, and the entire administration placed in sure hands. He explained to them how resolutely Oxford had withstood any of the proposed changes, and how reluctant the Queen was to lay aside the good opinion she had formed of him. But he assured them that now the work was as good as done ; the treasurer would be dismissed ; and when Parliament was prorogued there would be no power in being to interfere with the Queen in the plans they all had so much at heart. "He did not," says Lockhart, who was present at this interview—"he did not expressly name the King's restoration, but spoke in hints and innuendoes ; and he concluded by asking me to reason with my friends and *induce them to promise an ample supply.*" The explanation in fact was felt to be a lame one—its terms were too vague, and its motives too apparent ; and though the Jacobite leaders agreed to "trust him once more," it was with many misgivings, and an uneasy conviction that he was "sailing on the other tack." *

But the Government vessel can hardly be said to have been sailing on either tack. She lay drifting with the tide, uncertain how to steer her course, beset on every side with perils, but so formidably manned that all attempts to board her failed. During the warm and busy session which preceded the Queen's death, Bolingbroke's whole energies were absorbed in asserting his own position, and in assailing that of his different rivals. The vigour of his party opponents, and the dissensions amongst his friends forced him to act constantly on the defensive ; and his mortification at seeing the precious moments slipping away is reflected in every page of his correspondence. "If my grooms," he writes to Swift (July 13)—"if my grooms did not lead a happier life than I have done, they

* Lockhart's Commentaries, 477.

would quit my service." "The four or five months last past," he writes to Prior (July 9th), "have afforded such a scene as I hope never again to be an actor in. All the confusion which could be created by the dissension of friends and the malice of enemies has subsisted at court and in Parliament. Little or no public business has been transacted in domestic affairs; and as to you and your continent, we have not once cast an eye towards you." "The affairs of our court," he writes to the Lord Primate of Ireland (July 27th), "have been in all that confusion which has in a manner suspended all business, except debates in Parliament and the intrigues of party." "My own situation has been particularly nice. For several weeks before the session rose there were new plots day after day concerting against me, and new confederacies, the cement of which was to be my ruin ; and the utmost I could do has been little enough to ward off the stabs which were levelled at me, and to discover the mines which were daily wrought under my feet." "I know but one way of re-trieving these disadvantages—that is to act a clear game with the Tories, and on that foundation to establish the Queen's Government."

At length, but not till near the close of the session, after enduring for more than a month the severest inquisition into his conduct, and being put on his defence not only for everything that had been done during the past three years but for every step in the process, Bolingbroke suddenly took heart, seized the helm of power, and made that stand which, as he says, occasioned such remarks abroad, and for which he never expected to be forgiven by some people at home, to inspirit his followers and rouse them to a sense of their danger. The combined attack on his foreign policy was beaten off. Resolutions were passed sanctioning the peace and praying the Queen to complete the settlement of Europe on the lines laid down ; and then, with a view of animating the Church interest for the rough work before it by first blooding them well in the entrails of Nonconformity, he brought in his famous measure for preventing the growth of schism, and for the further security of the Church of England as by law established.

It was entrusted to Sir William Wyndham, then Chancellor of the Exchequer. But Wyndham was throughout his life the most devoted of Bolingbroke's friends ; and the measure was Bolingbroke's—Bolingbroke, who had no sort of belief in the religious system which he proposed to make absolute and enforce with stringent penalties, who had been bred in a Puritan household, who had been educated himself by Nonconformists, and who was in his own religious views an advanced Unitarian. The bill had in fact a political object, and a political object only. It was to be the beginning of Swift's policy of Thorough. It was designed to make the members of the Church of England "lay aside their little piques and resentments and cement closely together," to renew a "confidence with the Tories" and a "spirit in them," and to give a "regular motion to all the wheels of Government." *

The vermin thrown down before the pack on this occasion consisted of the schools and colleges recently set up, under shelter of the Toleration Act, by the munificence and enterprise of the Presbyterians, as some compensation for their sons, excluded as they were by. the bigotry of the State from the national seats of learning. The bill provided that every schoolmaster or tutor, whether public or private, must, on pain of imprisonment, conform to the Anglican Church. It required that every schoolmaster

* Bolingbroke to the Lord Chancellor of Ireland, April 13, 1714.

or tutor, whether public or private, should procure, as a preliminary to teaching, the license of an Anglican bishop. It made it a crime for any schoolmaster or tutor, whether public or private, to attend any religious worship except that of the Anglican body. It was inevitable that a measure conceived in such a spirit should be warmly welcomed by a Parliament so largely composed of zealous Episcopalians. It received, as its author hoped, the unanimous approval of all sections of the Church interest. That want of union amongst the Tories, and of concert between the court and party, which had produced, as he tells the Irish Chancellor, "such mischief," was for the moment at an end; and he was followed by Hanmer and Anglesea and the refractory archbishop as cordially as by Bromley and Buckingham. In the House of Commons the bill passed rapidly and by a great majority.

But there remained, unfortunately, the House of Lords. In the House of Lords, though the High Church prelates returned to their allegiance, the contest was sharp. Here the snake of religious freedom was only scotched, and could still bite at the heel that tried to crush it. The weight of argument and reason was, as might be expected, on the side of the opposition peers. But besides their moral victory they extorted some substantial concessions. One of Bolingbroke's objects in drafting the measure was to embarrass the Prime Minister in those newly formed confederacies, "the cement of which was to be my ruin;" and a measure to which Oxford was secretly hostile was never safe, however strongly supported. Encouraged by his sympathy, and strengthened by the votes of some of his personal friends—of Foley, for example, and Mansel, two of the famous twelve whom he had ennobled two years before to carry the treaties of peace—the Whig leaders set themselves vigorously to the work of mutilating the bill in committee. They cut down its penalties. They deprived the hotheaded country justices of the right of inflicting them. They confined this right to the superior courts ; and they provided that, though all higher education should be denied him, merely to teach a young Dissenter to read and write should not be penal. Finally the bill passed, but shorn of its harshest features, and by a majority so small as to be hardly distinguishable from defeat. It was in fact the expiring effort of the old Cavaliers to govern England in accordance with the old ecclesiastical policy of 1662. On the very day on which this new Act of Uniformity was to take effect, the dynasty of the Stuarts came to an end ; and the Church ceased to be the moving power in politics.

The Schism Bill, the most drastic of all the penal remedies against dissent, had been invented by Bolingbroke, partly with the view of putting his great rival on the horns of a dilemma between the High and Low Church bodies ; and in the same week in which it received the royal assent, the Lord Treasurer revenged himself by a return blow at his colleague. The chiefs of the opposition, having succeeded in blunting the edge of this attack on their nonconforming allies, had resumed their inquisition into the working of the treaties of peace. They had taken up the case of the English merchants trading with Spain, whose business, as they maintained, would be altogether destroyed by three new articles in the commercial treaty, which the court of Madrid had lately substituted in the room of those concluded at Utrecht. The Lord Treasurer, throwing over his colleague, expressed his concurrence. He joined in a representation to the Queen, praying that the terms of the arrangement might be modified ; and he is said to have dropped certain broad hints as to the real reason of the hasty ratification of a compact so clearly injurious, as he confessed, to English interests.

Wharton was conducting the inquiry. Near twenty years before, he had first won distinction as a Whig debater by exposing the peculations of Leeds and Seymour. He remembered with bitterness, as did all the statesmen of the Whig junto, how, when the tide had turned, two of their foremost colleagues had been driven from office on a similar charge of jobbery; and it must have been a keen pleasure to him in his old age to put the torch to the most formidable of the many mines which were sprung at that time under Bolingbroke's feet, and which made his situation "so particularly nice." He pressed for information as to certain reserved profits which the King of Spain had, at first, kept in his own hands out of the Assiento contract, and which, at the time of the ratifying of this treaty of commerce, he had made over to the English Government. The commissioners and secretaries of the Board of Trade, the directors of the South Sea Company, to whom the Assiento contract itself—the contract for the sale of negroes to the Spanish colonists—had been assigned by Government, were examined at the bar of the House. The inquiry continued for several days. On the whole, the evidence, extracted with difficulty from the lips of reluctant witnesses, tended to show that in the original Assiento contract a certain proportion of the anticipated profits had been reserved by the Spanish court, but that, in consideration of the unfavourable changes made at its instance in the general treaty of commerce, this share also had been conveyed, like the rest of the contract, to the Queen and her assignees. It further appeared, first, that the three new articles in the commercial treaty so introduced and now complained of had never been really submitted to the Board of Trade, but simply laid before them by Arthur Moore, as already agreed upon by the two Governments; secondly, that the reserved profits of the

King of Spain, so vested in the Queen and her assignees, had not been made over, like the rest of the Assiento contract, to the South Sea Company, but retained ostensibly in the hands of the "Treasury;" that in arranging the terms of partnership between the South Sea traders and the "Treasury" much delay had taken place in consequence of the solicitude evinced both by Bolingbroke and Moore for the public interest; that Bolingbroke in particular had put great pressure on the directors to obtain for the "Treasury" special advantages in the matter, and that Moore, himself at once a director of the company and a leading commissioner of the Board of Trade, had even urged upon his colleagues the policy of excusing the "Treasury" from advancing its proper share of the capital to be employed in their common trade of slave dealing.

Then Wharton mentioned the rumour which had come to him. He asked whether the public exchequer was to benefit by all this solicitude; whether the "Treasury," on whose behalf both Moore and Bolingbroke professed to be acting, really represented the nation in this matter; and what truth there was in a scandalous story now going about to the effect that the share of profits ostensibly reserved for the "Treasury"—which had been first purchased, it seemed, by sacrificing the interests of the merchants trading with Spain, and which had been augmented by thrusting on the South Sea Company the whole expense and risk of their common slave-trading ventures—was to go, not to the Treasury at all, but into the pockets of a ring of courtiers, comprising the Minister who had negotiated the amended treaty, the lady-in-waiting who had extorted the Queen's consent, and the Commissioner of Plantations who had forced the arrangement on his doubtful colleagues. It was notorious that the South Sea directors so far believed this scandal as to have threatened in their indignation to throw up their contract, and that they had dismissed Moore from his place amongst them for his gross breach of trust.

The Secretary of the Treasury was then summoned to the bar and examined. The Secretary was that William Lowndes who had, some years before, in the currency discussions of 1695, distinguished himself by suggesting how much the burdens of the State might be lightened if every ounce of silver were coined into seven shillings instead of five. Lowndes admitted under close examination that the Treasury had really no interest in this matter, and that he, its secretary, was simply acting as trustee, nominated by and representing the Queen, but bound to pay over her share of profits to certain private assignees. Their names he professed himself unable to give, and he was not pressed; for on further examination he was able to assure the House that the objectionable grant had now been cancelled, and the whole of the Government interest in this great contract made over to the South Sea Company. On the motion of Anglesea, a high Tory, but now a strong opponent of Bolingbroke, the House unanimously resolved to present an address to the Queen, thanking her for taking this step, and praying that "any other advantages" which might be vested in her should be "employed for the public service." It was time to put an end to these constant inquisitions and damaging revelations. On the following morning Parliament was abruptly prorogued, and the contest between the two ministers transferred to the closet and bedchamber of the Queen.*

There at last, by the help of his female confederate, Bolingbroke triumphed. On the morning of Tuesday, the 27th of July, after a stormy scene in the presence chamber,

* House of Lords Journals, July, 1714; Bothmar to Robethon, July 10, 1714; Lewis to Swift, July 6, 1714; Ford to Swift, July 10, 1714.

in which the falling minister, forgetting his dignity and his self-respect, condescended to bandy recriminations with the faithless kinswoman who had betrayed him—swore that he would be revenged and would leave some persons as low as he found them, and was assured in reply that he had never done the Queen any service and was incapable of doing her any—Anne resumed the white staff; and at a council held the same day she laid before the assembled lords her reasons for doing so—characteristic reasons, such as the mistress of a domestic household might give for turning off with a month's wages an insolent and tipsy butler.*

Meanwhile a statesman of greater experience than either of the two rivals had been an interested spectator of their quarrels. The conduct of Shrewsbury in the events preceding and following Oxford's removal has been an enigma to the historians. But the most probable explanation is, that he was acting throughout with the sympathy and, perhaps, the direct connivance of the Queen herself. It is to be remembered that the Queen was as much opposed as Harley to a mere partisan Government. It is certain that, even when convinced at length by Lady Masham's expostulations that a change in the chief office was necessary, she hesitated greatly about yielding herself and her kingdom entirely into Bolingbroke's hands. To do so was to abandon altogether her favourite policy, in pursuit of which she had dismissed Godolphin, and to revert to her old state of vassalage—this time not to a grave and experienced statesman who had once enjoyed her

---

* They will be found in Lewis's letter to Swift. Having a great respect for the institution of hereditary monarchy, I forbear to quote them. We learn from Lord Palmerston's correspondence, as published by Mr. Ashley, that even in our own enlightened court "subserviency of demeanour" is thought the most useful qualification in a minister, and that the late Lord Derby's "off-hand sarcastic manner" made him very unpopular at Windsor.

entire confidence, but to a young patrician adventurer, bankrupt alike in fame and fortune.

In the preceding winter, indeed, at the time of her great illness, Bolingbroke had, by his artful misrepresentations, so excited her anger against the Low Church leaders as to divert her for a moment from her moderating counsels. Had he been able to strike whilst her temper was hot, it is not improbable that vigorous measures might have been taken, with her full concurrence, for securing to the High Church party their monopoly of power. Swift, as we know, never ceased to lament the folly of his friends at letting such a chance escape. For the opportunity passed away. With time her resentment cooled. With reflection her old inclinations came back. On the very day of the Lord Treasurer's dismissal, Bolingbroke was still in doubt as to what the result would be, still in doubt how far his own power of directing events would be extended by the change now resolved upon, though he "hoped," as he tells his Irish correspondent, that the Queen would be at last induced to "act a clear game with the Tories," and on that foundation alone establish her Government.

Now in this policy of reconciling the two interests, governing by "gentle treatment," and persuading by "reason" rather than force, Shrewsbury concurred. Four years before he had associated himself with Somerset and Argyle in extricating the Queen from the dominion of Godolphin and the Whig junto. But none of the three friends, any more than the Queen herself, had then intended that the High Church leaders should become supreme, or that the rival faction should be altogether exterminated. As the Tory complexion and policy of the new Government gradually disclosed itself, Somerset relapsed into opposition, and was, after much delay and with the greatest reluctance on the Queen's part, removed from his place in the royal household. Argyle followed a few months later. But Shrewsbury remained. He did not indeed approve of the manner in which the peace of Utrecht had been brought about, but he consented at length to support the treaties; and he represented the Queen for a time with his customary grace and urbanity at the court of France. The winter of 1713 he had passed in Ireland; acting a part, in the opinion of his High Church colleagues, directly against their interests; carrying out his instructions to support the Protestant settlement, more unreservedly perhaps than was intended; drinking in public to the immortal memory of King William; retaining about his person Wharton's old adherents; endeavouring to bring the turbulent Whig Commons into order by means which Bolingbroke describes—with a slight touch of satire—as "agreeable to the mildness of the Queen we serve and the goodness of your own nature," and which certainly presented a striking contrast to those recommended by the vehement secretary.*

With these antecedents Shrewsbury had come over in the spring of 1714 to take part in the labours of the parliamentary session. His return had been eagerly anticipated by all the ministers as a means of putting an end to their fatal divisions and dissensions. Both the contending rivals had bidden high for his support; but he had shown no great anxiety to assume the post of mediator. He had delayed his voyage as long as possible. When, at length, he arrived, he maintained his counsels with the impenetrable reserve of Monk on his famous march from Scotland. By the public he was ranked among the adherents of the Lord Treasurer; and it is certain that he took sides, both in Parliament and in the closet, with the moderate Churchmen whom Oxford

* Bolingbroke to Shrewsbury, December 22, 1713, and January 19, 1714; Swift's Works, vi. 37; Froude, "English in Ireland," i. 352, 360.

essayed to lead.   He advised the issue of that proclamation
against the Pretender which so exasperated the Jacobite
leaders.   He discountenanced and defeated the attempt
of Ormond to remodel the household troops in the interest
of the Jacobite party.   He opposed and nearly defeated
the motion of Bolingbroke for extending the Schism Bill
to Ireland ; and he joined in the parliamentary condemnation, so damaging to Bolingbroke, of that minister's
commercial treaty with Spain.   But he seemed more disposed to resent certain slights to which he fancied himself
exposed than to try and reconcile his colleagues.   He had
sagacity enough to see, as Swift justly says, how their
disputes might be turned to his own advantage, and to the
advantage of the cause which he had at heart.   He opened
through one of the royal physicians a private channel of
communication with the Queen.   He made no attempt to
break Oxford's fall, recognizing no doubt that his influence
and usefulness were gone.   He regarded that catastrophe,
in truth, with such complacency as to arouse in the mind
of Bolingbroke's enthusiastic followers the pleasant belief
that he was not at heart unfavourable to their master's
elevation.   Even Bolingbroke himself seems to have been
doubtful.   "How I stand with that man," he said to
Arbuthnot a few days before the crisis came, pointing first
to the Lord Treasurer with whom Shrewsbury was talking
—"how I stand with that man I know ; but as to the
other I cannot tell." *

Such were the young statesman's relations to the
accomplished minister who now, in the interest of constitutional freedom, interposed to frustrate his designs.   In
the arrangements which he contemplated Bolingbroke had
abandoned, if he had ever entertained it, the idea of him-

* Arbuthnot to Swift, July 15, 1714 ; Ormond to Swift, July 22, 1714 ;
Ford to Swift, July 15, 1714 ; Swift's Works, vi. 37.

self holding the white staff. In the pithy words of Lewis, his character was too bad and his bottom too narrow to carry the great ensign. He aspired to direct the Government as Secretary of State. But it was essential to the success of his scheme that all the great departments should be confided to men whom he could trust, and especially that he should have entire command of the Treasury. At the council which met on the night of Oxford's dismissal, he proposed that Sir William Wyndham should be the First Commissioner. Wyndham was a man of parts and character, an extreme High Churchman, indeed almost an avowed Jacobite, but connected by close domestic ties with a great Whig house, and a favourite son-in-law of the Queen's most intimate personal friend. His name passed with general approval. But the remaining proposals of Bolingbroke were received in a manner which showed that the divisions in the Government had been by no means healed, and the obstacles in his path by no means removed, by his triumph over the Lord Treasurer. Every suggestion was opposed and resisted to the last. At length, long past midnight, the council broke up, after an angry and bootless discussion, which drew from the Queen the remark, as she left the room, that "she should never outlive these scenes." Next day the question was resumed. But again nothing was determined ; and again the council rose in great disorder.

But now, as she had foreseen, under the strain of this prolonged anxiety, the Queen's strength gave way. Her manifold difficulties, the stormy scenes she had witnessed, the bitter rivalry amongst her servants, the furious quarrels which still divided them, had done their work on a constitution prematurely shattered by domestic troubles and enfeebled by self-indulgence. Her gouty humour, deprived of its usual vent, attacked her brain. Fatal symptoms appeared; and the power for which Bolingbroke was vainly striving passed into stronger hands. When, on the morning of Friday, July 30th, three days after Oxford's fall, the Queen's condition had become so alarming that the great officers of State, informed of the approaching end, ventured to meet in council in her absence, and without the royal summons, Somerset and Argyle, who still retained their seats at the board, though they had long since ceased to attend its meetings, presented themselves and claimed the right as Privy Councillors to share their deliberations. It was one of those conjunctures which test the characters of men—when the destinies of the English people, the future of a great party, perhaps the fate of an ancient line, all hung upon a word. Shrewsbury, prepared no doubt for the scene, at once took the lead, thanked the two intruders for their timely attendance, and motioned them to their old places. Their presence turned the scale against Bolingbroke's influence, and in favour of those moderate Churchmen whom the gravity of the public danger was driving into the comprehensive policy he disliked. It was moved and unanimously carried that, in this hour of national peril, Privy Councillors, without distinction of party, ought to be summoned; that the great place of Lord Treasurer ought not to be left vacant; and that, as a guarantee and a security for the revolution settlement, the Queen should be advised to confer the staff on the veteran minister who in his youth had borne so large a share in framing it, and who was now in his old age to consummate the work of his early manhood.

And Bolingbroke acquiesced. Nay, he so far acknowledged his defeat as to press Shrewsbury's appointment, and to put himself at the head of the deputation which conveyed the resolutions of her council to the Queen's bedside. She was then fast sinking into the lethargy which preceded death. But she roused herself at the news, which doubtless lifted a load from her heart, and passing the staff to Shrewsbury with her failing hand, bade him "use it for the good of my people." It was the fitting close to a public life, darkened indeed by ignorance, disfigured by passion, and mistaken in all its aims, but redeemed by a sincere patriotism. On the morning of Sunday, August the 1st, she died.[*]

V.

It is said that Atterbury, who had been intended by Bolingbroke to fill the same great place in the new administration which the Bishop of London had filled

---

[*] Ford to Swift, July 31, and August 5, 1714; D'Iberville to De Torcy, August 14, 1714. Whether Bolingbroke himself proposed Shrewsbury, as Ford afterwards asserted, or merely "begged him to accept the charge" when offered, as D'Iberville, a better authority, seems to imply, is really immaterial. It is certain that Bolingbroke acted under compulsion, and was simply covering his own retreat.

Lord Stanhope's account of these transactions is not marked with his usual accuracy. Subsequent writers have corrected some of his mistakes. But neither Mr. Wyon nor Mr. Lecky, though they have examined the situation with laudable care, has perceived the fundamental error in Lord Stanhope's statement, the assertion, viz. that by Oxford's removal "the whole power of the State with the choice of the new administration passed to Bolingbroke." So far from this being the case, Oxford's removal left Bolingbroke with very little more power than before, still so weak in fact that at two protracted meetings of the council he failed to secure the lead, and that the addition of two new councillors, hostile to him, reduced him to complete impotence. A writer in the *Quarterly Review* for January, 1880, generally well informed as to the events of Bolingbroke's life, advances the singular theory that Bolingbroke proposed Shrewsbury as Treasurer in the hope of being able, through "his son-in-law Wyndham," to influence the new minister to his own Jacobite views. The Reviewer is, of course, confounding Shrewsbury with Somerset; and he forgets, besides, that the council had already decided to summon the Whig Lords. Was this also proposed by Bolingbroke in the interest of the Pretender? Yet if Bolingbroke was then master of the council and in the Pretender's interest, how came he to allow a motion so fatal to that interest to be carried?

under Harley, implored his leader with tears and impreca-
tions to take a bold course and proclaim James III. But
he had to deal with a man whose fortitude could never
bear the strain of a great crisis. If, indeed, Bolingbroke
had been able to forecast accurately the events of the next
few weeks, it is not improbable that Atterbury's advice,
desperate though it was, might have been followed. But
he was still quite uncertain how those events would shape
themselves; uncertain how far his late representations
at Hanover had purged from the Elector's mind the delusion
that the Whigs were his only friends; uncertain, too, how
far the spirit of Jacobitism had leavened the Tory ranks,
and how much they were ready to risk in the way of
actual rebellion. He suffered himself to be thrust aside.
In the Privy Council the vigour of the Whig lords, with
the new Lord Treasurer at their head, carried all before
it. Already the military experience and energy of
Stanhope had devised a scheme for opposing force to force
if it should become necessary to defend the Protestant
settlement by arms. But the bold manœuvre of Somerset
had placed the resources of Government itself in the hands
of opposition. Every precaution was taken to insure the due
observance of the law. The outposts were secured; troops
were moved up to London; the guards at the Tower were
doubled; an embargo was laid on the shipping; the fleet
was equipped and placed in sure hands. Notice was given
to the States-General that the British regiments in their
service, together with the armed convoy which they were
bound under treaty engagements to furnish, would be
required for the new King's safety. No resistance was
attempted. The Parliamentary Sovereign was proclaimed;
and the Lords Justices nominated by him, in accordance
with the Act of Regency, took quiet possession of the
State.

Whatever faint hope may have lingered in Bolingbroke's mind as to the secret preferences of the Elector and the success of his late embassy was quickly dispelled. The eighteen regents who, together with the chief officers of State, were charged with the duty of administering affairs till the new King's arrival, proved to be either great Whig nobles like Devonshire and Orford, or High Churchmen of the stamp of Nottingham and Anglesea, who had on the two questions of the peace and the succession separated themselves from their party. Shrewsbury—and the circumstance is very significant as showing the interpretation which the Court of Hanover had put upon his conduct in the party struggle of the last few weeks— Shrewsbury was the only one of the late Queen's ministers whose name appeared in the Elector's list. One of the first acts of the new Lords Justices was to order that all the business of Bolingbroke's office should pass through the hands of their Secretary Addison ; and in their intercourse with him no mark of disrespect and even contumely was omitted. Still Secretary of State, the doors of that council chamber where he had been for the moment the most conspicuous figure were rudely shut in his face, and he was left to wait his turn of audience in the ante-room, standing amongst the clerks and messengers with his bag of papers in his hand. Early in August came a letter from the King dismissing him ; and the seals were taken from him by two of his old colleagues with an ostentatious show of harshness and personal incivility which · affected him less as an indication of " Whig malice and power " than as filling his soul with grief at the thought that " the Tory party was gone." " The men who have broken from me continue still, notwithstanding all efforts to reclaim them, to act and speak on the old principles and with the old passions." " Numbers are still left ; but where," he mournfully asks, "are the men of business who would live and draw together?" *

When Parliament reassembled, a last despairing effort was made by Wyndham and Bromley, still at the head of a great party following, to win the favour of the new court. Every resolution of the preceding session which might be thought likely to annoy it was rescinded. The arrears of pay so long due to the Hanoverian regiments were ordered to be discharged in full. A heavy price was set on the Pretender's capture. A civil list was offered to the new Sovereign larger by near one-half than poor Queen Anne had ever enjoyed; † and when at length he landed at Gravesend, the very men who had chuckled at Bolingbroke's stories about his domestic naughtinesses, who had sneered at him over their wine as a low German boor, and who had openly expressed the hope that he would "never come to the throne," now crowded round with emulous servility to kiss his hand.

But they were to taste the bitterness of knowing that they had humbled themselves in vain. When the new arrangements were made public, it was found that his ministers were, with scarcely an exception, Whigs, and were specially noted for the zeal which they had displayed, and for the dangers which they had incurred, in support-ing the Whig foreign policy. Halifax was the most experienced, and Sunderland the most active of the Low Church leaders. But they were both passed over in favour of a younger statesman, the negotiator of that Barrier Treaty by which Great Britain, at some sacrifice of her commercial interests, clinched the bargain which bound the United Provinces to the support of the Revolution polity,

* Bolingbroke to Atterbury, September, 1714.

† On the motion, be it observed, of Bromley and Wyndham, not of the Whig leaders.

and a man whom the Parliament of 1710, in the first flush
of the Tory triumph, had denounced as an "enemy of the
Queen and country." With Townshend was associated
as Secretary of State General Stanhope, the victim of the
"glorious disaster" of Brihuega, the first fruit of the Tory
ascendency, a man whose indignation at the treaties of
peace and the desertion of the Austrian cause had impelled
him to put a personal affront on Bolingbroke, and who
had narrowly escaped a State prosecution in consequence
that would have reduced him to penury. Cowper was
the new Lord Chancellor; Wharton, Privy Seal; Orford
returned to the Admiralty. The High Churchman Nottingham, whom the Whig lords had put forward in December,
1711, to move their famous vote against the peace, was the
new Lord President. Marlborough's name, much to his
own surprise, had not been included in the list of regents.
To him more than to any single man had been due the
preservation of the reformed settlement from the perils
that beset it. But between Marlborough and the Elector
there was a grudge of old standing. He had shown a disposition, too, to trim in the final struggle; and he had
refused four years before to set his hand to that treaty
with Holland to which the new premier owed his distinction
and his rise to supreme power. He was now named
Captain-General of the Forces. Halifax, with the title
of earl and decorated with the garter, became First Commissioner of the Treasury; Sunderland, Lord Lieutenant
of Ireland. Shrewsbury, retaining the gold key of Chamberlain, relinquished the Treasurer's white staff, which
had made him at the critical moment the arbiter of the
national destinies—the last in the long line of English
nobles who have borne, in the train of princes that were
monarchs in something more than name, that ancient
symbol of ministerial power.

Such and so complete was the triumph of the Whigs, the triumph of statesmanship and organization over a divided and undisciplined majority. "We have more heads and hands than our adversaries," is Swift's bitter comment on their success; "but, it must be confessed, they have stronger shoulders and better hearts." * The new ministry contained, indeed, in the elevation of Townshend and the depression of the older Whigs, seeds of future misunderstanding which seriously weakened the party, and of which the effect might be traced in the statute-book down almost to our own time. But during the first few months personal rivalries were forgotten in the nearness of the common danger. The Government addressed itself with admirable vigour to the work of consolidating the reformed polity. It soon appeared that the lessons of the past four years had been taken to heart, and that the weapons forged in the arsenal of clericalism were to be used for "fortifying" and "establishing" a very different system. "The art of the Whigs," wrote Bolingbroke afterwards with equal truth and candour—"the art of the Whigs was to blend as indistinguishably as they could all their party interests with those of the Succession; and they made just the same factious use of the supposed danger to it as the Tories had endeavoured to make some time before of the supposed danger to the Church." † It was by such representations that the new Sovereign had been induced to forego his original purpose of giving a share of power to each of the contending factions; and it was by such arts, by an unscrupulous use of the cry of "Jacobite," "tools of France," "enemies of native industry," co-operating no doubt with the natural desire of armchair politicians to support the successful dynasty as the best security against disorder,

* Swift to Bolingbroke, August 7, 1714.
† Works, iii. 138 (State of Parties at the Accession of George I.)

that a Parliament was now got together which in no sense represented the relative strength of the two parties, a Parliament as thoroughly Whig as its two predecessors had been Tory.

And when, early in March, the two Houses met, the occasion was seized upon to pursue the same retaliatory system with greater union and increased spirit. The King's speech from the throne was accurately modelled on that with which Harley and St. John had opened their first session in November, 1710. It was a party manifesto of the bitterest kind. His Majesty was made to express, through the silvery voice of his chancellor, his " concern " that the conditions of peace had not corresponded with the successes of the war ; he was made to remind his hearers that of these conditions many had not been executed, whilst all were precarious ; he was made to point out that the Pretender still resided in Lorraine, openly boasting of the good intentions of the late Queen and her advisers towards him ; and whilst repudiating all thought of breaking faith with the public creditor, he was made to comment in strong terms on the " surprising increase " which the debts of the nation had undergone even since the conclusion of the war.

The address in answer to the royal speech was conceived in a similar strain. It was modelled on the lines of an address passed twelve years before, under Bolingbroke's own auspices, in the session which followed the death of King William, and in the ferment of High Church enthusiasm which welcomed the accession of Queen Anne. The Lords stated their conviction that his Majesty would, when assisted by a Parliament really zealous for his government and for the honour of their country, be able at last to secure what was due to it, ease its debts, preserve the public credit, restore trade, extinguish the hopes of the

Pretender, and " recover" the reputation of the kingdom, the loss of which, their lordships remarked, was not to be imputed to the nation at large.

It was in opposing this last clause, which he now maintained to be an outrage on the memory of the dead Sovereign, that Bolingbroke made his last speech in Parliament, leaving there at the age of thirty-seven the reputation of being at once the readiest and the most finished of all the great speakers who have, during its long life of six hundred years, adorned the most renowned of modern senates.   Nor was the opposition confined to Bolingbroke.   The clause was vigorously denounced by all the late Queen's ministers : by Shrewsbury, with the weight derived from his recent services ; by Trevor, whose political judgment and legal knowledge had earned him an authority such as afterwards belonged to the equally unprincipled Thurlow ; by Anglesea, one of the regents appointed by George I. and by the Archbishop of York, a High Churchman, but always a warm supporter of his title.   And yet, so keen was the feeling of relief as at a great peril momentarily escaped, so universal the desire to strengthen at such a conjuncture the men into whose hands the public welfare had been committed, that in an assembly singularly free from popular caprice, an assembly which twelve months before had passed, though with some reluctance, a vote approving of the Peace of Utrecht, and had denied, though with some diffidence, the assertion that the Succession was " in danger" under a High Church administration, this address, censuring the peace of Utrecht in the strongest terms and denouncing the authors of it by implication as traitors to the Protestant cause, was carried, in spite of the opposition of some of its foremost statesmen, by a majority of no less than two to one.*

* Sixty-six votes to thirty-three.

In the Commons the address was stronger still. It was moved by Robert Walpole, as yet only a subordinate member of Government, but already noted for skill in debate and knowledge of finance, his naturally humane temper embittered by the treatment he had just undergone, and eager in the name of the public weal to retaliate on the men who had tried to build up their own authority on the ruins of his fame and fortune. He declared the intention of Ministers to trace out the measures on which the Pretender had founded the hopes he now expressed, and to bring the authors of them to condign punishment. And the threat was confirmed by Stanhope, the leader of the House.

Thus the policy of proscription on which the Government had resolved to enter was fully disclosed ; and it remained for the two fallen ministers against whom the attack was chiefly laid to consider how they ought to meet it. They decided in a manner characteristic of the two men. Oxford, his clear judgment showing him the true path of safety, faced the storm with the same tranquil courage which he had opposed to the knife of Guiscard, defended himself before his peers with temper and dignity, endured with fortitude a long imprisonment, and having lived down the rancour of party, ended his days in lettered repose, which the glorious flattery of Pope has made immortal. But Bolingbroke succumbed. His restless and unscrupulous ambition required a support which nature, bountiful to him in a hundred lavish gifts, had withheld—tough and vigorous nerves, nerves strong to withstand the pressure of a long impending danger. His temperament was mercurial ; and his impulse always to rush forward or shrink back, never to stand still and wait. The feeling that he was in the hands of men whom he had cruelly injured ; the uncertainty

how much of his dallyings with St. Germains was known
to them; the bitter thought that he must stand at the same
bar and frame a common defence with the hated rival who
had brought all their party interests to ruin; above all,
perhaps, the "panic terror" produced by Marlborough's
insinuations, which at a calmer moment he would have
treated with the contempt they deserved, that his "blood
was to be the cement of a new Grand Alliance," and that
innocence itself would be no security now that his life
had been demanded from abroad;—utterly dismayed and
unmanned him.   On the evening of March the 24th, three
days after Walpole's speech was made, he appeared with
his usual air of careless nonchalance at the theatre in
Drury Lane, bespoke a second play for the next evening,
and on that very night in a mean disguise stole away to
France.   He left behind a letter in which he tried to
palliate his flight.

The course of his enemies now lay clear before them.
A fortnight later a secret committee was formed for the
purpose of digesting the papers relating to the peace and
reporting the substance of them to Parliament.   It was
composed of twenty-one members, all of them staunch
Whigs, with Walpole at their head.   For the sake of greater
despatch they distributed the work into three parts, and
early in June presented their report—an elaborate indictment of the fallen ministers, altogether weak and incon-
clusive as regards the technical charge of treason based
upon it, but setting in a clear light their offences against
Europe and the dishonour they had brought on the English
name.   Oxford, Bolingbroke, and Ormond were at once
impeached of high treason; Strafford, of high crimes and
misdemeanours.   Early in August a bill was introduced
attainting Bolingbroke, confiscating his property, and con-

demning him to death, unless he should return by the 10th of September to stand his trial. No one was bold enough to defend him. His flight was universally taken as a tacit confession of guilt. The bill passed easily into law. On the 17th his name was struck from the roll of peers.

CHAPTER IV.

I.

WE have now accompanied Bolingbroke to the end of his legitimate career. We have witnessed his efforts to "fortify and establish" Toryism under the Revolution Government by rendering it superior to those vicissitudes to which in an open parliamentary system all political parties are subject. We have seen the ground laid for this purpose in his foreign policy—the external bulwarks and guarantees of free institutions removed, and a clear space made for the re-erection of that " Tory system " of which peace was, as he justly said, the only solid foundation. We have seen and examined in the light of his own copious annotations the domestic policy which was to be built on the foundation so laid ; the measures for excluding from political power the statesmen by whose exertions and the classes in whose interest representative government had been established ; the measures for securing to the friends of the Church and the landed gentry the same exclusive privileges under the new constitution which they had possessed under the old. And we have witnessed the failure of these efforts, and noted the cause of this failure—the protracted and doubtful issue of those preliminary negotiations on which the whole depended ; the unpopularity even in England of many of the arrangements made ; the resulting insecurity of the Government, its dissensions, and his own want of influence to accommodate them ; and finally the sudden death of the Queen, with these differences unhealed, with the "body" of the Whigs still unbroken, and the "machinery" for perpetuating the Tory power still incomplete.

We have now to attend him into a widely different scene. During the remainder of his life Bolingbroke was an outlaw, and during a large part of it an exile—deprived of all legitimate means of making his voice heard and his influence felt, his attainder always kept prudently in force, even when his property was secure and his person no longer in danger. During the rest of his life, therefore, though his ends remained the same, his means were necessarily more shifty, and his general politics more crooked. His first attempt at retrieving the fortunes of his party, and replacing them in that position of supremacy of which the Revolution had deprived them, was to reconstruct Toryism on the basis of Jacobitism, to overturn the Parliamentary settlement by force of arms, to undo the work of the Revolution in letter as well as in spirit, and to restore the displaced system under the discarded monarchy.

That attempt failed, failed in spite of Bolingbroke's most strenuous exertions on its behalf. For reasons not wholly unintelligible—human nature being what it is—he was expelled with contumely from the service of the disappointed prince whom he had confessedly taken up as the instrument of party ambition and revenge ; and the shock at once sobered him. *T* nceforth he accepted the change of dynasty as plainly inevitable, and once more addressed himself to the task of so remodelling the new constitution as to transform it into a virtual reproduction of the old. We shall have to witness his third and most

famous attempt at reconstructing Toryism, this time on
the basis of "Patriotism," of popular rights confided to
the arbitrary will and judgment of the Revolution sovereign
(the patriot king being a Tory and a patron of Bolingbroke's party); how, unseen himself, he was the soul
and moving spirit of the great coalition formed against
the Whig minister and ostensibly against the Whig system,
the instigator of the political convulsion which shook
that minister's power, the accomplice and victim of the
political treachery which, by continuing that system,
betrayed the hopes he had excited. We shall see him
in private life identified with great movements of the
European mind, with science, with letters, with the progress
of free thought; the inspirer of men of genius, the leader
of a religious school. And we have finally to accompany
him into the melancholy retreat of his declining years,
to see him returned to the lonely manor house by the
Thames, crippled by disease, the effects of vicious indulgence; crippled by debts, the effects of youthful extravagance; estranged from his family and early friends; still for
a while the centre of a small society of rising politicians,
who preserved the traditions of his statesmanship; but
with his last prospects of personal distinction dissipated;
with the consolations of female friendship at length denied
to him; and with his hopes limited by a religious faith
which taught that man reaps his just deserts in this world,
and that death means annihilation.

II.

It was on the evening of the 24th of March, 1715, that
Bolingbroke quitted the theatre in Drury Lane for the
post-chaise that was waiting to convey him to Dover. His
flight, betraying as it was held to do the consciousness of

guilt, was the very step which his opponents most desired, and against which his best friends had warned him. But Bolingbroke chose to fancy that his life was aimed at, and that it behoved him to take precautions. Catching a hint, perhaps, from some scene in the comedy he had just witnessed, he dressed himself for the journey in a footman's livery, and pretended to be the servant of one De Vigne, a messenger travelling with despatches for the court of France. He was suffered to reach Paris unmolested. After a short stay there he retired into Dauphiny, and reviewed the position to which baffled statesmanship had brought him.

Here, in the first days of July, an agent came to him, professing to speak the sentiments of his political friends in England. He was assured that the reaction had now come; that the people were everywhere exasperated against the Government, the army disaffected, the city even ready to rise. He was told that in Scotland the difficulty was to hold back the movement; that the whole Tory party, now openly Jacobite, would join on the first blow struck; and that all its principal leaders were even now concerting with Ormond the details of the projected rising. He was gently chidden for lying neuter at such a time; and a letter was delivered to him from James III., warmly inviting him to the court at Bar.

If his own statement is to be credited, Bolingbroke was not convinced. It did not escape him that nothing was said about the actual measures taken for improving these good dispositions, and that the facts related were after all a mere repetition of assertions made to him three months before on landing, when leaders had been named, their engagements specified, and persons mentioned for particular services to whom, as he perfectly well knew, no overtures at all had been opened. But his temper

was sanguine; he was weary of exile and inaction; he
was possessed, too, with the natural fear that, unless he
risked something, he might be anticipated in the services
he hoped to render, and deprived of the rewards he hoped
to get for them. He determined to make the plunge.
In passing through Paris he had seen Lord Stair, the
British ambassador; had opened through him a negotiation with the Whig Government; and had formally
promised in the meantime to enter into no Jacobite
engagements. And in after years, when the memory of
these transactions perhaps was growing dim, Bolingbroke
was in the habit of taking credit to himself that he was
never tempted into breaking this promise till the ministers,
by attainting him of his offences, themselves released him
from it. "The act of attainder in consequence of my
impeachment," he writes in his pleasant imaginative way,
"had passed against me for crimes of the blackest dye."
"The smart of it tingled in every vein." "It set me free,
according to my apprehension of things, from the engagement which I had taken before to the Government, and
from which I would not have departed if this act had
not passed, as I never did depart till it had passed."*
Unfortunately these assertions, so circumstantially made,
so often afterwards repeated, that he was in fact driven
into rebellion in his own despite by the injustice of being
condemned unheard, will not, like some other of his
assertions, bear the test of an appeal to dates. The act
of attainder of which he speaks, fixing on Bolingbroke
the penalties of his impeachment, did not come into force
until the 10th of September, and would, had he returned
before that day to stand his trial, have been invalid. Nay,
the articles of impeachment themselves, on which this
attainder was afterwards founded, were not presented to

----

* Works, i. 36, 39. Bolingbroke to Lord Polwarth, July 12, 1739.

Parliament till the 4th of August. He accepted the seals of the Pretender in the first week of July.*

He soon repented his rashness. His first interview with the chevalier, of which he has given us a lively and perhaps a highly coloured description, answered in no respect, we are told, to the expectations he had formed. "The prince talked like a man who expected every moment to set out for England or Scotland, but who did not very well know which." As to the particulars of his affairs, he had nothing positive or circumstantial to go upon. The assurances of success were quite general, their authority seldom satisfactory, verbal for the most part, conveyed by doubtful messengers when professing to come from good hands, and when distinct and reliable coming from men whose fortunes were as desperate as their counsels. Scotland, indeed, was fully prepared for the enterprise, had planned all its details, and knew on whom to depend for every part of the work. But Scotland was not precisely the field of ambition on which Bolingbroke was anxious to enter; and with respect to England and the English Tories, the country gentlemen, the country clergymen, no principles whatever had been laid down on either side for their common action, no necessary assistances had been specified, no certain methods of correspondence even established.

But it was too late now to draw back. It was Bolingbroke's opinion that the rising in both kingdoms ought to be simultaneous, reciprocally supporting each other, and combining to distract the common enemy ; and he agreed

* It is commonly charged against Bolingbroke that an interview he had with Berwick in the month of March, directly after seeing Lord Stair, was in itself a violation of the promise just given. But this is a mistake. In that interview he carefully guarded himself against making pledges. And, in justice to Bolingbroke, it must be remembered that though the act of attainder had not passed when he joined the Pretender, it was still abundantly clear that the Whigs intended to proceed against him.

with Berwick in thinking that a considerable amount of French help—troops, ammunition, means of transport—was indispensable. He accepted the seals at Commercy; and then, towards the middle of July, hurried to Paris for the purpose of soliciting the French court, and disposing them to grant these necessary succours as soon as he should learn from England what form exactly they ought to take.

To induce the ministers of Lewis to violate the treaties so lately and so solemnly concluded under his own auspices, this was Bolingbroke's mission; and it was, as he justly says, a bold proposal for the negotiator of those treaties to make to a Government which war had reduced to the lowest ebb of poverty and weakness, and which peace was beginning to restore to some show of its old prosperity. Nor was his task made easier by the condition of things which he found on arriving amongst the Jacobite refugees in Paris, and which, fresh as he was to their peculiar habits, struck him with respectful astonishment—a multitude of people at work, each imagining himself a general or a minister of state; no order, no concert, no subordination; every man doing what seemed good in his own eyes; care and hope on every busy Irish face; those who could read running about with letters, the rest chattering and whispering secrets; women over their tea discussing the position of every sloop in the little armament that was to transport the chevalier to Britain; no sex, in short, and no profession, either male or female, excluded from these strange counsels, and all their proceedings perfectly well known to the vigilant ambassador of King George.

Bolingbroke, however, exerted himself most strenuously, and at first with considerable success. The French court would not indeed hear of any open engagement. He had not expected that they would. But he succeeded in obtaining some direct and much indirect help ; and he was well aware how easily under his skilful management the unfriendly steps they were willing to take and their general connivance in the whole conspiracy might be, as he says, "improved," till the two nations, always so suspicious of each other, should be set once more by the ears. From Spain he obtained the distinct promise of both money and officers. He enlisted in his cause the sympathies and, for a time, the active exertions of the eccentric King of Sweden. Nay, he even found means, through one of his young lady friends, to assail on his weaker side the licentious Orleans, making, as he ruefully said, the very pleasures and amusements of his life subservient to James's interests.

But he found the task of constructing a new coalition against the liberties and religion of his country less easy than that of dissolving the old coalition which had been formed to defend them. The long and chequered reign of the great monarch was now drawing to a close. The King was by far the best friend that the chevalier had ; and his ruling passion, strong even in death, was for the moment revived by the representations made him. Had his life been spared for six months longer, it was Bolingbroke's confident belief that the efforts he was making would have succeeded, and that England and France, possibly the whole of Europe, might have been again at war. But Fate darkly interposed. Lewis was not in a condition to exert his former vigour, and the men about him were occupied with matters more personal to themselves than the extension of French influence and the propagation of the true faith. All his ministers, all his courtiers, all his priests, were straining their eyes to pierce the future, then, owing to the youth of his successor and the uncertainty of his own dispositions, more than ordinarily dim. On the 1st of September the great King died; his will was set aside; and the whole supreme power passed to his nephew, Philip of Orleans, a man careless of the traditionary policy of France, and not unfriendly to the new order of things in England. His elevation shook down the house of cards which Bolingbroke was laboriously building up. He saw that the game was over. In his own words the hopes of the Jacobites, which had languished with the King's illness, sank when he expired.

III.

Unluckily· the rebellion in Scotland was already in full progress. Mar, obeying, if his own statement is to be believed, the express orders of James, orders carefully concealed both from Bolingbroke and from Berwick, had, on the 2nd of August, quitted London for the north, had held the famous hunting match at which the last details of the insurrection were planned, and had set up the rebel standard at Braemar. The call to arms was cheerfully obeyed, the sharp spur of their local jealousies coming to the aid of that deep sense of loyalty and that chivalrous attachment to the fallen which has always characterized the gentry of the Scottish highlands. But the cause of the Stuarts, at a conjuncture in many respects unusually propitious, was ruined by the complete want of concert amongst the leaders of their party, and by the gross incompetency of their military chiefs. In 1645, Montrose, with a handful of raw soldiers, unprovided with horse and ill supplied even with the commonest implements of war, gained victory after victory, broke the mighty power of the Campbells, traversed Scotland from end to end, and wrested it for a time even from the iron grip of the Covenanters. Forty-four years later Dundee, at the head of half a dozen ragged Jacobite clans, scattered at a single onset the disciplined army of the Revolution Government, commanded by a veteran Whig general. Again, in 1745, at a time when the Brunswicks were strong with the strength of a long prescription, the personal fascination of Prince Charles Stuart, co-operating with the military skill of his lieutenant, Murray, won from them one of their three kingdoms, and went far to win a second. Yet in 1715, Mar, with a force almost as large as those of Montrose, Dundee, and Charles Edward joined together, did literally nothing; wasted the autumn months ingloriously at Perth, yet neglected to fortify the town for winter quarters; stood by a helpless spectator whilst his adversary Argyle gathered together with difficulty at Stirling the troops necessary for dislodging him; allowed the certain victory of Sheriffmuir to slide out of his hands; and then, without striking another blow, retreated to Montrose, shipped himself and his master back to France, and left his army to disband itself in the wilds of Aberdeen. Forster, with the insurgents of Northumberland and the Scottish border, wandered aimlessly as far as Preston, and there, after a victorious engagement, pusillanimously surrendered to Wills. The great rising of the western counties, from which so much had been anticipated, was strangled at its birth. The unmeaning flight of Ormond had in fact utterly quenched the hopes of the English Jacobites; and in his tardy efforts to reanimate them with his presence, this idol of the people was refused a lodging in the very country where he had expected to be met by a nation in arms and welcomed by multitudes as their deliverer. Berwick was the ablest soldier in the party; and his military experience was studiously disregarded.

Bolingbroke was their ablest statesman and diplomatist; but his diplomacy proved unavailing to sustain the movement which his statesmanship had condemned.

It was natural that hopes raised so high, ending in disaster so overwhelming and ignominious, should stir the rage of the Jesuit priests and Irish adventurers whom Bolingbroke calls the rabble of St. Germain's. It was agreed to make the secretary their scapegoat, loaded with the evil consequences of their own follies and sent adrift. He was accused of treachery, of incapacity, of wilful mismanagement, of having entered James's service with the express purpose of betraying him, of having squandered on a courtesan the moneys entrusted to him to buy powder and arms for the expedition, of having in his cups blabbed secrets, ridiculed his colleagues, and even, dreadful to say, made game of their august master. These and similar charges were noised abroad in all the coteries of Paris into which the Jacobites had access.* They were deliberately adopted by the chevalier on his return. But they have never found credence with any reasonable man. That Bolingbroke disapproved of Mar's adventure is perfectly true. He thought the moment ill-chosen for a descent on England, with the Government now thoroughly on its guard, national troops raised, foreign forces sent for, and France, like the rest of the continent, against them; and he believed that without a successful descent on England no victories in the northern kingdom, however skilfully improved, would avail them. It is true, also, that he regretted his own precipitance in joining a body so shiftless as the Jacobites, and that after midnight, when the Burgundy was mounting to his head, he was but too ready, under the blandishments of a fair companion, to speak his mind on men and things with imprudent frankness.

* Lord Stair to Horace Walpole, March 3, 1716.

But that either his lively habits, or the belief which he soon formed of the uselessness of his efforts to procure the extensive foreign succours which Mar was constantly demanding, had the effect of damping the ardour with which in the daytime he addressed himself to the ungrateful and unprofitable task, this—and it was the main count in the indictment against him—has been distinctly refuted by Berwick, an unexceptionable witness who had no motive for concealing the truth and every means of learning it.

But it suited Mar and Ormond to thrust on Bolingbroke the odium of their own incompetency ; and James, always blindly submissive to the favourite of the hour, had been living in the most intimate communion, first with Ormond and then with Mar. The blow fell without any sort of warning. It was at the end of February, 1716, that the discomfited Pretender landed in France after his two inglorious campaigns, determined to vent his spleen on the one man of genius who had adopted his cause, whose best energies had been devoted to making his enterprise successful, and whose advice, if he had condescended to take it, would, there is every reason to believe, have put him in quiet possession of the kingdoms he had failed to conquer. On the evening of Monday, the 26th, the two men met in a long and confidential interview. They discussed with perfect amity the place of the Prince's retreat, agreed to the Regent's suggestion that he should proceed with all possible diligence to Bar and take possession of his old asylum whilst it was still open to him, and parted with the hope expressed on both sides of meeting a few days later in the neutral territory of Lorraine. On the following Thursday a note in James's writing was put into Bolingbroke's hand. It was a curt dismissal from the Pretender's service.

He was bitterly mortified. In an obscure corner of

Paris he possessed a retired lodging, lent him by one of his friends, and here during many days he hid himself from all eyes. When at length, in order to silence the clamour of scurrilous tongues, he appeared once more in the brilliant circles in which he had filled so large a space, he came forth the deadly and implacable enemy of that cause for which he had sacrificed his fame, his birthright, and his whole public career. He welcomed loudly, as was his wont, his newly recovered liberty. To Mary of Modena, who courteously expressed the hope that the misunderstanding between him and her son might be set right, he made answer that he was now a free man, and that he wished his hand might rot off if ever again it drew sword or held pen in James's service. He went at once to Lord Stair, bewailed his folly with tears of mingled rage and contrition, and besought the ambassador to plead for him once more with the Government at home. In the first heat of his resentment he offered to earn his pardon by any task or service they might demand from him. Was it desired that the Tory gentry should be put on their guard against Jacobite plots and snares? He would write a letter to his friend Sir William Wyndham, whose influence with the party was scarcely inferior to that of Ormond; would paint the St. Germain's rabble in their true colours; would show him what the chances of a restoration under the present management really were; and would send his letter unsealed under cover to the minister himself, who would thus be able to judge of the sincerity and efficacy of his repentance.

But with time passion began to cool and sounder judgment to reassert itself. In the elaborate apology for these events which, a few months later, Bolingbroke put on record, it is interesting to notice with what a magnanimous air he waves aside the notion that he ever made advances to the Whigs or entertained for a moment the thought of trafficking with them about his restoration. His solicitude was not to obtain either pardon or revenge—these were minor matters—but to promote the good of the English people by using on their behalf the unfortunate experience he had just gained. To undeceive his friends in England so grossly and so dangerously deluded both as to the state of foreign affairs and the management and character of the Jacobite interest in France, this was a plain duty demanded of him by "honour" and "conscience," and, it was a duty which he intended to perform at all hazards. The obligation was altogether unmixed with any personal or sinister motive. If the Government thought that in fulfilling this duty he should be in fact contributing to their stability, if they thought that the restoration of his family honours might give greater effect to the blow which the Pretender's treatment of the whole Tory party in his person put him under the necessity of dealing at the Stuart cause—well, that was their affair, not his. For himself he was anxious to leave no room for any doubtful construction of his conduct. "The notion of a treaty when first propounded shocked me." *

The truth seems to be that the negotiation broke down on the important question of price. Between what the Government asked and what Bolingbroke was ready to give there was a substantial difference. The British ambassador had been informed by Stanhope of the dismay which Bolingbroke's disgrace had caused amongst the English Jacobites, and had been authorized, "if he seemed in the disposition to return and tell all," to strengthen his purpose by giving him on the King's part "all suitable hope and encouragement." † This was not precisely the "unsolicited, unconditional" offer of favour which he claimed

---

* Works, i. 84.   † Stanhope to Lord Stair, March 28, 1716.

to have received, but an offer of favour clogged with an
onerous and unpleasant condition to which Bolingbroke
on reflection declined to submit. He was still ready to
earn his pardon by betraying the Jacobite interest and
breaking up the Jacobite party. He wrote and sent through
the minister the epistle to Sir William Wyndham which
was to be the medium of converting the gentlemen of
England from Jacobitism. * But he refused to inform
directly against individual Jacobites, which would, as he
justly pleaded, have " damaged his reputation."

It was on this point no doubt that the treaty failed.
Lord Stair, whatever he may have thought of Bolingbroke's
disinterested patriotism and refined sensibility, held that
his hatred of James was a passion sufficiently strong in
itself to be relied on, and counselled ministers to open
their arms to the repentant prodigal. And at one time,
owing to a temporary schism in the Whig ranks, his
prospects looked bright. Walpole, who had borne the
chief part in his impeachment, and who distrusted his
restless ambition and insatiable propensity for intrigue,
had resigned in consequence of the dismissal of his kinsman, Townshend ; and the chief power · had passed to
Sunderland and Stanhope, who, bitterly assailed as they
were by their old colleague, were not unwilling to purchase
the support of their old opponent. But unexpected difficulties arose. The temper of their Whig following could
not be trifled with. Year after year passed by, and their
autumnal promises always ended in vernal excuses.

* Bolingbroke to Wyndham, September 2, 1716 ; Townshend to Stanhope,
September 15, 1716.

IV.

The tedium of exile and the weariness of hope deferred were relieved by Bolingbroke with pursuits more congenial to his better nature than the intrigues of faction. He resumed those habits of close and arduous study which political success had interrupted, and which had dignified his first two years' retirement at Bucklersbury, caused by his grandfather's death and his father's estrangement from him. It was now that he wrote his characteristic " Reflections on Exile." In answer to the Pretender's manifesto from Avignon, he put on record, in the masterly Letter to Sir William Wyndham, which was published after his death, a powerful and, on the whole, a fairly trustworthy account of his own short administration. He lost himself in the mazes of metaphysical inquiry, and laid the foundation of that system of philosophical Deism which he afterwards elaborated at La Source, and which, though a perfectly legitimate contribution to the advancing science of theology, has with ignorant men done more to blacken his fame than the many errors and offences of his public conduct. In the intervals of these graver matters he prepared himself for the retired, abstemious life on which he was shortly to enter by taking a surfeit of the delights of Paris, and was for a while a conspicuous figure in those brilliant orgies of the Regency wherein vice, in losing its grossness, lost, we are told, half its evil.

But about this time a salutary change took place in Bolingbroke's habits. Like other men of the world who have experienced the discomforts of an uncongenial marriage and sought relief in temporary connections with a succession of frail ones—green-room beauties, women of the town, and fine ladies of fashion—he at length found in one of the objects of this desultory attachment qualities of mind and person which might, he thought, bear the strain of a firmer union. In March, 1720—his first wife having died some eighteen months before—he married the Marquise de Villette, a niece of Madame de Maintenon's, whose acquaintance he had made three years before in Paris, and who had since been living for a time under his protection. The event gave a new meaning and a new interest to Bolingbroke's life. On her personal charms Time had laid his hand; but her lively wit, her finished grace of manner, and her entire unselfish devotion to his fortunes, soon concentrated on Lady Bolingbroke the roving attentions which the statesman almost from his boyhood had been used to distribute "with such profusion" amongst the "dear thoughtless Claras" who inspired his earliest muse. Like the rest of the world of Paris, he had speculated a little at the time of the great Mississippi bubble; unlike the rest of the world, he had realized before the crash came, and had wisely laid out his gains in the purchase of a life interest in the small estate of La Source, a chateau near Orleans, in the grounds of which the river Loiret takes its rise. Thither he now retired with his wife. In this hermitage, where, as he describes it in a charming letter to Swift, the hoarse voice of party was never heard, whence gazettes and pamphlets were rigorously banished, and where the insects of various hue that had hummed and buzzed about him in the sunshine had no longer power to vex and tease, the days passed tranquilly away in the domestic endearments which he then first learnt to prize.*

But the fresh and unlooked-for happiness which Bolingbroke now found in retirement and obscurity was not incompatible with a desire to win back the trinkets and baubles which he affected to despise. In his country

* Bolingbroke to Swift, July 28, 1721.

retreat, amidst the pleasant surroundings which he had made, immersed in the absorbing pursuit of knowledge, and enlivened by the occasional presence of a few congenial friends, life seemed, as he said, to move back upon its steps like the sun on the dial of Hezekiah, and his philosophy grew daily more confirmed by habit. But when he entered into the world the illusion passed away. There the insecurity of his position as an attainted man, exiled from the country of his birth, living by sufferance amongst strangers in a foreign land, with no other support than the consciousness of his own "integrity," forced itself upon him. His health, too, was beginning to decay. He was entering into the latter scenes of life. The small fortune which he had saved and acquired abroad had been exposed to abundance of diminutions and losses, and was no longer adequate to his needs. Anything certain and determined seemed preferable to a suspense the burden of which neither his temper nor his purse could stand.

Accordingly, in the winter of 1722, seven years nearly since the first conditional promise of favour had been given him, Bolingbroke brought to bear all the influence at his command to obtain from Government, if not a complete restoration, at least the power of communicating with his friends, the privilege of visiting England, the right of enjoying, when they should fall to him, the family estates which his father held. The circumstances of the time were not unfavourable to him. The unlucky South Sea Company, a legacy left by Harley's administration of the treasury, had indeed dragged down in its fall those chiefs of the Whig party by whom originally the offer of pardon had been made. Sunderland and Stanhope, Aislabie and Craggs, had disappeared from the scene. The whole party, invigorated by a recent election in which the public voice had confirmed and justified the doubtful policy of the

R

Septennial Act, was drawn up in a firmly united body behind Walpole. In 1719, no doubt, when Bolingbroke's restoration had been last mooted, Walpole, then engaged in attacking all Sunderland's measures with impartial acrimony, had denounced the proposal as an insult to Parliament. But many things had happened since then. Walpole himself was minister, occupied in consolidating that power which accident had given him, and exposed to the same solicitations by which his predecessors had been assailed. In the spring of 1723, amidst the excitement caused by Atterbury's treason, Bolingbroke's pardon formally passed the Great Seal, chiefly owing, it is said, to the exertions of his old colleague Lord Harcourt, then on confidential terms with the minister, and long since purged, like Bolingbroke himself, from all taint of Jacobitism. The exile was now at liberty, if he chose, to return home ; and in the same summer he took advantage of this privilege to pay a short visit to London. But the Act of Attainder which deprived him of his property, and of what he valued more, perhaps, his honours, was still in force. To the repeal of this Act the consent of Parliament and of the Whig party would be necessary ; and this consent the minister, like his predecessors, did not see his way to asking. It was in vain that Bolingbroke, during his short sojourn in England, attempted to remove the minister's difficulty by bringing about a formal coalition between Walpole and the small body of Hanoverian Tories which followed the lead of Sir William Wyndham. The attempt was coldly repulsed. It was based on a misconception of Walpole's character and political objects. But before the close of the same year Bolingbroke was able to confer upon the Whig leader a substantial service in a matter which he had greatly at heart—this time by narrowing instead of widening the base of his administration,—and it

is not a little remarkable that the first step in the work of
creating the modern office of Prime Minister, with his
paramount authority over his colleagues and his exclusive
monopoly of political power, should have been skilfully
furthered by the very statesman whose bitterest invectives
were afterwards directed against that main feature of
Walpole's system.

V.

The story is a curious illustration of the politics of that
age when changes in the form and composition of Government, imperatively called for by the exigencies of the
public service, had to be worked out for the most part
through some closet intrigue, or the corrupt manipulation
of votes in Parliament. At the King's accession Townshend, a man honest indeed and sensible, but violent in
temper, and hardly qualified by experience for the duties
of his great place, had been raised above the recognized
chiefs of the Whig party through the friendship of Bothmar,
and Bothmar's influence at the Electoral Court. His
elevation had caused much murmuring. During the first
months of the new Government personal rivalries had been
banished by the nearness of the dangers threatening it ;
but towards the close of 1716, when the success of the
Revolution Settlement seemed secured, Sunderland, who
had then succeeded by the death of his principal colleagues
to the leadership of the Whig junto, made a determined
effort to assert in his own person the authority of which,
two years before, they had been deprived. The attempt
succeeded. The learned and eloquent Republican, bent
on securing for the privileged order to which he belonged
and for the hereditary chamber in which he played his

part a perilous, because an unmasked, ascendency in the
State, condescended to use for this purpose the same
courtly arts on which he believed his rival's power to rest.
Townshend was pulled down by the hands that raised
him, was deprived of the premiership, and, after a few
months, was dismissed from office.   Sunderland, the natural
leader of the Whigs, became first minister.   But a schism
was formed in the party fatal at the moment to the
political objects which he had at heart.   Townshend was
followed into opposition by Walpole, whose parliamentary
experience made his support invaluable ; by Methuen, the
depository of the commercial traditions of the Whigs ; by
Pulteney, their most rising speaker ; and by the heads of
the two great Revolution families of Cavendish and Russell.
The new Government, weakened by these defections, was
powerless to carry its great domestic measure of reform,
that bill for limiting the prerogative in the matter of
creating peers which the minister believed to be essential
to the welfare of the State, and which his strongest
opponent admitted to be a remedy, though too severe a
one, for a serious and growing distemper.

But Sunderland's administration was saved from the
consequences of this failure by the vigour and success of
its foreign policy.   It was the old foreign policy of
adventure which made England the moving spirit in
the Liberal cause throughout Europe, the policy of Cromwell and William of Orange, which Somers and Montague
had inherited with their Puritan traditions, in which
Townshend, under the influence of Walpole's novel theories
of free trade and non-intervention, had shown signs of
faltering, and which Walpole himself was finally to
abandon.*   Under Stanhope's superintendence a close

---

* To the student of politics the change of government which took place
in the spring of 1717, and which is generally represented by the historians as

alliance was formed on the basis of reciprocal guarantees with the Regent's Government in France, rendering Great Britain to a great degree independent of the continued hostility of her old allies, depriving the Jacobite conspirators of their foothold on French soil, and giving a new meaning to those articles in the recent treaties which sought to provide against the virtual union of the French and Spanish crowns. By Stanhope's exertions the Government of the United Provinces was drawn into this policy of sustaining the Orleans rule in France against the efforts of the old nobility to restore the ancient system. The Emperor, in return for a guarantee of his actual possessions and an intervention in his domestic troubles, was induced to renounce those nebulous pretensions to the crown of Spain which still kept Europe at war. And thus France herself, merging her traditional ambition in the personal interest of her new ruler, became, through the influence of the English minister, the main instrument in frustrating, perhaps, the most formidable of all the many schemes matured by the House of Bourbon for gaining the mastery of Western Europe.

In the face of achievements such as these, recalling

a mere personal struggle between self-seeking rivals, is interesting as the first indication of that remarkable change in the foreign policy of the Whigs which had led before the close of the century to a complete transformation in the two party creeds—the Whig adopting the financial and political heresies which Bolingbroke had learnt from Moore, the Tory taking up the abandoned system of entangling alliances and lavish expenditure. Townshend's fall was undoubtedly caused in the main by his reluctance to second cordially the vigorous course of action with regard to the Northern Powers, on which Stanhope and Sunderland were bent, and which the King had greatly at heart. It is a curious fact, which I do not remember to have seen mentioned, that Arthur Moore, the real author of Bolingbroke's commercial treaty with France, and the promoter of the economical policy of Harley's government, had become, at the time of Bolingbroke's return in 1725, a close ally and party follower of Walpole, whose policy, both foreign and financial, presents, especially in his later years, so many points of resemblance to Bolingbroke's. A life of Moore, written with adequate knowledge, would be a most interesting contribution to the secret history of the eighteenth century.

the best days' of English statesmanship and securing to
the ministry the cordial gratitude of the Electoral Court,
parliamentary defeats, and victories hardly to be distinguished from defeats, mattered little ; and after three
years of fruitless opposition the malcontent Whig leaders
tacitly acknowledged their failure. A reunion took place
between the two sections of the Whig party. Stanhope
and Sunderland retained the supreme power ; Townshend
and Walpole consented to support Government in subordinate places.

But then had come, all in a moment, a surprising turn
of fortune—the collapse of Sunderland's commercial policy,
the death of Stanhope, the expulsion of Aislabie, the timely
epidemic which saved the generous Craggs from the like
degrading fate, the removal of the Prime Minister on the
unjust suspicion that he too had been implicated in the
frauds ; and Walpole, amidst the wreck of so many great
reputations, was called to the head of affairs as the only
living statesman competent to put into shape the disordered finances. It was in the spring of 1721 that he
first entered on his long career of official supremacy,
designated as minister by the unanimous voice of the
trading classes. In opposition he had closely allied
himself with the Hanoverian Tories. But in office he
determined to stand on what he calls a " Whig bottom ; " *
to put aside Bolingbroke's offer of a coalition with Wyndham and Anglesea ; to create such a borough interest
as might secure his own authority against the fluctuations
at once of royal favour and of popular caprice ; and to use
the official patronage in his gift as the means of procuring
not lively speakers or skilful administrators, men who
in proportion to their achievements would increase their
own pretensions at his expense, but votes, brute votes

<hr>

* Walpole to Townshend, July 23, 1723.

whose support might be relied on with confidence and manipulated at pleasure. Such was the aim of Walpole's system. At the close of 1723—the office of First Lord of the Treasury, which he now held in place of Sunderland, not then carrying with it of necessity the supreme direction of affairs—he was still engaged in the preliminary work of gradually making good his own position as chief minister against such of Sunderland's colleagues as seemed inclined to dispute it.

Foremost amongst these was the gifted and versatile Carteret. Carteret was Secretary of State. His appointment had been the last official act of Sunderland before laying down his power. He claimed to represent the famous Whig junto of Queen Anne's reign, to be the arch-Brahmin of the holy Whig caste; and he aspired to direct the policy of England through his command of her foreign relations, leaving to Walpole only the dry subordinate details of finance and parliamentary management. In influence and weight of character he was decidedly Walpole's inferior. But he was a man of extraordinary energy and resource, an accomplished intriguer, a master of those Machiavelian arts by which ascendency at courts is won. His knowledge of German had gained him the King's ear; and his continental policy, which aimed at extending the power of Hanover in Germany as a security for British interests abroad, and by the united strength of the two countries swaying the destinies of Europe for their joint benefit, had roused the patriotic ambition and earned him the unbounded confidence of the King's Hanoverian ministers. One condition of success, however, was wanting. The Duchess of Kendal was the leading personage at the court of George I. The duchess had for value received taken Walpole under her august protection. In Carteret's judgment it was necessary to balance the duchess's influence by help of a rival beauty equally devoted to himself, and for this purpose he was paying assiduous court to Madame de Platen, the second lady, so to speak, of the Electoral bedchamber, by furthering a marriage which she had in view for one of her "nieces." He had staked his whole credit with these dispensers of royal favour on being able to thrust the father of the young Count de St. Florentin, to whom the lady's hand was pledged, into the highest rank of the French nobility.

Such was the delicate and momentous question on which the struggle came to a head—whether by the persistence of the British envoy in Paris, in opposition to the strong repugnance of the French Government and to the indignant remonstrances of the peers of France, a dukedom could be procured for a rising French official as a sort of bribe or dower for taking to his house a lady whose family antecedents were so equivocal ; and on this issue depended the ultimate authority of two great ministers, the triumph of two rival policies, the existence, it may be, of that parliamentary system which Walpole consolidated, and which, resting as it does on party attachments rather than on the personal claims of statesmen, has bequeathed its character and even its methods to the political life of our time. Walpole had no means of directly traversing Carteret's negotiation. His kinsman Townshend was also Secretary of State. But the court of France was, as Townshend confessed, the "strength and heart" of Carteret's province. Sir Luke Schaub, the British agent at Paris, was an old protégé of Stanhope's, and devoted to Stanhope's successor ; and the instructions under which he acted came straight from Carteret as King's secretary, and were not, as they would be now, first submitted to the cabinet for its joint approval. All that could be done was to instruct Horace Walpole, then in

Paris on what he calls a roving commission from his two brothers, to impair so far as he could the authority of the legitimate minister. And the task was not an easy one. Horace Walpole indeed was a skilful diplomatist; but his manners and accomplishments were not exactly those of the polite society in which he was now called to move. He had no recognized position at the French court, where, till a happy thought struck Townshend, he filled the *rôle* of a mere passing tourist. He was quite inexperienced in the wiles of French diplomacy; and he was known to be in the interest of a minister whose star was believed to be on the wane.

It was in these circumstances that Bolingbroke's assistance was invoked. It was strongly represented to the minister by Harcourt that his great diplomatic experience, his familiarity with the many-sided life of the Parisian coteries, the intimacy in which he lived with the companions of Monsieur le Duc—now on the Regent's death Prime Minister of France—and the personal esteem which his highness was known to bear for him, made the exiled statesman peculiarly fitted to correct the inexperience of the unofficial envoy and put in his hands the clue to the tortuous jumble of French politics. Bolingbroke accepted the mission in his most characteristic manner, unable to conceal from the shrewd observer now associated with him his delight and exultation at such a proof of confidence, yet affecting an air of indifference, a doubt how far he was competent after so long an absence from business to deal with a matter so delicate, and a fear lest, as a "proscribed man" with no other support but his "integrity," he should exert himself to little purpose. He could indeed easily become acquainted with Madame de Prie, a lady who would no doubt, under the new *régime*, exercise on the politics of France and of Europe all that influence to which her personal charms entitled her, and he would, "if it was thought proper," see what could be done.

In a couple of interviews with the Duke of Bourbon, Bolingbroke accomplished the mission on which Horace Walpole had been sent. He explained the state of English parties at the time. He showed that this matter of the De la Vrillière dukedom, which was causing such embarrassment in France, was being pressed by the English secretary more as a means of securing his own favour with the King's mistress than to please the King himself, who by no means desired such a trumpery question to be elevated into an affair of State as Schaub was representing; he combated the prevailing notion that Walpole, as head of the Treasury, had no voice in foreign affairs; he showed that Townshend had by virtue of his office, an equal share with Carteret in the management of them, and by his authority with Walpole a much greater; and he strongly advised the French court to take their cue from the unaccredited diplomatist who knew the sentiments of the two leading ministers wherever he and Schaub should differ.

Then he sought an interview with Horace Walpole, and with his accustomed vivacity pointed out to him the glorious opportunity he now had of entering on this business with the path to success made smooth for him. Nor was Walpole the man to allow such a chance to escape. The French Government, fortified by his secret encouragement, rejected the demand of the English envoy. Carteret, his authority destroyed at the court where the chief part of his business lay and on a matter on which he had staked his credit as minister, was compelled to exchange the office of Secretary of State, with the constant access it gave to the royal presence, for the Siberian exile of Dublin Castle. A close ally of Walpole's, a man altogether

Carteret's inferior in parts and acquirements, but the greatest boroughmonger in England, succeeded him. Schaub was recalled. Horace Walpole himself was promoted to be ambassador at the court of France, where during several years he contributed with eminent skill to bring the general politics of Europe into harmony with the pacific objects of his chief. The reward of Bolingbroke, the real author of the diplomatic triumph to which the new minister owed his elevation, and of·which in his despatches he calmly appropriated the entire credit, was delayed for some months. But he had taken the wise precaution to administer, through Madame de Villette, out of property belonging to her then in the hands of an English banker, a heavy bribe to the Duchess of Kendal, with an intimation that the fund from which the gratuity came was not exhausted by it. Gratitude, as Bolingbroke elsewhere reminds us, means, in the language of courts, the expectation of future favours ; and the great lady honourably enshrined Bolingbroke's services in her heart, gave her friend the minister no peace till he also had recognized them, whispered his name even in the August Presence amidst the silence of the night-watches, bore him, so to speak, in the folds of her robe into the empyrean in which she dwelt.*

It is pleasant to think that these offices of sisterly friendship proved successful. In the session of 1725, Lord Finch, the son of his old antagonist, Nottingham, introduced and, with the help of the Government, passed into law a bill which bestowed on Bolingbroke the forfeited interest in his family estates, and the right of holding and purchasing landed property in England. But the Act was not passed, omnipotent as Walpole then was, without difficulty, and

---

* Townshend to Walpole, September 26 and October 23, 1723. Horace to Robert Walpole, December 15, 16, and 29, 1723.

much murmuring on the part both of sturdy Whigs like Methuen and Onslow, who objected to reverse a State prosecution on the importunities of a courtesan, and of timeserving Jacobites like Musgrave, whose idea of pleasing their vagabond and mendicant prince was to insult at his bidding all who had incurred his enmity.* And Bolingbroke was forced, after all, to content himself with what he calls a " two-thirds " restoration. To the end of his life Walpole would never consent to remit the remaining penalties of his attainder, or reopen the doors of Parliament to that eloquent voice whose persuasive power he had had such bitter cause to dread.

In justice to Bolingbroke it is necessary to remember this. He was under no obligations to Walpole. Had Walpole felt strong enough at court to follow his own unfettered judgment, not one of the penalties of Bolingbroke's attainder would ever have been remitted at all. When, therefore, failing to move the minister by flattery and offers of political service, Bolingbroke suddenly changed his tactics, and looked about for some means, open or secret, of overthrowing him, and marching to a complete restoration over the ruins of his power, he is in no sense open to that charge of ingratitude which Walpole's adherents have brought against him. Nor is he to be seriously blamed, so far as I can see, for his first unsuccessful endeavour to upset King George's minister by means of the influence which his wife's money had given him over the mercenary affections of King George's mistress, perfectly in keeping as it was with those constitutional theories of government by court favour, by " sovereigns and statesmen," of which he was through life the consistent inter-

* Lord Bathurst, as might be expected, was superior to this baseness. "I have not yet learnt," he said, "*jurare in verba magistri*" (Duke of Wharton to James Stuart, February 3, 1725).

preter. The lamented death of our first Hanoverian deliverer nipped this plot of the bedchamber in the bud, just as it showed some promise of opening out into flower. But before this time the inordinate craving of Walpole for an undisputed authority in his own government had thrown in Bolingbroke's way an accomplice of a very different stamp from Madame de Schulenburg, as fond of money, perhaps, as void of principle, but with gifts and acquirements and connections which made him a far more formidable instrument for assailing a minister whose fastest stronghold was parliamentary power.

VI.

Among the younger leaders of the Whig party none filled or deserved to fill a larger space in parliamentary circles than William Pulteney; for he possessed in a remarkable degree that peculiar combination of internal qualities and external advantages which, under a popular constitution administered by an aristocratic society, wins applause and attracts followers. His family was honourably distinguished both by its high descent and its devotion to the cause of liberty. Himself a simple country squire, proud of his position as one of the untitled gentry, he had inherited possessions equal to those of the greatest noble. To these advantages of birth and wealth he united the accomplishments at once of a man of fashion and a man of letters, polished manners, scholarship graceful and easy if not profound, admirable quickness of wit, perhaps an unrivalled facility of expression. Of all the public men of that time, the time which began with the fall of Bolingbroke and ended with the rise of Chatham, none certainly equalled Pulteney as a debater, none approached him perhaps in the readiness with which, without preparation and following strictly the course of the preceding discussion, he applied to every subject its appropriate turns of phrase, entertaining, explanatory, persuasive, or pathetic, passing with perfect ease from mood to mood as the occasion served. Like Carteret, he was many-sided in his tastes, and played with success widely different parts in life— the scholar, the orator, the poet, the fine gentleman.

But, as in the case of Carteret, the brilliancy and versatility of Pulteney's gifts were accompanied by a conspicuous absence of those more solid qualities of character and judgment on which an enduring reputation is built. He was capable of displaying on great occasions a misplaced disinterestedness and an ill-regulated public spirit. But his nature was sordid and vindictive, his principles were lax, his attachments unsteady, his passions impetuous and uncontrolled. As a man of business, he was unmethodical and untrustworthy, industrious by fits and starts, prone through restlessness of temper to throw aside his work half done. In statesmanship, in political insight, he was wholly wanting ; nor is there any evidence that he detected the true meaning of the political changes at work before him, or estimated the real nature and issues of the party struggle on which wounded vanity and baulked ambition now impelled him.

Such was the man with whom the chances of political life now threw Bolingbroke into the closest companionship. Hitherto they had borne the relation of bitter and rancorous party rivals. In the late reign, with characteristic impetuosity, Pulteney had carried his partisan resistance to Bolingbroke's policy beyond the limits of fair party warfare, had exhausted every artifice of intrigue to hinder the treaties of peace, had even strained his private credit to enable the Emperor to continue the war in spite of them. In the session of 1712, when Secretary St. John, by way of retaliating on his chief assailant, had procured Walpole's expulsion from Parliament on a trumped-up charge of corruption, Pulteney had warmly supported that victim to the intemperance of factions run mad. He had sat by Walpole's side in the Secret Committee which practically fixed the terms of Bolingbroke's impeachment, had helped Walpole in the work of frightening Bolingbroke into exile, and had resisted with Walpole all the efforts of Bolingbroke's friends to procure the reversal of his attainder. Nay, he had supported Walpole against the chiefs of his own party, and, in the schism of 1717, had resigned a valuable appointment to follow the malcontent Whig leader into opposition. Unfortunately, though included in the reconciliation which took place three years later by the offer of a peerage and afterwards of a considerable post in the royal household, Pulteney had not been consulted by Walpole in the settlement of its terms ; and in his vain and irritable nature the slight rankled into a permanent sore. According to his own account he resented those terms as too degrading ; and it is possible that Pulteney, under the influence of passions which always bore the semblance of public virtue, really disapproved of a compromise, which was certainly a humiliation for his friends, an acknowledgment of defeat, if not a surrender of public principle. And yet if this charitable explanation of his conduct be accepted, it must be confessed that Pulteney's manner of marking his respect for political consistency was at least singular. For four years later, after holding for a few months his place at court, on the elevation of Newcastle to succeed Carteret as Secretary of State, Pulteney suddenly resigned, broke away from his allegiance, repulsed all Walpole's efforts to win him back, and at length, about the time of Boling-

turn, through the mediation of a kinsman, Daniel
an old follower and near connection of Lord
Sunderland's, whose career had been arrested by that
minister's fall, put himself at the head of the small remnant
of Sunderland's party which Walpole had failed to conciliate, that party to which eight years before he had
vowed an undying enmity.

It is to the genius of Bolingbroke that this opposition,
which was afterwards so widely celebrated as that of the
Patriots or Discontented Whigs, owed its renown and the
attractive power which drew eminent men into its ranks.
As in the case of the great regenerator of old, an opposition,
bred entirely out of personal resentments and having for its
object simply the satisfaction of personal grievances, was
organized by him into a legitimate party, and endowed
with living principles of political conduct. It was Bolingbroke's merit to see more clearly than his contemporaries
not the faults only and shortcomings of Walpole, but his
achievements—the silent revolution which he was effecting
in our constitutional system, and which makes his ministry
so great an era in its annals ; the organization of Parliament
into a real governing assembly, its division into parties
drilled and officered for the work before them ; the substitution of a united Cabinet formed out of the prevailing
majority, and responsible to its chosen leader, for the old
heterogeneous council presided over by the King in person.
He saw that Walpole's plan of concentrating in the representative body all the different powers of the State was an
innovation, with no warrant in the expressed traditions
of the older Whigs. He saw, therefore, that it might be
made the ground and subject of an opposition which should
not confine itself exclusively to Tories ; which should take
its stand avowedly on the soundest Revolution principles ;
which should appeal in the interest of those principles from

a usurping faction supporting itself, as he said, by novel methods, establishing novel maxims, introducing novel customs in government, to the conservative instincts of the nation at large, on one side of its character, practical, utilitarian, progressive, but, on the other, reverent of the past, distrustful of violent changes, capable of enthusiasm for a tradition and an idea.

By Pulteney and his immediate friends, intent simply on revenging themselves on Walpole, the high sentiments of constitutional morality which Bolingbroke put into their mouths were expressed with tongue in cheek as so much common form. The "principles of the opposition," as he afterwards very justly said, "were the principles of very few of the opposers;" and their affectation of "patriotism" on the part of the leading patriots, their recantation of latter-day Whiggism, the new-born desire for that "union and coalition of parties meeting together on a national bottom," which under Bolingbroke's tuition they proposed to substitute for Walpole's exclusive system, was in the great majority of cases a mere pretence, a mere "scaffolding, nothing else, which they showed the greatest readiness to demolish whenever they had a glimpse of hope that they might rise to power without it." * But Pulteney and his friends were men of wisdom in their generation. They knew the use that might be made of sentiment in politics, and the value of a specious political cry. They knew that Bolingbroke was a consummate master of political strategy as well as a great constitutional moralist. Their idea was to enlist him into their ranks as a sort of confidential and literary adviser, in much the same position in fact which Swift had occupied under his own and Harley's Government.

His party connections not less than his personal

* Bolingbroke to Lord Polwarth, April 6, 1742.

qualities marked him out for this position. By the great mass of the old monarchical party which retained its dislike to the House of Hanover and held itself aloof from public affairs, choosing to play the part, as Bolingbroke said, of an outcast race like the Jews, vainly waiting for a Messiah who never came, he was cordially hated as a traitor and renegade. But over the parliamentary followers of Sir William Wyndham, who accepted the Revolution dynasty without further question, and confined their antagonism to the Whig ministers, he exercised through his old friend and colleague a strong and growing influence. The authority of Speaker Onslow has conferred on Wyndham a high reputation for eloquence and statesmanship. But with many fine gifts of character he shines chiefly with the reflected light drawn from the stronger intellect of his friend; and it was this connection, so honourable to Bolingbroke, that marked him out to the two Pulteneys as a valuable coadjutor. His function was to bridge over the space which separated the two sections of what was now to be a joint opposition, and to erect what the Americans would call a platform for their common appeal to the nation. It was not an easy task: to blend together two parties naturally hostile to each other, governed by different traditions, starting from different principles of public conduct, looking on to a different future as the result of their joint efforts, and united only by the common knowledge that each without the other was powerless to attain its ends. Bolingbroke, moreover, was incapable of sitting in Parliament. He could only direct the party by his counsels and assist it with his pen. But in that age, when debates were unpublished and platform oratory unknown, a parliamentary conflict involving the fate of ministers was always accompanied by a literary conflict, conducted for the most part by the same public men who daily confronted each other in the Legislature ; and of the two the literary conflict was apt to produce the most result, to exercise the greater influence in forming and shaping parliamentary opinions. It was his pre-eminent skill in this part of the work of governing which had made Addison, who never opened his lips in Parliament, a Secretary of State ; and it was in this necessary part of the work of opposing government that Bolingbroke now found an adequate field for the exercise of his brilliant gifts. In the weekly pages of the *Craftsman*—a paper which Pulteney had set up at the close of 1726, and which soon attained under the impulse of Bolingbroke's genius a circulation that brought its words into the household of every politician in the kingdom—he published during the next seven years, in the intervals of organizing the new confederacy, political writings as finished, as easy, as ingeniously persuasive as those in which Addison had pleaded the cause of the new dynasty before the Jacobite freeholders, or endeavoured to win the assent of Parliament to the enthronement of the House of Peers. The apotheosis of pure constitutional monarchy of the old Elizabethan type, they formed the ostensible case of the Patriots against Walpole presented to the nation as in an extended Midlothian campaign. And they undoubtedly contributed largely to Walpole's overthrow, though not until he had succeeded in his main objects, and had established Parliamentary Government substantially on its present lines.

CHAPTER V.

I.

THE Whig system in its pure form was an attempt to establish a popular government in the hands of a particular order in the State—a government under which, by the free choice of the people, a particular order should exercise power as being of all other orders the fittest for power, the most familiar with the nation's wants, and the most likely to pursue its true interests. Their favourite scheme of polity was an aristocratic republic, a commonwealth in which a free Parliament should govern through the agency of responsible ministers connected by close party ties with the great class of nobles. Just as the rival system of hereditary monarchy, bound but not fettered by constitutional restraints, presupposes a Patriot King more qualified for the work of government than any man in his dominions, and subjects sufficiently enlightened to recognize and acquiesce in this superiority, so the Whig system also presupposed two similar conditions—a body of aristocratical statesmen identifying their interests with those of the nation, and a nation freely acknowledging their claim to rule and willing to entrust its interests to their guidance.

In the case of the Whigs, one at least of these conditions was often wanting. As a party they had many titles to public confidence. Forming in themselves the most highly placed, the most progressive, and the most intelligent representatives of the great landowning class, collected into an order of nobles which had no exclusive privileges, into which the meanest peasant in the kingdom was free to enter, and whose great historic achievements had been won in asserting the constitutional rights of the people at large, they had in an unusual degree the virtues of a popular aristocracy, a body of men marked out by character and position for the work of parliamentary leadership. Their patriotism, their political training, their freedom from sordid cares, their superiority to local jealousies and intrigues, the responsibilities attaching to their conspicuous station, their readiness to sacrifice ease and comfort to the public good, the refined habits, delicate discrimination, and anxious judgment which their mode of life tends to foster, all combined to give elevation to their public objects, and to set before them a loftier standard and ideal of national greatness than is contemplated by leaders sprung directly from the people. With all their faults they have furnished the finer tissues in the corporate body of our national life, and given to our political system its characteristic unity and coherence— its unbroken fidelity to the essential principles of public freedom ; its capacity for assimilating new ideas without any outward change of organic form ; its power of reconciling in government the two antagonistic tendencies, the disposition to distrust novelties and live by precedent with the restless expanding energy of individual impulse, transforming each achievement of the past into a step for higher conquests in the future.

But in seeking public confidence, the Whigs were subject to one grave disadvantage. They were not, and they hardly professed to be, a popular or democratical party. Their pride and their independence alike revolted from the dictation of a superior power, whether the prince upon his throne or the people in their polling booths. The ideal government which they favoured was not in fact a popular government, not the sort of government which the people, if left to themselves, would establish. A popular government subjects minor classes and interests to the absolute rule of the largest and the most powerful; and this was almost the reverse of what the Whigs desired. The Revolution was their great achievement. It was brought about by their favourite methods; it embodied their characteristic principles; it resulted in the establishment of their ideal system of polity. And the Revolution was in no sense a popular or democratical movement. It appealed to the sense of national justice and national duty, not at all to the passions and interests of the multitude; appealed to that sense of national justice and national duty from which the multitude, as a rule, is almost entirely free. It was a movement of the weak against the strong, of the towns against the country, of the middle class against the upper, of the counting-house and the chapel against the justice-room and the church. Its principle was to break down the exclusive dominion of the two greatest and most powerful interests in the kingdom— the priesthood and the landed gentry; to admit all sects and classes, however small, however unpopular, to their just share of political power; and to frame under the forms of the old constitution new institutions which should guarantee the stability and permanence of their freedom.

The Whigs had sought to effect this object in the first place by transferring the balance of power from the Crown to Parliament, and virtually to the House of Commons. The House of Commons was then an assembly returned by every kind of franchise, from household suffrage to pure nomination by a single voice. It provided, therefore, in theory for the most complete variety of representation.* But in practice it was still dominated by the old ideas of political and religious exclusiveness. In assenting to the Revolution the mass of the people had intended no change in the system and very little in the aims of government, had desired simply to vindicate the national independence and Protestantism of England against the danger threatening them from France and Rome. The rights of civil and religious liberty, the claim of all sects to equal justice and of all classes to equal privileges,—these were matters about which the people at large were at best indifferent ; and the free parliamentary institutions designed for securing them, the institutions which took from the Crown its liberty of action and from the Church its religious ascendency, were not the desire of the nation generally, but the work of a small body of leaders, wiser and more far-sighted than their fellows, skilfully turning its necessities to their own purpose. Three times since the Revolution the Whig statesmen, engaged in consolidating parliamentary government, had found themselves deserted by the nation, their policy repudiated, their majority scattered, themselves driven from the helm with contumely, their party rivals enthroned, and their political achievements endangered. Three times since the Revolution, in 1690, in 1698, and again in 1710, the country gentlemen, the class hostile to all the political and ecclesiastical ideas of the Revolution, the class against whose exclusive dominion the movement had taken place, had been returned by the free voice of the electors to power, and on every occasion had laboured, with no sign of disapprobation on the part of their constituents, to undo the work of the Revolution, to replace the old exclusive system, to build up round the

* This is well put by Canning in one of his Liverpool speeches (i. 325).

power so given them the old rampart of tests and penalties. The Sacramental Test excluding all but Churchmen from municipal and electoral privileges, the Qualification Bill excluding all but landowners from sitting in Parliament, the Schism Bill confining the entire education of youth to the ministers of one selected and favoured communion,— all these measures, so foreign to the spirit of the new polity, were the direct result of the unfettered action of the electoral body which the new polity had made supreme. If the principles of the Revolution were to be preserved and its objects attained, it would be necessary for a time to protect the weaker sects and classes against the stronger, to give to the trading and dissenting bodies, in whom the reforming spirit and the influence of progressive opinions were most felt, a voice in the State to which their numbers and their popularity did not entitle them, and to exert the weight of Government against those powerful interests which were bent on restoring the old system of monopoly and exclusion.

Thus the Whig statesmen, after the accession of the Hanover line, having opposed to them the force of ancient traditions and associations without having at their back the force of democratic enthusiasm, were driven into the very same system of party consolidation which the High Church leaders had practised during the last four years of the Queen. They entered on it with many advantages which those leaders had wanted. They were the ministers of a Prince who was at first, from the necessities of his position, altogether amenable to their influence, much more amenable to their influence than Queen Anne had been to that of their Tory predecessors. His natural sympathies were with the party of reaction and prerogative. Like William of Orange, he had intended to govern as he thought "fairly," by dividing his favours evenly between the two contending factions ; and more than once he exerted himself to save from punishment Tory assailants of his Government whom its policy, at once proscriptive and republican, had driven into rebellion. But the extreme insecurity of his title, his obligations to the Whig leaders, his entire and beneficent ignorance of the circumstances, the interests, the wishes, even the language of the people he was supposed to rule, practically transferred the kingly power to his advisers; men bound together by close party ties, intent on well-defined political objects, and far more anxious to conciliate the representative body, now supreme over the nation, than the dependent Prince, whose tottering throne they bore upon their shoulders. It was necessary sometimes to humour the parliamentary Sovereign, just as it was necessary to discipline the parliamentary majority ; and much the same methods were employed in both cases. If any symptoms of fractiousness or disaffection began to show themselves in the palace or its surroundings, ministers allayed them by means of a subsidy judiciously expended in relieving the finances of Hanover, or a few pensions and blue ribands scattered about amongst the royal mistresses and boon companions. But on questions of public policy they no longer even summoned their titular chief to their deliberations ; * and it was only in the internal disputes that once or twice arose out of the conflicting pretensions of rival Whig leaders that either of the two first Brunswick Kings was able to assert any of that personal authority in government which their predecessors had carried into every department of the State.

Besides the advantage of a Prince upon the throne who

---

* Since the accession of the House of Brunswick the Sovereign has never attended any of those cabinet meetings of the Privy Council at which the policy of the State is determined.

frankly accepted his true position under the new system, and whose own political leanings, if he had any, might be safely disregarded, the new ministers, in the first Parliament of King George, could rely on a compact majority in both Houses, and were freed from the necessity under which Oxford and Bolingbroke had laboured of nursing up their strength in one House for the purpose of covering their weakness in the other. The House of Lords was the natural stronghold of the great Whig magnates. At the time of the Revolution indeed the two parties had been very evenly balanced there; but in the generation that followed, the successive creations of King William, the influence of the larger proprietors amongst their fellows, and the authority exercised by the statesmen of the Whig junto had gradually secured for the party of progress and public liberty an ascendency which, when the pressure of the late Government was withdrawn, rose to a greater height than ever. In the House of Commons the balance of parties, though swaying from side to side with the impulses and passions of the moment, naturally leaned to Toryism. But even here, in the first Parliament of King George, the dissensions among the Tory chiefs, their mismanagement, the abstention of their followers at the polls, coupled with the desire of the time-serving unpolitical part of the nation to support the successful dynasty, the dynasty which at the critical moment had managed to get itself established, gave to the Whig ministers an accidental majority out of all proportion to any natural strength which they possessed in the constituent bodies. The two most typical divisions in the first session of this Parliament took place, in the Lords, on the Address which distinctly foreshadowed a policy of proscription, and in the Commons, on the motion for impeaching the late ministers. The first was carried by 66 votes to 33; the second by 280 against 125.

With these signal and in many respects fortuitous advantages on their side, the Revolution statesmen entered on the heavy task of consolidating parliamentary government in the teeth of the most powerful interests in the kingdom. When the inevitable reaction set in, due in part to that natural law which regulates the ebb and flow of public opinion, but largely promoted also by the very vigour and success with which they addressed themselves to this policy, they were driven to choose between their principles and their objects—driven to defend against the nation by arbitrary courses those rights of national self-government which they had wrested from the Crown. Being before all things statesmen, men who saw clearly their aims and were deterred by no sentimental scruples from reaching them by the readiest methods, they chose their course without hesitation. They entered with resolute tread that path of despotic repression in the interest of constitutional freedom which has been so often falteringly pursued by their modern successors when administering in the face of Irish discontent and disaffection the same liberal institutions. State prosecutions were set on foot under cover of which the most formidable opponents of their policy were driven from public life. The military forces in their pay were largely augmented, nominally, as the Mutiny Blil in its preamble still states, " for the better preserving of the balance of power in Europe," really as a support for the Revolution polity against domestic disturbances. The right of personal liberty was suspended, and the power of arbitrarily imprisoning men without cause shown was vested in the new Government. In order to deal more effectively with the popular tumults which broke out all over England, and which, stimulated and directed in many places by the local clergy, almost always ended in the destruction of some meeting-house of the Nonconformists, the Riot Act was introduced and passed, making this method of propagating the State religion a felony, and throwing on the township in each case the duty of making good the damage inflicted in its interest. Royal proclamations were put forth, warning the disaffected priesthood to keep off politics in their sermons. In the charges of the Low Church bishops stress was laid on the necessity in the present divided state of religious opinions of avoiding all questions of disputed doctrine in the pulpits paid for by the nation ; and Convocation, the hotbed of sacerdotal intolerance, when it showed signs of proving troublesome, was promptly crushed. The Jacobite rebellion was vigorously stamped out, and the chief victims to a delusion with which half the nation was in sympathy punished with a severity that effectually cooled its courage. To avoid the hazards of a general election at a time when an adverse majority would almost certainly have been returned, the duration of the existing Parliament was prolonged by its own act for four years beyond its natural term. The plan of bolstering up the Parliamentary Settlement by foreign guarantees was revived in the statesmanship of Stanhope, and those unexecuted provisions in the recent treaties which were favourable to the allies of England were carried out under his direction.

These measures answer to the modern Coercion Acts, the Peace Preservation Acts, the Westmeath Acts, the Insurrection Acts, the forcible suppression of patriotic associations, the imprisonment without a trial of Land League orators guilty of no offences of which a popular tribunal would take cognizance—to the whole series of unconstitutional exertions of authority by which the Liberal minister in Ireland, confronted with the same problem of ruling over a nation largely disaffected to the political system which he administers, seeks to chastise it into loyal citizenship,

and secure a clear field for the operation of his chosen
policy. By these means the external dangers threatening
a new and unfamiliar constitution were kept at arm's length
till its roots could strike into the soil, and the natural
strength derived from legitimacy and prescription give
vigour and toughness to its fibres. But in the judgment
of the Whigs something more than this was wanting.
They valued the change of dynasty not simply as substituting a Parliamentary in the place of a Legitimist line
of Sovereigns, but as the symbol of a change in the aims
and methods of government, the breaking down of the
old system of privilege both in politics and in religion. To
that system the Conservative instincts of the landed caste
were strongly bound ; whilst the constituent bodies, even
where the suffrage was most popular, were indifferent,
leaning first to one side and ' then the other in the
wantonness of their new powers, expressing in their actions
the perplexities and indecisions of a divided nation rather
than its deliberate judgments. If Parliament were left free,
it was almost inevitable, judging from the experience of
the past, that the old system would sooner or later be
restored, though not perhaps under the old monarchy.
To preserve representative institutions, and give weight
and dignity to the deliberations of the ruling chamber,
it was necessary, therefore, as the reforming statesmen
held, to modify in some degree the constitution of
Parliament itself, until, with the growth of political knowledge, and the spread of sounder and juster ideas, power
might be safely left to the classes numerically the most
powerful ; and accordingly, under successive Whig ministers,
there was gradually built up, partly in the hands of the
Revolution families themselves, partly of the Government
responsible to them, an extended system of parliamentary
influence, which was admirably effective for its purpose,

under which England rose to the highest point both of internal prosperity and of external glory, but which lasted long after all occasion for it had ceased, and which was even in its inception as opposed to the spirit of the new polity as the tests and penalties of the High Church-men.

It was chiefly the work of Walpole. Walpole had procured the rejection of Sunderland's famous scheme for giving to the great Whig Houses an unmasked ascendency in the State. That measure, conceived in the bold and haughty spirit of its author, would have effectually secured the object on which the friends of the Revolution were then bent. It would have vested the supreme power once for all in the House of Lords, that House in which the ideas and principles of the Revolution had their rise; would have emancipated the Liberal chamber from all political control, either on the part of the Crown, or of the nation; and would have transformed it into an isolated and privileged oligarchy, estranged from the sympathies and interests of the community at large. Walpole had opposed this scheme as he had opposed all the other measures of Sunderland's Government. But he entirely agreed with Sunderland, that some change was necessary for the purpose of securing to the most advanced opinions then current a means of determining the type and ensuring the permanence of the new institutions; and on coming to power he sought to effect their common object in a less invidious way, by strengthening the authority of the leading patrician families under the forms of the existing Government.

This was the cardinal feature and essential aim of Walpole's constitutional policy, the object to which the methods of his parliamentary system were all directed. He was not of course the inventor of that system commonly associated with his name. The practice of welding together a party majority by appealing to the self-interest of its members was as old at any rate as the reign of Charles II. The practice of procuring a parliamentary majority in the first instance by appealing to the self-interest of the electors was as ancient as the very foundation of Parliament itself in the old Plantagenet days. Both these practices Walpole brought to extreme perfection. The expense of county elections was increased in the interest of the great capitalists and large proprietors. The guineas of the city merchant were everywhere brought down to counteract the intimidation of the country landowner. In those large and growing constituencies, where the suffrage was open and popular, electoral organizations based on the principles of the modern caucus were established for the purpose of influencing and directing the representation in favour of selected candidates.* But the most fruitful field of Walpole's labours was found in those close and decaying boroughs, then thickly studded over our southern and western counties, in which the right of voting had become confined by custom to some select and irresponsible body—a local proprietor in virtue of manorial rights, a town council of struggling tradesmen, a dozen or so of the leading citizens who had gradually stereotyped their own authority by a sort of natural selection ; and here, coming to the aid of the natural influence in such places of the trading and dissenting classes, the wealth of the great Whig peers, the patronage of the Government, the secret service money at its disposal were all unsparingly used for the purpose of securing, generally by direct barter, the power of designating their parliamentary nominees. The representative institutions of England were in fact

* These organizations were first employed to any large extent at the general election of 1722.

consolidated by carefully nursing and extending the most corrupt and decrepit parts of her parliamentary system.

By such devices as these, aided by the systematic abstention of large numbers of Jacobite freeholders, select Whig majorities were returned at every election for many years—majorities which did not, there is no doubt, accurately represent the mind and temper of the English people. And on these majorities the minister brought to bear without scruple all the familiar arts of party discipline, of mingled cajolery and menace, which have since been consecrated by the constitutional practice of five generations of whippers-in. He applied them, no doubt, in a coarser form than is agreeable to the manners of our more squeamish age, and with the increased pressure rendered necessary by the greater secrecy of parliamentary proceedings. The good things in the gift of the Government were strictly confined to the party supporters of Government.* Every Whig member was made to feel that his

* This practice continued down to our own time. Sir Robert Peel is generally credited by his biographers with being the minister who first purified our political parties. In an instructive letter to his brother, the Dean of York (April 5, 1843), Sir Robert explains how on first forming his great administration he laid down a new principle for the disposal of his official patronage. He divided that patronage into two equal parts. One part he determined for the future to "regard as a public trust," and apply to the "reward and encouragement of public service." One part only he continued to devote after the manner of Sir R. Walpole, to what he calls "the less praiseworthy but still necessary purpose of promoting the party interest of his own Government." He was thus obliged through sheer lack of means to refuse the request of his own brother, that offices might be provided out of the spoils of victory for that brother's three children, who had "in the borough where they resided" exerted considerable influence in "returning the Government members." It was not, the Dean assures us in his memoir, that Sir Robert had no affection for his own nephews. He invited them to his shooting quarters, and was fond of finding them amusement. But so strict was he in his adherence to the self-denying ordinance he had just laid down, that he "steadily refused," notwithstanding their party claims on him, to "enrich them out of the public purse." And in this interesting way, beginning as charity should begin, at home, the first step in the purification of one at least of our great political parties was taken.

interest lay in keeping true to his party standard, and in redeeming the pledges by which his election had been secured. No attempt was made to seduce a political opponent from his allegiance. This was foreign to the whole spirit of Walpole's system, the "exclusiveness" of which was its main feature and the main charge brought against it by his literary assailants. On the other hand, though the privileges and emoluments of the State were confined within the narrowest party limits, its public policy was conceived in the general interest of the entire nation, and so far from being exclusive was perhaps unduly directed towards respecting the grievances and lightening the burdens of classes hostile to the minister.

II.

In this way during many critical years, without any startling constitutional change or unpopular restriction of national privileges, the most competent opinion in England, then strongly in favour of Representative Government as the surest guarantee for political and religious freedom, was enabled to assert itself without dispute, at a time when the mass of Englishmen were lukewarm or hostile, and when under any scheme of diffused suffrage it would have been outvoted. That this system of parliamentary influence was continued and extended until it had become an unmitigated evil, a mere clog and hindrance to the natural development of the very institutions of which, originally, it was the safeguard ;—this was due to a danger inherent in it, which Walpole always foresaw, and against which during his lifetime he was always carefully on the watch. The cardinal principle of his system was that the great Revolution Houses should govern, not through an

invidious pre-eminence in their own House of Parliament,
but by means of confidential agents and delegates chosen
to represent them in the popular chamber. " A combination
of more or less intelligent noblemen, all of liberal ideas
and aims, living and acting together, a combination partly
aristocratic, partly intellectual, cemented by the common
possession and common use of political power, engaged
men of trained political capacity to develop their ideas
and help them to attain their aims." And at first, under
Walpole's precept and example, they chose these confidential agents with the same solicitude, the same close
attention to their personal interests which they displayed
in regulating their domestic affairs — in choosing the
steward who managed their households, the bailiff who
let their farms and received their rents, the lawyer who
drew their leases, their marriage settlements, and their
wills. Nor had they any difficulty in finding men of
character and intelligence to serve them in these political
employments on their own conditions. For the immense
prizes of public life, the large income assured to any one
willing to profess Whig principles and competent to serve
the Whig party in the House of Commons and in the
Government, the enormous opportunities given for finding
a livelihood for friends and dependents in the public service,
made politics at this time the most honoured, the most
lucrative, and one of the most certain of the great professions, and drew into political life the most promising
adventurers of the day. They gave it, not as such men
now do, the lees and dregs of intellectual powers of which
the prime and freshness have been exhausted in more
profitable occupations, but the same industry and method,
the same energy, the same entire devotion which win
success in other walks of business.

And thus there was gradually formed, as a result of

Walpole's system and of the machinery for working it, a powerful class of professional debaters and politicians, highly trained and educated for the duties required from them, thoroughly informed on all questions of government, connected with the upper classes by early ties of patronage and keenly alive to the interests of their patrician employers, but socially distinct, united with each other in the bonds of a strong professional *esprit de corps*, and regulating their conduct by the artificial standard of a professional code of morals. Of this class perhaps the most typical example is Henry Fox, a trained administrator, a practised debater, a master of every detail of parliamentary government, insatiable of power but valuing power as a professional man values practice solely as a means of accumulating riches, perfectly unscrupulous in raking together public plunder for himself and his family connections by every artifice of peculation recognized as legitimate in the trades-union he belonged to, absolutely indifferent to the vast and growing mass of public odium which his character and proceedings were bringing upon him, but acutely sensitive to the good opinion of his leading professional rivals, and holding high the principle of honour as honour is understood in a fraternity which lives upon its neighbours.

This system, under Walpole's careless and feebler successors, produced its natural effect. In the course of time, as the Parliamentary Settlement and the institutions bound up with it gathered to themselves the strength of an assured and legitimate polity, and the great Whig magnates, satisfied that their work was done, gradually relapsed into dignified retirement and more congenial occupations; as wealthy country gentlemen not of the orthodox persuasion became reconciled to the new system, and began themselves to cultivate borough interest as a

means of rising in the social scale; as needy and embarrassed peers began to recognize the fact that a family
borough was a marketable commodity, like a gallery of
family portraits or an avenue of ancestral oaks; as the
old party connections became weakened by the practice
of letting out seats in Parliament to the highest bidder,
and by the admission of new men careless about preserving
the old party exclusiveness;—the ties which originally bound
this class of professional politicians to the great patrician
houses were suffered to fall loose; the relation of principal
and agent between them, on which Walpole had always
insisted, ceased to operate; and they gradually built up
and consolidated an immense political authority, independent both of the patrons they had served and of the
people they were governing. They took possession, so to
speak, of the political estate of the Revolution families
of which they had been hitherto the overseers and administrators, much as the knavish lawyer in Scott's novel,
enriched by thirty years of legal pilfering, absorbed the
patrimony of his easy-going employer. They always
called themselves Whigs. When, as the reward of a life
of successful industry and lucrative devotion to the public
service, they were made peers themselves, they essayed
to enter the hereditary chamber as members of the
privileged circle of the Revolution oligarchy, skilfully
using as occasion served its venerable signs and passwords,
affecting a respect for toleration, for civil liberty, for the
popular origin of Governments;—just as Gilbert Glossin
in the story saw to the strict preserving of all his coverts
after his elevation, as one of the necessary obligations of
a Galloway laird. But they had no political opinions of
their own, except a stolid conservatism as widely removed
from the generous loyalty of the old historic Cavaliers as
it was from the best traditions of the party they disgraced;

a reverence for the existing constitution by administering which they had risen to fortune ; a strong professional desire to hand down its beauties and advantages unimpaired for the benefit of their still struggling brethren ;—the feeling, in short, which induces a retired attorney to resent, as a sort of personal reflection on himself, all attempts at reforming in the interest of the outside lay public the time-honoured customs and recognized devices for swelling out a bill of costs. The rise of these men, the position they originally held, the position they ultimately attained, closely resembled that of the zemindars of Bengal when the great agrarian measure of Lord Cornwallis, recognizing and confirming a state of things which their own tact and energy had brought about, transformed a body of public tax-collectors, middlemen between the Government that owned and the peasant who tilled the fields, into a powerful independent caste of landlords, applying to their own use as their lawful property the entire agricultural produce of the soil, beyond a modest quitrent to the State and a bare subsistence for the cultivator.

In this way the Parliamentary system, as developed by Walpole's successors, lapsed into one of pure Toryism—government by a privileged class exercising power for its own benefit. It was the same system in fact which Danby had meditated in 1675 for securing permanent authority to the Cavalier party, which Bolingbroke had attempted to put in force in the interest of the High Churchmen, and which Swift had in his mind when he urged upon his friends the completion, before it was too late, of their " machine of four years' modelling." The consummation so earnestly desired by these three great masters of Tory politics, Walpole unwittingly effected by establishing methods of government which ultimately vested power, not as he intended with the Revolution Houses, the

Pelhams, the Cavendishes, the Wentworths, in whom the high traditions of Whig policy still lingered, but in the Hollands, the Rigbys, the Jenkinsons, men who, beginning life as their hired retainers, ended by usurping the prerogative of the masters they served, and using it solely as a means of exalting their own fortunes. The growth was, of course, a very gradual process. When, about the time of the rebellion of 1745, George II., chafing against his thraldom, broke loose for a moment from the chains that bound him, he found the hand of the independent magnates of the old Whig party still too heavy, and after an interval of struggling once more submitted to their rule.

But half a generation later a startling change had taken place. In 1760 George II.'s grandson came to the throne fresh from the lessons of Leicester House, burning with patriotic ardour to exterminate party and overthrow with his doughty arm the giant of parliamentary privilege. But the young Quixote was held back by the canny Scotchmen who formed his court. They showed him that he was setting his lance in rest to tilt against a windmill. The plan of government which he had been taught to fear and hate was one which imposed on the Sovereign the will of an independent party, embodying distinct and recognized principles of national policy, and which made a Parliament elected to support them the arbiter of the national destiny. The Parliament which then existed was made up of a number of self-seeking connections having no object in public life but their own advancement, each owing allegiance to some ambitious chief, for whom they were ready to fight in their mutual interest without regard to the cause he represented. A Parliament so happily constructed, claiming absolute power as the mainspring of a popular constitution, exercising its functions in secret as a necessary protection to popular privileges, completely irresponsible, to a great extent self-elected, and largely composed of men who made political life a "business," could hardly, as these advisers assured their young master, have been felt as an encumbrance by the most arbitrary Stuart or Tudor king; while for a prince in his position, a prince of foreign extraction who owed his throne to the vote of Parliament, to destroy such a representative body, because he was anxious, forsooth, to emancipate himself from popular control, was to throw aside in the mere wantonness of autocratic purism at once the most invaluable shield for covering, and the most effective instrument for extending the prerogative he sought to revive.

George III., with all his faults of character and breeding, was himself a shrewd and practical man of business. A very little reflection showed him the force of these considerations laid before him by Lord Mansfield and Lord Bute. At the instance of these advisers from North Britain, men to whom such words as honour and public faith had lost all meaning, he determined to turn his back on whatever was wisest and most righteous in the lessons of his political training. The parliamentary methods of Walpole were "improved" to an extent at which Walpole would have stood aghast, and used for objects the very opposite of those for which Walpole had designed them. The policy of proscription and exclusion against which Bolingbroke had warned Prince Frederick—the policy which placed beyond the pale of court favour all but the members of the one prevailing party—was continued. But it was now directed against the friends of the Revolution Settlement and of the ideas and principles it represented. Before long a huge spider's-web of illicit influence overspread the whole political system of the English people, all its minute filaments centering in the royal closet, being spun out of the royal entrails, and for the gratification of the royal appetite. The Irish pension list was tripled. The recipients of the royal bounty in England increased in nearly the same proportion. Every grant so given, every salaried office in the kingdom, every sinecure, every reversion was made strictly contingent on serving the political pleasure of the occupant of the throne. The private estates of the Crown were administered for the sole purpose of multiplying places and extending political influence, till their revenues were swallowed up, and they became a charge upon, not an assistance to, the national exchequer. The royal household, the public services, the courts of judicature were all managed on the same evil system ; ill-paid deputies to do the work, principals in the receipt of large emoluments, and earning those emoluments by servile dependence not on the minister but on the Sovereign. Burke, in a single short sentence, pictured the vast mass of mingled prodigality and corruption which constituted the Government of George III., and which rendered futile all attempts at reforming it. " Sir," he said, " the very turnspit in his Majesty's kitchen is now a member of the House of Commons." * Before a generation had elapsed, in the assembly which governed England, a clear majority of her so-called rulers were nominated by less than fifteen thousand electors, carefully distributed in little malleable parcels of votes—often the grooms and serving-men of some court favourite—exercising their functions under duress in the rottenest boroughs in the kingdom ; and there was hardly one of the ruling majority so nominated who did not receive in the form dictated by the King, and too often direct from the royal hand, the wages of his prostitution. In the House of Lords, that House of Lords which a hundred years before had been the sanctuary

* Speech on Economical Reform.

of public freedom, at the death of King George III. it was proudly calculated in his household that more than half the existing peerage of Great Britain owed their mushroom coronets to his creation, and that nearly half enjoyed some pension, some sinecure, some lucrative possession or expectancy determinable at his good pleasure. That system in short which had been originally devised as a protection for free institutions, in the interest of all classes and under the direction of the wisest statesmen of the time, had been turned by an unscrupulous misuse of its own methods into a means of advancing the personal whims of one self-willed and ignorant recluse, the representative of a line of parliamentary Sovereigns inserted in the Act of Settlement as contingent remainder-men, without an idea that they would ever exercise any of the functions of independent royalty.

All this, however, was long after Bolingbroke's death. In his time the worst evils resulting from Walpole's system had not begun to show themselves, whilst its many advantages for the object it was designed to further were becoming day by day more manifest. There is a well-known passage in Gibbon which fixes the age of Trajan and the Antonines as that period in the world's history when the condition of the human race was generally the most happy and prosperous. For then the vast extent of the Roman empire was governed by absolute power, but under the guidance of wisdom and virtue; the dangers inherent in an imperial polity were in great measure suspended; the forms of civil administration being preserved by men who, delighting in the image of liberty, were pleased at fancying themselves the accountable ministers of the law.

I think that the modern historian, if called upon in like manner to choose that period in the history of the English people when their condition most nearly resembled that of Rome in the golden age which Gibbon celebrates—when the " ideal restraints " of the senate, not yet abused to the destruction of all liberty, served but to display the enlightened policy of its ruler—he would point to the reign of George II. and the long administration of Walpole. Government under Walpole was reduced almost to its ideal function of protecting national and individual independence. The practical well-being of the people at large was made the chief aim of statesmanship; and the fittest methods for ascertaining and executing their wishes were seen and applied. Thus while the identity of parliamentary with party government was fully established, it was shown how the aims of party might be made to conform to the general interests of the entire nation. Parliamentary management in the hands of a responsible minister was developed into an art; the party majority was moulded and fashioned into an effective instrument for governing purposes; and the representative chamber was made the acknowledged centre of our parliamentary system. It was the systematic moderation of Walpole, administering in the interest of all classes an extremely strict and exclusive party organization, which reconciled the nation as a whole to the rule of an elected dynasty, and to the free republican constitution of which it is the symbol. Through Walpole's exertions the old ferocity of our political factions was moderated, and the old antagonism of sects and parties softened down. Thus the burning question of religious toleration was settled on what, for an age of religious intolerance, was the only feasible plan. The privileges of the Anglican Church were preserved ; for their roots lay deep in the sentiments of the English people. But under the wise treatment of a minister, himself perfectly free from all denominational bias, the epileptic fits of sacerdotal zealotry grew rarer year by year, and each recurring paroxysm was milder than the last. Convocation was never revived ; and the country was spared the degrading sight and the evil example of its proceedings. Latitudinarian bishops, scholars and men of the world rather than ecclesiastics, gradually imparted a new and more tolerant tone to the teaching of the parochial clergy. In their ministrations all inflammatory matter, all questions of doctrine and controversy at issue amongst the various Churches, were systematically avoided ; and the weekly exhortations addressed from the State pulpits to the divided nation made to consist of plain practical suggestions on the proper conduct of life, or instruction in those fundamental principles of morals which all Christian sects alike inculcate. At the same time the disabilities of the Nonconformists were maintained in the eye of the law ; for the great disabling statutes which condemned them to isolation and inferiority were cherished by all church-going Englishmen as essential to their personal comfort. But the whole practical effect of these time-honoured symbols of ascendency, so far at least as affected offices held directly under the State, was quietly taken away by a device thoroughly characteristic of Walpole's methods of government. From the accession of George II. down to its final abrogation a hundred years later, though the Test Act indeed remained, Bills of Indemnity were annually passed as regularly as the Appropriation Bill, exempting all who infringed it from the penalties attaching to the offence ; and the demand of the Dissenters for its repeal became, therefore, no longer a just claim to the removal of a substantial grievance, but an ambitious desire for an express recognition by Parliament of that full civil equality with Churchmen which Parliament by the dispensing power in its hands was already according them.*

* Between 1727 and 1828, these acts of indemnity were only omitted on

The same principle of wise and liberal innovation, concealed as far as possible from the public eye—the principle of the Toleration Act, and indeed of all the constitutional changes which accompanied the change of dynasty—the minister carried into every department of the State. In doing so he was bound by no superstitious respect for the ancient traditions of his party. The policy of the older Whigs was one of protection to native industry. It was by them that the first germs of a free trade system, tentatively introduced by Bolingbroke in his commercial arrangements with France, had been ruthlessly crushed in the interest of the great commercial monopolists who formed a main strength of their party. Walpole abandoned this policy, so far at least as party spirit and popular prejudice would allow him. It was by this rough sportsman and farmer, who never opened a book after his fall, and the favourite part of whose correspondence when in office was his gamekeeper's weekly letter, that the first serious attempt was made—anticipating the beneficent reforms of Huskisson and Peel—to allow the industrial forces of the nation to expand after their natural bent. The monopoly of the mother country in the products of her colonies was relaxed where it proved oppressive. Export was made practically free. Import duties on raw materials were year by year diminished ;

seven occasions ; and on all these occasions, the Whig party being in power, the omission was no doubt accidental.

Down to the year 1866, the same Walpolean practice prevailed with reference to another supposed bulwark of orthodoxy. The standing law required from every minister of State a formal declaration that he would not use the power of office to the injury of the Church Establishment. But the requirement was abrogated in practice by the device of an annual indemnity. Mr. Gladstone, when Chancellor of the Exchequer, always declined to make the declaration legally enjoined upon him, in the consciousness that the default of which he was annually guilty would be thus legally condoned. At length, on the motion of a Nonconformist member, and not without some clerical protestations, the solemn farce was discontinued by the repeal of the standing law.

and the principle of warehousing in bond was introduced as part of a financial measure which, under the plea of removing two commodities from the customs to the excise for the greater convenience of collecting revenue, would have revolutionized the entire fiscal system of the English people, and made their ports the chief markets for the commerce of all nations.*

The policy of the older Whigs, again, was one of lavish expenditure, incurred in the first instance, no doubt, with a view of spreading as widely as possible a material interest in the stability of the new Government. This system Walpole altogether reversed; but he did so in such a quiet unostentatious manner that to the end of his life lavish expenditure was charged against him by his literary opponents. As a matter of fact, this corrupter of Parliaments was the first finance minister who has inculcated, as one of his primary duties, the practice of systematic economy in the interest of the whole tax-paying public. By pruning down the different establishments, by fiscal rearrangements which made the exchequer a sharer in the growing prosperity of the nation, by setting aside certain fixed and increasingly productive taxes to meet the interest on its engagements, and form a sinking fund for their redemption, the credit of the State was raised to a height seldom reached even in our time. Its obligations, many of which had been incurred at no less than eight per cent. interest, were gradually consolidated into a general three per cent. stock, which, notwithstanding this

---

* Thus realizing the prophetic vision of Pope, a vision itself inspired, the reader will recollect, by Bolingbroke's commercial policy which Walpole was now following out.

> "The time shall come when, free as seas or wind,
> Unbounded Thames shall flow for all mankind,
> All nations enter with each swelling tide,
> And seas but join the regions they divide."

small return, was more than once quoted at a premium.
The surplus revenue set free by these operations was
devoted partly to lessening the body of the public debt,
but mainly, with a truer financial and political insight, to
lightening such annual burdens as seemed to press unfairly
on special industries and special classes, and in particular
to successive reductions of the land-tax, the tax which
weighed on the great class hostile to the State, which
Walpole at one period of his prudent administration
succeeded in bringing back to its old pre-revolution level.
Thus one of the main objections of the country gentlemen
to the new dynasty, that it took more money out of their
pockets than the old, was removed. Several years' purchase was added to the selling value of their land. Rents
and the profits of agriculture rose together; and with
the spread of comfort and material well-being amongst
the farming and land-owning populations, dissatisfaction
with the order of things under which they lived steadily
died away.

And this salutary change in the internal stability of
the reformed Government brought about, as it was in
its turn promoted by, a change equally salutary and
characteristic in its foreign relations. The policy of the
older Whigs was one of great continental alliances against
France, designed to form an artificial barrier and support
for the Parliamentary Settlement against the efforts of
France to overthrow it. It was a policy which involved
England in heavy expenditure, and constant dangers and
sacrifices; a policy unavoidable perhaps in the time of
King William in face of the unscrupulous ambition of
France and the slight hold which the Revolution Settle-
ment then had on the affections of the people. But since
the time of King William a generation had passed away.
The new constitution was gradually working its way into

acceptance with all classes of Englishmen. To the continuance of that material well-being and individual freedom which had so largely contributed to this salutary result, peace was an almost necessary condition ; and it was owing to Walpole's keen insight into the change which his domestic administration and commercial policy were effecting in the sentiments of the nation, to the singular freedom of this dissolute cynical country squire from party and class prejudices, above all to his courageous and enlightened patriotism in withstanding, alone amongst his colleagues, the warlike impulses of both court and people, that England enjoyed, amidst European convulsions, in which so many of the landmarks set up at Utrecht were shifted, twenty years of peace and prosperous industry, and this without sacrificing one of the solid benefits secured to her by Bolingbroke's treaty.

Walpole recognized, in fact, as completely as Bolingbroke, and no doubt under the same secret inspiration, that the peculiar geographical position of England imposed on her special duties and invested her with special privileges. He aimed, like Bolingbroke, at disengaging her Government from all those foreign entanglements which impeded her freedom of action. He held, as all great economists have held, that the plan of involving her beforehand in every European complication on the plea of preserving a shadowy balance of power was incompatible with any large industrial progress, exposing her to constant apprehension of immediate dangers (with the result of limiting her gains and increasing her expenses) for the purpose of averting others, greater perhaps, but more remote and more uncertain ; and that in particular the closer intercourse with France which had resulted from Bolingbroke's policy, though purchased in the first instance by withdrawing England from engagements which tended to limit the power of France, was now in its turn, through extended commerce and material advancement, so largely augmenting the general resources of her people as to be worth on the whole the high price given for it.

Thus, though the power of this great minister rested exclusively on party attachments, the policy of the State combined under his guidance whatever was most characteristic and most advanced in the policy of both the contending factions ; and that Walpole was enabled so easily to manipulate a close and narrow party organization in the interest of the nation generally, and with scant respect to its own recognized traditions, was due in no small degree to those peculiarities of his party management which are now brought against his memory as matter of shallow and ignorant reproach. The parliamentary system as administered by its original founder differed in two important respects from that of his modern parliamentary successors. As the strength of a chain is measured by the weakness of its frailer links, so the power of a modern minister is too often bound and limited by the average opinions that pervade the lowest ranks of his party following. He translates into legislative enactment their crude political fads and theories as a means of winning from them that daily and nightly support in Parliament on which his tenure as a minister of State depends. If, rising above the narrow groove of party tradition and party conventionality, he desires to transform the policy furnished to him by his supporters into conformity with some change in the requirements of his party which his keener intelligence first detects, or, it may be, with the larger exigencies of the public service ; if, for example, being a Protectionist, placed at the head of a protected interest, he wishes to introduce absolute freedom of trade, or, being an anti-Reformer, pledged to resist all " degradation " of the franchise, he seeks to establish through the hands of the men associated with him in these pledges a measure of bare unmitigated household suffrage ;—he can only do so by practising manœuvres akin to those by which a seaman makes a given port in the teeth of an adverse wind, by steering for a time an oblique course and bending himself to things in some degree contrary to his main design, with a view in his case of concealing from the party followers, whose help in navigating the vessel of State is indispensable to him, the particular harbour to which their combined efforts are guiding her.

Walpole was exempt from this necessity. The votes of members, the propelling power of the Government vessel, he obtained by means simpler, more direct, if you like more unprincipled ; but then, in the consciousness of an assured support, on which he could rely without regard to the strict party orthodoxy of his measures, he was free from these numbing and paralysing limitations, free to govern according to his lights for the benefit of all classes, borrowing without fear the best ideas of his opponents, throwing aside without scruple the obsolete traditions of his friends.

In the next place, though the power of the minister for carrying even an obnoxious measure was complete, without any of those fancy devices we have seen adopted in our time for veiling its naked monstrosity from his followers, he never attempted to enforce, if the nation really disliked it, even a wise and useful reform, on which his party following was united. The opinion of Parliament was no exact measure, as he knew, of the national judgments it was supposed to express. But speech and writing were perfectly free ; political agitation was not discouraged ; the popular element in Government, checked and controlled in its natural channels, found vents for itself in new and irregular ways; and a public sentiment was generated outside the walls of Parliament to which the minister, however arbitrary in the closet and in the legislature, paid the most scrupulous attention, fully recognizing the truth that Government must have public sentiment at its back, and that a defective or incomplete enactment which respects the prejudices of the people is often to be preferred by the statesman to one more ideally perfect which fails to recommend itself to their prepossessions.   Thus his famous measure of Excise, the crowning effort and necessary completion of his financial policy, a measure every part of which has since his time been carried into effect with general applause, and which forms in its main feature undoubtedly the most valuable improvement ever introduced into our fiscal system, he at once and finally withdrew as soon as he found that it had roused throughout the country a real as distinct from a mere party opposition, though he knew that this opposition, however wide-reaching, was the result of pure ignorance of its scope and objects, though he had ample parliamentary means of carrying it, and though his strongest supporters urged him to persevere.   It was the same in the case of the Spanish war.   As soon as he found that the nation, scenting perhaps with a keener instinct the hidden purpose of Bourbon politics, was bent on wresting from Spain at all hazards a renunciation of the Right of Search, which Spain indubitably possessed, and of that commercial monopoly guaranteed to her by long-standing treaties of which the Right of Search was the symbol, from that moment Walpole made himself the instrument of a filibustering policy; though he looked on war with all an economist's disgust as a barbarous tribunal, to be shunned even in the most righteous cause unless the object sought was certain to outweigh in value the cost of seeking it; though he believed the war in this case to be one of aggression simply, unjust in its origin as well as doubtful in its issues, and not at all unlikely by the ambitious desires it would foster to wreck that commercial prosperity for advancing which it was undertaken.* But Walpole in this, as in all cases, regarded himself as the minister of a self-governing nation, bound to execute the national judgment when unmistakably expressed. His system differed in little in its effects from the ideal Tory polity which Bolingbroke was then developing for the instruction of the Patriots in opposition. It was liberal and enlightened monarchy tempered, and, in extreme cases, regulated by floating democratic opinion.

III.

It was this policy of peace, of low establishments, of lessened public burdens, of freely extended commerce, of extrication from foreign entanglements, of carelessness of the "honour" of England as compared with her material interests; this policy of Church privileges maintained and religious equality ostensibly at least refused, of close alliance with France and alienation from Austria, of party exclusiveness carried to his own extreme limit of "filling every employment in the kingdom down even to the

---

* The conduct of Walpole with regard to the Spanish war has been almost exactly paralleled in our time by that of Lord Aberdeen, Sir James Graham, and Mr. Gladstone in the case of the war with Russia, into which they were driven (like Walpole) by the compulsion of the newspapers, and the public, in spite of their conviction of its injustice and impolicy, and which afterwards (to repeat the words of Burke) "they condemned as freely as they would have done in speaking of any other proceeding in history with which they were totally unconcerned." (See the curious conversations between Lord Aberdeen and Mr. Cobden, Sir J. Graham and Mr. Bright, recorded in Morley's "Life of Cobden," ii., 174.) So does history repeat itself, and so shortlived are its sharpest lessons.

meanest" with party supporters; this Elizabethan polity
of personal power tempered by public opinion, modified
indeed to suit the exigencies of a time when the anointed
Sovereign was politically impotent, and vested by natural
selection in the survivor of a hundred parliamentary
conflicts; that Bolingbroke had now to assail, not in the
open field of legitimate parliamentary warfare—in anonymous newspaper libels, shooting like an Irish peasant with
blackened face from behind a wall; attacking principles
of government every one of which is associated with his
own career and his own reputation, in the service of a
political faction which consisted in one part of high
prerogative Tories hardly yet denuded of their Jacobitism,
and in the other of Revolution Whigs proud of their
ancient traditions and their party orthodoxy.   It was
certainly an occasion calling for the exercise of all those
intellectual powers of which he was confessedly a master.
And that Bolingbroke should have succeeded, even with
the help of the eminent talents associated with him, in
rousing the nation, or any large part of it, against a
minister who was successfully carrying into effect so many
of his own most characteristic principles of public policy,
is undoubtedly a proof of the extent and versatility of his
parts.

But the truth is, that the fall of an English minister
under a parliamentary system of government is rarely
due to the efforts of his party opponents to discredit his
policy, however powerfully organized and skilfully directed
these efforts may be.   It comes from personal faults of
his own—faults of character and manner for the most
part, always far more effective under a popular constitution
in arousing public odium than any administrative incom-
petence, and certain to excite public odium in the face
of any administrative triumphs.   Walpole owed his fall

to his coarse cynicism, his licentiousness, his want of public decorum, his insatiable greediness of authority. These faults affected his relations with the great Whig proprietors who held the reins of power, as well as with the general public. He had, moreover, from the first offended, perhaps designedly offended, an immense mass of public sentiment. He had striven to construct a Government in which plain men could live and labour and consume the fruits of their industry, which held strictly to the facts of this life and the wants of the passing generation. In that long period of peace and ordered liberty, of equal laws wisely conceived and justly administered, there was little room for the exercise of those high qualities of which History loves to speak, and for which the dark setting is furnished by the crimes and the follies and the misfortunes of men, for chivalry, or saintly aspirations, or patriotism of the heroic type. To all these Bolingbroke appealed. He made himself the exponent of the accumulated dissatisfaction of the literary and " cultured " classes with a time of material prosperity, and with the political content and indifference that it fostered. As he himself afterwards expressed it, he laboured to " enlarge the minds of men which the minister had narrowed to personal regards alone; to expand their views which he had confined to the present moment, as if nations were mortal like the men who compose them, and Britain was to perish with her degenerate children." *

And besides " enlarging their minds " from the sordid contemplation of their own freedom and prosperity, he sought to open the eyes of the people to the momentous constitutional change then in silent progress, on which so much of that freedom and prosperity depended, and which forms undoubtedly the most enduring of all Walpole's achievements—the establishment of representative institu-

* iii. 38 ("Letter on the Spirit of Patriotism ").

tions framed on the modern type, in which Parliament itself administers and governs, instead of simply checking the administration and government of others. He knew that this system, under which each party in turn, as the embodiment of prevailing opinion, "engrosses all power and profit in the State, exclusive of all other subjects under this establishment," was, as he expressed it, "a violation of the ancient and strict forms of the constitution." He knew that it was opposed to the interests of the complex parliamentary faction which he led, and in which from its peculiar composition no consistent public opinion on questions of policy could ever become embodied. He attacked it, therefore, in the double character of a party politician and a Conservative reformer. In place of it he proposed to substitute what he calls a "union and coalition of parties meeting on a national bottom," and taking their cue from the personal predilections of the Revolution Sovereign. Amidst all his current insincerity, this feeling of respect for the monarchical element in the constitution freed from all taint of the divine right heresy, for the doctrine of checks and counterpoises, for the political inferiority and due subordination of the three estates to the Crown, for the old Elizabethan polity, in a word, as opposed to modern parliamentary institutions, was undoubtedly sincere ; and in giving utterance to it he undoubtedly touched a chord in the nation which responded to his pressure. "Liberty," according to Bolingbroke, depended in the reformed as well as in the unreformed constitution on a "just balance of its different parts," and this balance again on their "mutual independency of each other." * He was fond of inculcating this doctrine on his most trusted political friends. " Remember," he writes to one of them after he had himself withdrawn from the

---

* Works ii. 388 ("Remarks on the Study of History").

active work of opposition,—"Remember that the opposition, in which you have engaged in your first entrance into business, is not an opposition only to a bad administration of public affairs, but to an administration that supports itself by means, establishes principles, introduces customs repugnant to the constitution of our government and destructive of all liberty." *   It is this feeling which gives to Bolingbroke's writings their enduring historical interest. For it elevates an ignoble struggle for place into a chivalrous effort to preserve by purifying the spirit of the old monarchy, and to stem the advance of the Revolution which, by concentrating power in the representative chamber, was making England in spite of herself a republic.

Take, for instance, his "Idea of a Patriot King." Like all Bolingbroke's tracts, it was framed originally to cover and promote a party manœuvre ; but, like all Bolingbroke's tracts, it had a higher object beyond and superior to the political requirement of the moment, an object which has given to it, in the eyes of the student, a permanent historical value. At the time when it was written, the heterogeneous opposition which he had done so much to form was again disintegrating into its component elements. The Whig statesmen who had rebelled against Walpole's paramount authority had no desire to be trammelled in office with the party connections into which Bolingbroke had led them, or with the political principles and pledges he was putting into their mouths. Their opposition was mainly, if not entirely, a personal opposition to Walpole himself, not at all an opposition to the scheme of party government which he was consolidating, and which they knew to be, under the rule of Parliament, the only expedient for carrying on an efficient administration of the national affairs. As

* Bolingbroke to Lord Lyttelton ("Letter on the Spirit of Patriotism," iii. 21).

the prospect of attaining office, therefore, grew nearer by the waning of Walpole's influence, they began to separate themselves from their Tory allies, to draw closer to the ministerial Whigs, and to hint to Bolingbroke "not obscurely" that his name and presence among them did them harm. Bolingbroke, on his side, not unnaturally, resented this treatment. In the summer of 1735, convinced that his chance of success for the present was gone, and influenced, no doubt, in the main by an acute sense of political failure, he suddenly broke up his establishment and quitted England for France, not, as he afterwards said, till some schemes which were then on the loom, though they never came into effect, made him one too many for these so-called friends.* The fine essay on the "Spirit of Patriotism" which he composed in the first months of this second exile—and which contains, it may be remarked, perhaps the most striking passage he ever wrote—an admirable delineation of the two great orators of antiquity by a master of modern oratory—is instinct from the first page to the last with this sense of failure ; with indignation at the continued success of Parliament in engrossing, contrary to all ancient precedent, the entire executive administration, and at the baseness of those opposition Whigs, the sole object of whose "pretended Patriotism" was to carry on the same methods of government in other hands than Walpole's.

But in 1737, about a year after this "Letter on the Spirit of Patriotism" was composed, an opportunity presented itself of outwitting these time-serving politicians who were turning "a virtuous defence of the constitution into an intrigue of low ambition." At this time Queen Caroline, the great support and mainstay of Whig power at court, was no more. The King's health was supposed to be

---

* Bolingbroke to Lord Marchmont, July 24, 1746.

breaking. The prince, his successor, was becoming daily more estranged from the party which upheld his father's throne, and more and more connected in society with the converted Jacobites whom Sir William Wyndham led. In these circumstances Bolingbroke saw a chance of supplying that of which, when in England, he had always lamented the want, and which was indeed a necessity of his political system—"a center of union, a superior authority under whose influence men of different views and different characters might be drawn together." Prince Frederick was to be the Messiah, as Bolingbroke characteristically expresses it, who was to rescue the Tory party from being any longer a distinct race in politics, hewers of wood and drawers of water for Philistine Whigs. He was, it is true, a young wastrel at war with all his kinsfolk, his judgment as weak as his passions were strong, unfitted both by nature and education for public duties, even of the simplest kind. But, then, "very uncouth characters" had, as Bolingbroke reminds Sir William Wyndham, been often in past times turned to very high purposes, and he was "not without hope" that a good use might be made of this one. "Is it not possible," he asks "to prompt by concert, and since his confidence is now well placed to prevail on him to listen to no other prompting?"*

It was to assist in this work, to draw the entire Tory party from its retirement round Prince Frederick as a "center of union," to detach him and them from the Whig followers of the treacherous Pulteney, to pay his own personal court as their leader to the young Messiah, and to frame for the party so formed new watchwords and an effective political cry,—that the "Patriot King" was written. It depicts a commonwealth in which the established orders and constituent parts of the State, with the different powers

* Bolingbroke to Sir William Wyndham, February 3, 1738.

and privileges anciently attributed to them, are being insidiously and essentially changed to the destruction of the old constitution. The change is so far advanced that the utmost private men can do is to keep the spirit of the old constitution alive in a few breasts, to protest against what they cannot hinder, and to claim on every occasion what they cannot by their own strength recover. In these circumstances they turn their eyes to the succession of a Patriot King. The possibility of such an event is the main advantage which monarchy has over other forms of free government. These are made up of different parts, and are apt to become disjointed by the shocks to which time exposes them; for absolute stability is not to be expected in anything human, and the best constituted governments carry in them the seeds of their own destruction. When so disjointed they must be constituted anew. All that can be done to prolong their duration is to draw them back on the first favourable occasion to the true principles on which they were founded; and to do this, to preserve the old system by new laws and new schemes of government whilst the indifference of the people continues and grows, is in such cases impossible.

But with a free monarchy this is not so. The monarch, like the keystone of a vault, keeps the whole building together. The accession of a new monarch of itself renews the spirit of the monarchy, draws back the Government to its first principles, restores the orders and forms of the constitution to their primitive integrity, and should be improved, like a snatch of fair weather at sea, to repair the damages sustained in the last storm and to prepare to resist the next.

And what an occasion is offered for reinfusing into the minds of men the true spirit of their constitution when the new monarch, whose accession is ardently longed for, is a Patriot King, "a sort of standing miracle, so rarely seen and so little understood, that the sure effects of his appearance will be admiration and love in every honest heart, confusion and terror to every guilty conscience, devout submission and resignation in all classes of his people!" The Patriot King is not a divinely appointed Sovereign in whom arbitrary will stands in the place of all rule of government, and whose attributes are the necessary accompaniments of his sceptre, as of old the gift of prophecy was conveyed by the mantle of Elijah. Nor is he, on the other hand, a mere puppet after the Venetian type, with power so "limited" that the essential form of government by a single person is altogether lost, a monarch stripped naked, or left at best with a few tattered rags to clothe his majesty. No ; he is a constitutional monarch in the true sense of the word, a popular Sovereign on whom Providence has impressed the character of a born ruler of men, obliged, no doubt, to exercise his power according to fixed rules established by the wisdom of the State and by the consent of the people, but with ample power notwithstanding ; holding in his hands the whole executive authority ; having in the Legislature a recognized right, both of initiative and of veto ; finding the "limitations" to which he is subject (designed to preserve liberty under a bad prince) no clog on his administration, but rather, if his patriotism be founded on great principles, a means of enabling him to govern with greater ease, security, dignity, and honour.

And in the very first steps of his reign the Patriot King will merit his noble title. He will purge and regenerate his court. He will cast off the men in power, the adventurers busy and bold, without true ability, or ambition, or even the semblance of virtue, who crowd the public offices under a system of party government, with their attendant swarm of spies, parasites, and sycophants. He will call into his service in place of them honest men, men who have given proofs beforehand of their patriotism as well as capacity, who are wise rather than cunning, who think of fame rather than applause. He will govern not in the interest or by the instrumentality of any particular set or order, however powerful in the State, but as the common father of a patriarchal family, in which the head and members alike are all animated by one common spirit, in which, if any are perverse enough to have another, they will be borne down by the superiority of those who are in agreement. He will rest his cause on the innocency of his administration, on the strength of the Crown, on the concurrence of the people in the Government they have established; espousing no party and proscribing none; pursuing his own true principles of government independently of all, and in his own chosen way.

Such was Bolingbroke's " Idea of a Patriot King," the most popular and in some ways the most finished of his writings, a party pamphlet devised for a temporary object an appeal from the statesmanship of the nation to poets and non-jurors and striplings fresh from college, an adroit piece of flattery laid at the feet of the Parliamentary heir, but with a graver meaning and purpose which have secured it a more lasting fame. For this little tract, carefully excluded from general circulation by its author till the eve of his own death, has influenced the speculations of four generations of Englishmen, formed the political creed of George III., created the faction of the King's friends, encouraged the conspirators who broke the power of the Whig nobility, inspired that mixture of the autocratic with the popular which distinguished the rival policy of Chatham and William Pitt, and in our own time fired the imagination of a great minister who aimed at reviving under the phrase *imperium et libertas* its distinctive qualities.

Take, again, the letters which Bolingbroke contributed to the *Craftsman* between September 1730 and June 1731, and which he calls " Remarks on the History of England ;" and the " Dissertation on Parties," written between October 1733 and December 1734, in preparation for the general election and the new Parliament of that year. In both these works Bolingbroke addressed himself to the task of exposing the vices of the parliamentary system of government as invented and practised by Walpole, with the view of showing that this system was a violation not only of the old monarchical constitution, but of those Revolution principles of which, writing now in the interest chiefly of the discontented Whigs, he expresses himself the warm admirer. The " Remarks on History " had the same sort of literary success which attended similar attempts at conveying satire in the form of analogue when directed by skilful assailants against the Third French Empire ; and they undoubtedly exhibit in the highest perfection the admirable merits of Bolingbroke's style. In these letters he begins by speaking of the ferment which the *Craftsman* had roused in the " dull uniformity of eternal assent," with which Walpole's proceedings had been hitherto received ; and he identifies this ferment with the " spirit of liberty " which his Puritan forefathers so carefully cherished, which in their time watched over public freedom with the hundred eyes of Argus, guarded the frontier of prerogative with perpetual jealousy, and resolutely withstood the earliest encroachments of power. This spirit of free, unbiassed, individual criticism, springing from information and from conviction, he contrasts with the spirit of party which estimates a given measure less by its intrinsic merits than by the source from whence it comes, which postpones the

public interest to the advantage and security of particular
men. He quotes Machiavelli's remark, that the best governments are those that by the natural effect of their constitution are frequently "renewed," or drawn back to their first
principles ; passes in review in his characteristic manner
the many excellent institutions which "among the
Romans" served to maintain in force the first principles of
their political system ; and then shows how small will be
the effect even of the best institutions and the most
admirable laws and customs when the spirit of liberty
which enacted and established them has been stifled by the
spirit of party. For the best laws are a dead letter unless
strenuously and honestly executed, executed, that is to
say, by magistrates and administrators who are possessed
by the spirit of liberty, and are chosen from the ranks of
a people who carefully tend it and keep it alive.

After this introduction he comes to the main part of
his work, an attempt to trace the growth and vicissitudes
of the spirit of liberty from the earliest times. Over the
first few reigns he passed rapidly ; but on the reigns of
Edward III. and Richard II. he dwelt at length, relating
the history and drawing the character of the two monarchs
in such a way as to suggest an obvious parallel between
Edward and King William, Richard and George II.
Through the succeeding reigns the same plan of treatment
is pursued. The whole work, in fact, is an attempt to
convert a sketch of constitutional history into an attack on
the methods of parliamentary government, to twist
particular epochs and incidents in the past into counter-
parts of others in the present, and to assail and insult the
minister, and less directly the Sovereign, in the person of
predecessors more or less odious or incapable.

Thus in the elaborate account which he gives of the
conduct of the Queen of Edward IV. in acquiring power

by conniving at her husband's infidelities, and in using
the power so acquired to form a separate interest of her
own by raising her immediate creatures and by banish-
ing and proscribing the old nobility, the reader is expected
to substitute the name of Queen Caroline for Elizabeth
Woodville, Walpole and his Whig crew for the creatures
raised up by her, and the Tory country gentlemen for the
proscribed nobility. The relations between Henry VIII.
and Wolsey, again, are so described as to show how a
prince, who had it in his power to be the arbitrator of the
Christian world, might be drawn into the most inconsistent engagements, and thence into complete isolation, by
becoming the bubble of a minister, "the most insolent
the nation had at that time seen ;" and what certain and
just retribution will overtake the statesman who, disre-
garding the sense of the people and trying to govern by
management and intrigue, makes his own political schemes
the hinges of his public policy. In like manner, the glow-
ing and in the main just panegyric on Queen Elizabeth's
reign is intended as a foil, not merely to the two following
reigns with which it is ostensibly contrasted, but to any
more recent times in which a separation of interests
between the governors and a large part of the governed,
making the limitations of the monarchy weigh like
shackles on the monarch and driving his servants to novel
expedients for maintaining his authority, had succeeded
to that wise impartiality and that sagacious observance
of the ebb and flow of national opinion which won for
Elizabeth the trustful affection of her subjects. "When
a prince has turned the spirit of a nation in his favour,"
says Bolingbroke in effect, "he need not be solicitous
about gaining particular men ; but when he knows that
the spirit is against him, he must employ all arts, even
the lowest, to detach particular men from the body of the

people, to form them into parties, to make them act by motives of party interest against the public sense. This is faction; and therefore, whenever a Government is industrious to seduce, to inveigle, to corrupt particular men, we may safely conclude that it stands on a factious, not on a national bottom." "Good government depends under our constitution on the unity of interest between the King and his subjects. A wise and necessary measure is certain to be accepted by the nation and its representatives. A judicious and enlightened minister, if he encounter systematic opposition, will recognize that his policy is mistaken, and will change it. Elizabeth understood this. Instead of struggling to bend the constitution to her own notions, she accommodated her views and character to it, feeling that she was made for the sake of her people, not the people for the sake of their Sovereign. She attached the nation to her by the ties of affection and confidence. She was jealous of her prerogative, but moderate in exercising it. James I. endeavoured to persuade men who had on their side the balance of property, and in their hands a great share of the supreme power, that they had no right to this power. He tried to govern without the concurrence of the nation. He imagined that the higher he carried his prerogative the more securely he should be seated on the throne, mistook the weight for the strength of the sceptre, and forgot that when it is heaviest it is most likely to fall out of the prince's hand. His successor, educated in these notions, came a party man to the throne. His prejudices, confirmed by habit, fortified by flattery, and provoked by opposition, led him to continue an invasion of the people's rights, while imagining himself to be concerned in the just defence of his own. The factions of the court tainted the nation, and gave life and strength, if not being, to the factions of the State. The spirit of liberty, trampled down by the one, could not make head against the other ; and at length the constitution, escaping the danger that assailed it on the side of prerogative, fell a victim to absolute anarchy."

In the " Dissertation on Parties " the same subject is continued, and the moral of the whole work is pointed against the existing administration. These nineteen letters were dedicated to Sir Robert Walpole, the Minister of Party, and were written in order to expose the artifices and point out the train of misfortunes which divided the nation into parties ; to revive in the minds of men the true spirit of the constitution which the contests and excesses of party had brought to the brink of ruin ; to vindicate the justice of the principles established at the Revolution, of the means employed in it, and of the ends obtained by it ; and to unite men of all denominations in support of these principles, in defence of these means, and in pursuit of these ends.

The principal end of the Revolution, according to Bolingbroke, was to secure the nation for the future against all the dangers to which liberty as well as religion had been exposed in the past. The chief of those dangers then arose from the dependent position which the two Houses held to the Crown in consequence of the recent unnatural growth of prerogative. Against this danger the Revolution effectually guarded liberty by curbing the prerogative, and by making the prince once more amenable to the law. But it made no provision for preserving the independence of the Houses, or the freedom of elections against the danger of party management, a danger indefinitely increased by the enormous growth of revenue, of debt, of offices, of the power to seduce by appealing to the self-interest. The conclusion which he draws is, that the ends of the Revolution have not all been obtained.

X

In what way and by what further changes the original plan of this noble work should be made complete, a private person would, he thinks, be presumptuous even to insinuate. This belongs to the wisdom of the nation assembled in Parliament. Private persons may, however, represent such things as they judge to be of use to the public, and may support their representations by the reasons which have determined their opinions.

And Bolingbroke then proceeded to represent how, in the opinion of an impartial spectator, the real difference of principles and designs which at one time divided the nation into parties had arisen; how the extraordinary pretensions of James I. to be the divinely appointed ruler of a people bound to receive his decrees with devout submission and execute them with filial obedience, instead of being buried in his grave with every mark of contempt, had drawn new life and strength from the temporary triumph of anarchy; how Roundhead and Cavalier, flourishing after the Restoration as vigorously as before, had given birth to the factions Whig and Tory, the one seeking to throw us back into confusion, the other to entail tyranny on the State and Popery on the Church; how the Revolution, brought about by a formal departure on each side from the principles peculiar to it, had saved us from these grievances and dangers, creating new interests, new obligations, new principles of government, giving to the Sovereign a new title, to the people a more solemn establishment and a fuller declaration of their privileges, to the Whigs whose principles prepared the way for it, and to the Tories who adopted them and assisted to carry them out, a means of laying aside their differences and of coming together on a foundation truly national; how the old bygone distinctions had been wantonly revived by the minister then in power, in order to serve his own personal ends by perpetuating these obsolete party divisions ; and how, therefore, it behoved all men of virtue and honour, all men possessed by the spirit of liberty, all men really anxious to draw back the constitution to its ancient lines, to rally in support of the Patriots in opposition, made up as these were of the bulk of both the old parties, engaged in defending the true principles of that Revolution for which both were responsible against an obscure remnant of the one and a mercenary detachment from the other.

IV.

In the "Patriot King," with its ideal conception of a constitutional monarch after the feudal type, deriving his title from popular choice, and transformed by the nature of his tenure into a popular Sovereign, we have Bolingbroke's remedy for the distempers of the State, addressed to those Tories who, retaining their old monarchical principles, accepted the Hanover line ; to the students and men of letters who almost unanimously opposed the minister ; and to the younger Patriots or boys, as Walpole called them, men like Lyttelton and Pitt, who, full of democratic enthusiasm, though they afterwards acted with the Whigs, always repudiated the party name and disliked the party system. Its leading principle is government by a limited monarch ; limited not by having all his power taken bodily away from him and put into the hands of men who should be simply his advisers, but by consenting to exercise that power subject to the acknowledged authority of public opinion, as manifested in a free Parliament, according to certain fundamental covenants forming the Trust Deed which defines its privileges, and by which he has voluntarily bound himself ; limited as God's government of the world is limited (according to Bolingbroke's favourite illustration), by laws which result from the various relations and various natures of the things he has himself created.

In the " Remarks on History," on the other hand, and in the "Dissertation on Parties" we have the indictment against Revolution principles, as developed by Walpole into the art and mystery of party government, addressed to the whole heterogeneous opposition before the great disruption took place, drawn at great length, illustrated with elaborate commentaries taken from history and constitutional law, and set forth with all the literary charm which brilliant eloquence, inflamed by keen personal animosity, could impart to it. That it contains a certain element of truth is undeniable. The Whig statesmen, following out what was undoubtedly the real meaning of the Revolution, had made England a progressive republic, a free commonwealth in which the hereditary chief magistrate set up by Parliament was no longer, as from his tenure he could not be, a Sovereign in the true sense of the word, but an imposing and dignified State official, whose duty it was to lend the cover and sanction of his name to acts of government for which ministers, possessing the confidence of Parliament and changing with the changes of Parliament, were alone responsible. And this system, as we now see it beginning to work in fairly complete operation, with the Crown stripped of all political authority and retained only for the more efficient performance of certain grave ceremonial functions, with the Estates of the Realm exercising a firm grasp on every part of the executive government, and with the nation at large controlling and directing each important movement of the Legislature, is probably, on the whole, the best which human experience and ingenuity, as applied to the art of politics, has yet developed.

But the Whigs had then only carried this system out in part. They had made the executive government practically responsible to the Parliament which created it; but they had not made Parliament responsible to the nation which it represented. On the contrary, they had laboured with success to weaken that responsibility, to subordinate large and powerful classes to others in which at the moment the love of freedom and progress was more marked, and which they raised up into an artificial prominence as a guarantee for the continuance of the institutions they were planting. That when once firmly seated in power they governed with admirable wisdom in the general interest of the whole nation, and with perhaps an undue regard for the special ideas and special wants of the men whose political privileges they abridged, is true, no doubt. But all arbitrary power, all power purchased by corrupt arts, is tainted at the source; and the taint soon spreads, infecting all who touch it. Even in the early days of Whig ascendency it was not difficult for an acute and vigilant assailant like Bolingbroke to discover abuses which gave point to his invective, and which made the charge of fomenting factions, of subordinating national to personal interests, of securing safety after misgovernment by systematic invasions of liberty, not altogether unmeaning. His error lay in supposing these abuses to be the inevitable results of the Parliamentary system which he disliked, and that system to be a perversion of the Revolution principles of which he supposed the Patriots to be the only true guardians. He failed to see that the Revolution itself was something more than a dynastic change, intended to restore the Elizabethan system in its integrity; that it transformed the very nature and character of the English Government, reversing the relative position of the Crown and the House of Commons, substituting representative in the place of monarchical institutions ; and that the Whig system of parliamentary management by the division of men into parties, each drilled into submission to its chosen leaders, and made to subordinate individual caprices to their judgment, though as yet imperfectly carried out and justly open to attack on the side of its abuses, was a necessary accompaniment of this change, without which under the rule of Parliament any reforming policy, or indeed any efficient administration, would, in face of the hostile interests it arrays against it, be impossible.

Moreover, the substantial grain of truth which Bolingbroke's argument contains is obscured and his speculations, except as fine samples of rhetoric, deprived of almost all lasting value by the necessities of his unfortunate position as the mouthpiece of a heterogeneous faction utterly at variance as to its political ends, perpetually torn with schisms, joined together in an alliance radically and essentially immoral, and dominated by a body of malcontent Whig place-hunters, shrewd statesmen, and men of affairs, who were in complete sympathy with the system he was attacking, even in its most corrupt and exclusive features, who were bent on continuing that system, and who, as a matter of fact, on attaining power at length by Bolingbroke's help greatly extended, strengthened, and degraded it. He was hampered in all he said by the knowledge, which he afterwards justly pleaded in his own defence, that the "principles of the opposition were the principles of very few of the opposers," and that the main body was simply turning a "virtuous defence of the constitution into a scheme of low ambition." This famous political party, in short, was in a condition of such unstable equilibrium as to require, on the part of its leaders, the most delicate and careful handling to prevent it from toppling over and breaking in pieces. Its component parts, united by no single bond of principle and by no common sentiment, except personal hatred of the minister, could be kept together only by constant appeals to that one touch of nature which made them kin. Hence the elaborate falsifications of history, the studious misrepresentation of current events, the unbridled ferocity of invective which disfigure Bolingbroke's tracts. However abstract in character or elevated in their general tone, however grave the constitutional theories discussed in them, or searching the treatment recommended, they are party pamphlets designed, not to instruct and enlighten, but to obscure and mislead. Like those contemporary Histories against which in one of his own letters he scornfully warns his correspondent, they are " to be read with suspicion, for they deserve to be suspected "—their assertions verified, their epithets and judgments put aside, their declamation disregarded.* And the admiration we justly feel for the great master of style, and for the consummate literary skill with which facts are tortured to his purpose, contrary statements reconciled, and awkward admissions slurred over, is constantly mingled with pain to see that fine intellect bound to the service of a mean faction, which accepted all its efforts with indifference and requited them with contempt. In truth, the fate of Bolingbroke in his later years and the contrast it presents to the hopes and promise of his early manhood irresistibly recalls that of the mighty deliverer of old as pictured by Milton in imperishable lines : a man pre-ordained for great exploits ; destined as by divine command to set the subject nation free ; failing to achieve his end because his heaven-sent powers were not conjoined with wisdom ; and condemned at last to prostitute his consecrated gifts,

* Bolingbroke to Lord Cornbury, ii. 500.

shorn of half their strength, in servile toil, at the bidding
of the very men at whose expense his youthful triumphs
had been won.

" Promise was, that I
Should Israel from Philistian yoke deliver ;
Ask for this great deliverer now, and find him
. . . . at the mill with slaves,
Himself in bonds under Philistian yoke.'

CHAPTER VI.

I.

IT is pleasant to turn from Bolingbroke the anonymous pamphleteer and leader-writer, the bondslave of Pulteney, the "scoff" and "gaze" of the discontented Whigs, to Bolingbroke the man of letters and society, the friend and familiar correspondent of Pope and Swift and Gay, the farmer and host of Dawley, the honoured guest at Twickenham. In his country retirement the political schemer and libeller is at once transformed into the judicious adviser and kindly patron of wit and genius. At Dawley he is a man supremely contented with his lot, at peace with fortune, glad to throw aside ambition and worldly cares in rural pursuits and the amenities of generous friendship. Just as at Marcilly and La Source he had affected the elegant trifler, whose highest exertion was to frame a symmetrical flower-bed or pen a happy inscription on his summer-houses, being all the time absorbed in the abstrusest labours of a hard student of philosophy, so now in his English homestead, whilst plotting the destruction of Government by every factious artifice in the company of grave and experienced statesmen, he liked to pose before his literary friends as an eighteenth century Cincinnatus, anxious chiefly about his crops in the uncertainties of this insular climate; dined on beans and bacon, with an occasional barn-door fowl; inscribed over the porch of his "sepulchre" the characteristic motto, *Satis beatus ruris honoribus;* and painted the walls of his entrance-hall with emblems of husbandry, after the uncouth embellishments of a farmer's kitchen.

In that brilliant circle of wits in whose society Lord Treasurer Oxford and Secretary St. John had been wont to forget the cares of State, time had made many inroads. Parnell had drunk himself into an early grave. The dissolute and accomplished Prior, shipwrecked by the storm which scattered his party, had died in poverty and obscurity. The turbulent life of Atterbury was drawing to a close in exile. Swift, after two brief visits to Twickenham and Dawley, had fled back to Ireland, overwhelmed by public and private calamities, his spirit broken by the consciousness of failure, his heart tortured by anxiety and remorse, to drag out his long days in misery; nor could any persuasion again draw him from his lonely banishment. Arbuthnot, indeed, was left for a while, and Gay. But it is with none of these friends of his happier days that the lasting reputation of Bolingbroke is most closely linked. Of the literary companions with whom he lived at this time, during the ten years of his own most prolific industry, at once the most eminent and the most closely associated with him by common pursuits and common opinions, were the two greatest writers of that age—Pope in England and Voltaire in France; nor would any review of Bolingbroke's public life be complete which did not at least refer, however briefly and inadequately, to the mighty influence which, in the midst of his own labours, he was preparing to exercise through these two disciples on the public mind of Europe.

Pope and Bolingbroke were now near country neighbours. Their acquaintance dated, indeed, from the early days when Bolingbroke was minister; but it was not until he came to reside at Dawley, within an easy drive of the little Twickenham villa, that their friendship ripened into that close and familiar intercourse the effects of which may be traced in all Pope's subsequent writings. Shut out from politics by his religion, and by feeble health from the world of business and society, the delicate and secluded poet, dazzled by Bolingbroke's reputation, flattered by his attentions, and always prone to endow with divine qualities those whom he admitted within the inner circle of his friendship, seems to have regarded the fallen statesman, who in his greatness had changed the course of history, almost as a "messenger descending from the Thrones above," as Adam received the "heavenly stranger," Raphael—

> "Not awed,
> Yet with submiss approach and reverence meek,
> As to a superior being."

He recognized in Bolingbroke, carried to the highest perfection, all that artifice, and vanity, and simulated indifference to the world's opinion which made up the essence of his own character ; and, subjugated by his aspiring spirit, his eloquence, his energy, his wide and various knowledge, was blind to the faults and weaknesses which so closely resembled his own. He thought his illustrious friend, as he confesses, "superior to anything he had ever seen in nature." He prophesied for him the fate of Elijah, loved and worshipped him with all the ardour of his warm and sensitive temper, and, after his custom, submitted the tendencies of his literary genius without question to the master at whose feet he sat. *

It was in 1732 and the two following years that the fruits of this singular collaboration first appeared in the publication of the four epistles which form Pope's " Essay

---

* The three great phases of Pope's literary career may be said to have been determined by three great prose writers, Addison, Swift, and Bolingbroke.

on Man," and in the four "Moral Essays" which Pope afterwards, with the help of Warburton, worked into the same
comprehensive ethical scheme. In the noble lines which
close the "Essay on Man," as in the dedication of the whole
poem, Pope has recorded with grateful appreciation his
obligations to Bolingbroke. He is the guide, philosopher,
and friend, the master alike of the poet and the song. In
a hundred familiar discourses, delivered amongst the hay-
cocks of Dawley and in the multiplied scenes of Pope's
little garden, with that unrivalled faculty of unpremeditated
expression, the art of which, as it steered from grave to
gay, from lively to severe, the poet has in these closing
lines so happily commemorated, Bolingbroke had gradually
unfolded before his admiring pupil his favourite and long-
cherished ideas, touching those high questions of philosophical meditation on which he had thought so deeply
at La Source : concerning man's proper rank in creation
and the nature of his relations to its Author ; concerning
the two principles contending for mastery within him—the
self-love which stimulates, the reason which restrains ;
concerning the ends of divine government in the production of general good, and the necessity of estimating
individual well-being according as it finds its place in this
general system and contributes to this beneficent aim.
For the purpose of preparing and assisting his friend in
introducing this philosophy to the world in such poetical
dress as should set off its most attractive features, he is
reported to have written for Pope's guidance a whole
volume, now unhappily lost, which contained the entire
scheme of the "Essay on Man" in prose, and which their
common friend Lord Bathurst thought not less worthy of
admiration than the poem founded on it ; whilst during
the long progress of the work he furnished him, from time
to time, in those "Fragments and Minutes of Essays"

which have come down to us, the germs of pretty nearly every doctrine, every argument, even every illustration contained in it. The brilliant Satires of Pope, again, were due to Bolingbroke's suggestion. To his fuller insight into the characters of public men the portraits enshrined in them owe all their distinctive form and colour. And it was by Bolingbroke's influence that Pope was drawn at length into the strife of parties, from which in his youth he had carefully kept himself clear, and with the spirit of which all his later works are tinged—drawn to substitute statesmen for poetasters as the objects of his invective.

On the other hand, Pope, on his side, succeeded for a moment in weaning his friend from politics and "low ambitions," and in drawing him back to those high trains of thought which alone were worthy, as he thought, to occupy the human mind. It was in answer to Pope's appeal that Bolingbroke addressed to him, in the thick of his public labours, those famous "Epistolary Essays" which in orthodox eyes have won for him a place in the seething pitch of Malebolge. In this work, written partly for his own satisfaction, partly for that of his friend, he takes up and develops in a more connected way than in the "Fragments," but still with the same unreserve and disregard of form, their common ideas touching the limits of human knowledge, its nature, extent and reality, thereby ultimately turning against himself, as he foresaw, the malice and obloquy of what he calls the theological stipendiaries of the State, "the condition of whose engagement is to defend the existing doctrines," and whose resentment Pope, by screening their common meaning in the safer generalities of poetry, had managed to disarm. The aim and purpose of Bolingbroke's philosophical essays is, however, precisely identical with that of Pope's "Essay on Man," though Bolingbroke, freed from the restraints of metre, is able to treat

the subject with greater precision, and to extend it into
ampler detail. That purpose is defined to be, in the words
of the statesman, to plead the cause of God against all who
assert that His dispensations are unequal, to prove His
existence against the atheist, to defend His attributes
against the theologian, to justify His providence against
both. In the words of the poet, it is to vindicate the ways
of God towards man by showing that the real cause of
man's error and misery, his failures, the contrast between
his far-reaching aims and his random achievements, lies,
not in any ancestral lapse from purity supernaturally
entailed upon his race from generation to generation, but
in his own pride and ambition, which will not be satisfied
with his own conditions, which aim at more knowledge
and aspire to greater happiness and perfection than is
consistent with his intended place in the providential order ;
to prove that this world is not, as the theologians say, out
of joint with the purposes of its Creator, but that in the
passions and imperfections of man no less than in his
virtues, in the inequalities and hardships of life no less
than in its blessings, the great scheme of universal benevolence, rightly understood, is being fulfilled. The method
employed by both writers is the inductive method, the
experimental method, of their great contemporaries Locke
and Newton—to study the works of God as exhibited in
that minute portion of the universe which human faculties
are qualified to examine, and by this help to try and lift
the impenetrable veil which hides the secrets of the moral
world ; to search out by patient inquiry and painful labour
some knowledge, however imperfect, of God's character, and
some insight, however faint, into His relations with man.

"The *philosophia prima,*" writes Bolingbroke in a letter
to Swift,* " is above my reach, especially when it attempts

* Bolingbroke to Swift, August 3, 1731.

to prove that God has done so and so by proving that the
doing it is essential to His attributes or necessary to His
design, and that the not doing it would be inconsistent
with the one or repugnant to the other. I content myself
to contemplate what I am sure He has done, and to adore
Him for it in humble silence. I can demonstrate that every
cavil which has been brought against the great system
of the world, physical and moral, from the days of Democ-
ritus and Epicurus to our own day, is absurd ; but I dare
not pronounce *why* things are made as they are, state the
ends of infinite wisdom, or show the proportion of the
means."

And the striking contrast between the fate of the two
works, which Bolingbroke foretold, was due, not to any
difference in their essential aims, but mainly, if not entirely,
to the fact that the one is a poem intended simply to please
and therefore shadowing truth for effect, the other a grave
treatise intended to instruct, to prove, to convince, developing principles fully, and omitting nothing that could
serve its purpose. The consequence has been that the
moral essays of Pope, in which truth is shadowed for
effect, have been edited by State clergymen, and extolled
even by a State bishop. They are admitted to be the most
striking example of his peculiar art of seizing so much
of general truths and principles as it is convenient to
acknowledge, arranging and illustrating them, setting them
in the clearest light, and expressing them in the condensed
and pointed style which at once stamps them into the
memory. For the philosophical letters of Bolingbroke,
on the other hand, in which principles are developed for
instruction instead of being " shadowed for effect," and
truth is pursued for its own sake, which contain precisely
the same system of Natural Religion, stripped of its
poetical embroidery and drawn out towards its necessary

conclusions, equally well written, equally elevated in its moral sentiments, equally unsatisfying perhaps to the mind, no epithet of saintly rancour and saintly intolerance is too abusive.*

II.

Scarcely less close was the literary connection between Bolingbroke and Voltaire. In many respects they resembled each other in character. They had the same mobility of mind and brilliancy of wit, the same sceptical and rebellious spirit, the same keen and lively sensibilities, the

* For example, "diabolical wickedness due to an excess of natural depravity," is the mild expression applied to them by Sir Walter Scott, a layman, a man of the world, and a member of the political party of which Bolingbroke is the greatest ornament. For curiosity's sake I reproduce the main features of the religious system thus violently and, let us trust, ignorantly denounced. That there lives and works, self-existent and indivisible, one Almighty God ; that the world is His creation ; that all we can discern of His nature and His attributes is to be deduced from the economy of His universe ; that this shows us the quality of infinite wisdom coinciding with infinite benevolence, and both operating not by particular but by general laws ; that in the harmony of the universe (where alone His voice is heard) there is to be discerned a fundamental connection between the idea of God and the reason of man, touching conduct with emotion, and elevating morality into something more than a conventional code ; that man's mental faculties, like his bodily, are, so far as we can see, adapted only for the practical functions of existence, his knowledge derived from sensation and reflection, his life in itself complete, virtue constituting as a rule its own reward, vice its own punishment ; that to man and the human race is assigned a small part only in the great drama of existence, just as the earth which he inhabits forms only a speck in the vast ocean of created Nature ; and that just as he controls and subjects to his own pleasure the animal life about him, so in his turn he himself ministers, in the pains and limitations at which he chafes, to the success of the general scheme and, it may be, to the enjoyment of higher creatures superior to him in its ascending scale ;—such was the depraved and diabolical creed of Bolingbroke. It must be observed that Bolingbroke did not expressly deny a future state for man, though his system, which rests on the providence of God in this world, does not expressly require one. The last words recorded of him, when sinking under the dreadful malady to which his life succumbed, are instinct with the true spirit of Christian humility and Christian resignation—"God who placed me here will do what He pleases with me hereafter ; and He knows best what to do."

same lack of fortitude and worldly wisdom. They had met at the time of Bolingbroke's first exile, and amidst the glittering society of the Regency had been mutually attracted by congenial tastes and habits. In the winter of 1721, Voltaire had visited Bolingbroke at La Source. In one of his early letters he has left us a characteristic description of his host, as a man who united the erudition of England to the politeness of France, who was perfectly master of the language of both countries, familiar with the history of both nations, an equal lover and discriminating judge of their literatures—so discriminating, indeed, that he rated the productions of his young guest higher than those of any living writer. When, in May, 1726, Voltaire came to England, he made Bolingbroke's house his home. In the library at Dawley he studied our literature, our history, our customs, our national character, learning from the comments of his host the application of his various studies. By Bolingbroke he was introduced to the distinguished body of statesmen and men of letters who were then setting up the standard of opposition to Walpole. In Bolingbroke's company he witnessed the first trial of their arms of precision ; observed the scrupulous fairness with which, on the side of Government, the attack was met and parried ; remarked the latitude allowed to enterprise and criticism ; and, as the result of his studies and his observations combined, derived that admiration for English liberty in speech, in writing, in action, which he afterwards taught to France, and through France to Europe.

Investigating the principles and character of English freedom, however, under the tuition of Bolingbroke, it was inevitable that Voltaire should see things to a great extent with the eyes of his master ; should view our constitutional forms, for instance, and the political changes then at work in them, not as they would appear in the unclouded light of truth, but coloured and distorted by that brilliant and misleading fancy. It was the theory of Bolingbroke that in England the spirit of liberty, the spirit of active, unbiassed, individual criticism, necessary to preserve all free institutions in their purity, was dying out. He held that under this decadence the ancient and historic English monarchy, the type of constitutional freedom, with its separate estates and orders, each acting as a check upon the others, and all combining by their rivalry and collision to preserve this freedom, was being transformed into a simple oligarchy, which essayed, against all constitutional precedent, to unite the different functions of Government; which kept itself in power corruptly for its own selfish purpose, in defiance of the national wishes; and which constantly sacrificed the national interests entrusted to it to secure its own safety or advance its ambitious aims. What Voltaire actually saw as the result of his own unaided observation, was a people enjoying an amount of prosperity and material comfort hitherto unexampled, going through all the business of life without let or hindrance, saying what they pleased in society, printing what they pleased in books, propounding any novel theories that occurred to them in speculative philosophy, taking the keenest interest in religious controversies, protected in all their different enterprises by the strong hand of equal justice, shaping at their pleasure the general course of the national policy, criticizing the ruling classes, the ministers of State, the very person and actions of the Sovereign, with a happy unconsciousness of their advantages, which to a Frenchman, fresh from the confinement of the Bastille, and still smarting from the canes of De Rohan's lackeys, seemed the ideal of public freedom. And it is not surprising, therefore, that Voltaire, in his endeavours to reconcile the facts which he noticed with the comments on them he was always hearing, should have failed to penetrate the meaning of the constitutional polity established by the Revolution ; failed to detect the close connection between the two ideas expressed by the common name of liberty—the absence of an arbitrary control by authority interfering in individual enterprise in its own selfish interest, and the presence of a general habit of watching over and moulding the nation's history ; failed to perceive that the material prosperity which so much struck him, the progress he observed in the civilizing arts of industry, and that independent vigour which he admired in speculation and in literature, were the direct result of a healthier spirit of political liberty quickening all the pulses of the national life, of that very spirit of liberty the loss of which his friend Bolingbroke was always lamenting.

So, again, in religion. Bolingbroke was the chief of the English school of Deists. At La Source, during Voltaire's visit there, he was engaged in bringing together, from many different sources, his " Thoughts on Natural Religion." He had already completed those philosophical letters to M. de Pouilly, of which a French edition was afterwards published, and that treatise on the " Limits of Human Knowledge," out of which he constructed the first of the four epistolary essays he addressed to Pope. The "Reflections on Innate Moral Principles " was actually written in part while Voltaire was staying in his house. After his custom, when in the society of a congenial friend, his conversation, so brilliant, so animated, so persuasive, constantly turned on the subjects with which his mind was full. And five years later, when Voltaire came over to England as the guest of Bolingbroke, he found "society," and especially the aristocratical circles into which his host introduced him, moved almost to excitement on the subject of these new opinions. The attempt of Toland to invalidate the canonical authority of Scripture, and disengage Christianity from mysticism ; the attempt of Shaftesbury to exhibit the inherent worthiness of humanity, and so destroy the doctrinal foundation underlying the Christian system ; the attempt of Collins to break the connection between the two Testaments, by showing that the prophecies on which Jesus and the apostles relied for their credentials would not bear the meaning ordinarily given to them ;— these and similar works, all of them bringing out in their several ways the fundamental principle of Bolingbroke's teaching, that the essence and vivifying power of a religion, its influence in shaping and perfecting human conduct, lies in its moral precepts, not in the dogmas and sanctions enforcing them, however much they might be officially condemned, were widely and eagerly welcomed. During the very time of Voltaire's visit, the attempt of Woolston to do for the miracles what Collins had done for the prophecies, and convert into allegories the most essential facts of historical Christianity, was published, had for those times and considering the nature of the subject an immense success, drew forth a warning pastoral letter from the ablest of the Anglican bishops, and was ultimately honoured at his instance with a State prosecution.

— Now, it was from Bolingbroke, as his spiritual pastor, that Voltaire derived, as he in fact confesses, nearly every article of his doctrinal creed. From the religious school of which Bolingbroke was the chief master, he drew the rationalizing spirit and borrowed the controversial weapons with which he commenced and carried on his long warfare against authority. It is to the social and literary con- nection, therefore, between Bolingbroke and Voltaire that France owes, not perhaps her emancipation from political and ecclesiastical oppression, but certainly the manner in which that emancipation was effected ; the fact that in France the assault on spiritual abuses was made to precede in point of time the assault on political abuses; the fact that in France the assailants of the most venerable and elaborate of all ecclesiastical despotisms took their stand on the simplest of all religious philosophies, a system which elevates private judgment to the point of discarding all dogmatic assertion touching the fundamentals of belief. In 1730, while Bolingbroke and Pope were together laying the foundation for the poetical illustration of this philosophy, appeared "Tract 90" of the movement, the famous attempt of Tindal to show that the God of Reason and Nature, the Eternal making for righteousness, whom all men in their hearts dimly acknowledge and silently worship, was not and could not be the rude, partial, humanized Deity of the Jewish and Christian Testaments; and in the characteristic methods of Tindal, in the elaborate contrast which he draws between the ethics of Scripture as priests expound them, and those that an eighteenth century lay moralist, if left to himself, would inculcate, may be found the idea of one of Voltaire's most subtle and effective ways of holding up the authorities who took their stand on Scripture to general reprobation.

After Tindal, the controversy declined in the hands of the Chubbs and Morgans; and it says much for Voltaire's interest in it, that he continued to receive from his English correspondents and diligently to study their contributions. For in England the discussion had by this time produced its main effect and was passing into a different phase. From the first the strong interest which it excited had been confined to a small part only of the public ordinarily interested in religious questions. In England, religious freedom has been won, religious equality promoted, and resistance to authoritative theology chiefly maintained by men who were no friends to religious progress, men in whom the spirit of religious fervour was intense even to bigotry, and adherence to orthodox dogma most un-qualified. To the mass of middle-class Englishmen, zealous God-fearing Nonconformists, swathed in the fetters of a narrow, soul-deadening Calvinism, all that was most attractive in the new philosophy, the beauty of its ethical teaching, its ennobling conception of the vastness of God's providence, only added to its dangers. To these men the self-seeking indifference of the privileged hierarchy was not more repulsive than the all-dissolving scepticism of the infidel writers. They resolutely closed their eyes to the spectacle of their controversy.

And here the controversy was seen almost from the first to involve no vital issues, to be on the part of the disputants on both sides a mere theological duel with blunted foils.* The Deist philosophers, on their part, had far too much culture and æsthetic refinement to join hands with Nonconformity. They accepted without question the principle of a dominant Church, and the rule of a State priesthood pledged to maintain the doctrines stamped with its authority. All that they attacked was the particular conclusions with which at the moment this Church and priesthood were held to be identified. And on these points the Anglican divines, on their side, were quite willing to meet them half-way. So far as the limits legally assigned them would permit, they were even anxiously desirous to modify both the theology and the ethics entrusted to them in the direction pointed out by these unruly supporters. Gradually they incorporated into their own system nearly everything that was most plausible in the reasoning of their assailants and most elevated in their ethical teaching, while denouncing and excommunicating (pardonably enough) the presumptuous

---

* This is well brought out by Mr. Leslie Stephen in the second volume of his " History of English Thought."

impostors who ventured on their domain. At length they boldly maintained, and supported the position with a vast array of learning and argument, that Anglican Christianity, rightly understood, *was* Natural Religion, accredited indeed by historical proofs, armed with necessary sanctions, confirmed by positive laws, and endowed with lucrative privileges, but appealing to the believer with a force independent of, and superior to, these carnal accompaniments. The consequence was that when, many years later, Bolingbroke's own attack on the "theological stipendiaries of the State" was published, the matters in dispute had been already settled by a happy compromise. Society had turned to a new branch of the same theological study. Speculations about the religion of Nature, attempts to conceive an ideal Providence by collating the works of His hand, attempts to educe a moral law by contemplating the eternal verities, were out of date. Historical investigations into the truth of the alleged facts which testify to the Christian system were now the mode. Butler, adopting Tindal's premiss, though demurring to his conclusions, was held to have finally proved that the God of Nature and the God of Anglicanism were substantially the same; that each works in the moral, precisely as in the physical, order by slow development, not distinct enunciation ; and that, in the judgment of Anglicans themselves, all that is sound and reasonable in advancing speculation may be read into their vague and loosely drawn formularies ; whilst Middleton, the typical Broad Churchman of those days, had personally shown (what, after all, was the great point) that a man might hold the entire Deist position, if he liked, and still continue, with a little care in expressing himself, to enjoy the comforts and advantages of the Establishment.

The Anglican divines, therefore, found little difficulty

in turning the weight of social condemnation against the posthumous indiscretion of Bolingbroke. It was held to be an unnecessary raking up of painful questions just happily settled by mutual compromise ; and this wanton thrusting of intellectual and moral difficulties in the way of the hard-pressed administrators of the State system, with the essential principle of which he was in complete agreement, was felt to be as unfair as his personal strictures on them were ungenerous.

But the same religious philosophy, which in England produced its main effect in a short generation, and within the limits of the privileged Church itself, was destined to a longer life and a far wider influence when transplanted by Bolingbroke's great disciple. Here it was the first introduction of the liberal and Protestant spirit into a country dominated by authority, and the result was a deadly struggle between the two principles which in England had come to terms. In the more genial soil of France, in the hands of men burning with the enthusiasm of Knox and Calvin, amidst the anathemas of a Church that scorned to whittle away its theology at their bidding, and in presence of an eager, keen-witted, sceptical people, with all whose aspirations it was in tune, a people impatient of worldly compromises, prone to draw principles to their conclusions, and lending themselves easily and with rapture to the influence of great ideas, the religion of Nature, no longer pruned down and shaped by official hands into the semblance of orthodoxy, flourished and vegetated in wild luxuriance—flourished as it never had flourished, as it never could flourish, in free, practical, unspiritual England. From Paris, as from a centre of civilizing light, the new heresy spread beyond the Alps, interposing everywhere its shield between the oppressed and the oppressor, encountering principalities and powers in the cause of justice and mercy and toleration, inculcating that charity towards alien creeds and races which orthodoxy had failed to teach. Unhappily, it developed also, in its stronger and ranker growths, some qualities of a more dangerous and noxious kind. But for this Bolingbroke and its earliest teachers can hardly be held responsible—no more responsible than the man of science who, intent on advancing physical knowledge, invents in his laboratory some new compound capable of being made, in the hands of men maddened by oppression, an instrument of crime and vengeance. The religion of Nature which Bolingbroke taught Voltaire was a fertile closet speculation, pregnant with good or evil, according to the mind and purpose of its propagator. In itself it was a perfectly legitimate product of that restless energy of private judgment which, in the words of a great Catholic writer, "thrives and is joyous" under the rough buffets of authority, and the manifestations of which, in constant conflict with authority, are necessary to preserve religion in its vigour. Even in constructing it he was, perhaps, unseasonably anxious to warn against the dangers inseparable in his view from any sceptical philosophy when suffered to spread itself abroad unchecked. For himself, fond as he was of "posing" the Anglican divines and putting them on their mettle, he was satisfied with the *conditions* of religious progress as they existed under the Anglican system. He held that in a State-regulated Church, from which the essence of the theological spirit had been excluded, a Church based on the principle of historic development and natural expediency, there was as large a capacity for religious growth, both in thought and practice, as was consistent with human welfare and human institutions. In his familiar letters, he pointedly disclaimed all sympathy with those "pests of society," the *esprits forts*, the fanatical, proselytizing free-thinkers, who in their

hurry to pull down the pompous structure of revealed
religion would endanger the common foundation on which
also their own humbler building stood ;* and in the
midst of his most advanced religious speculations he paused
to lay down and defend the political theory on which
a State Church is founded, and which, twenty years
before, when minister, he had first employed for justifying
his own policy of repression towards Nonconformists—
the theory that man, though he has the right as a
rational creature to think and judge in religious matters
for himself, stands under restraints as a member of
society, and can no more be suffered to speak than he is
to act with the full licence of his desires.†

The religious philosophy of Bolingbroke, therefore, and
the position he claimed for it towards the older systems,
differed essentially in character from many of its lineal
descendants—from, for instance, the aggressive materialism
of the modern French *littérateurs*. In its doctrinal parts,
too, it is far more akin to the mild and gentlemanly
unbelief of our own savants, our

> " Huxleys and Tyndalls apt at priests to jeer,"

who experiment on the properties of Omnipotence, in the
intervals of scientific inquiry, with the same intelligent
interest, apply to spiritual problems the same philosophical
methods, subject the gross conceptions of Holy Writ to
the same cleansing and evaporating processes, and ethe-
realize the Almighty Power revealed there into the same
attenuated divinity.

Scepticism of this sort, conceived in the groping
search after truth by men who in tastes and sympathies
are on the side of orthodoxy and respectability—conservatives in politics, for the most part, like Hobbes, anxious

---

* Bolingbroke to Swift, September 12, 1724.
† Works, iii. 334 (Introductory letter to Pope).

that creeds and churches should survive though faith
may perish ; opportunists in morals, like Hume, ready to
recommend his young free-thinking friends to "take
orders," *—for how otherwise could a man of letters be
provided for by an English Government ?—the scepticism
of men who, in losing their hold on the old religious
ideas, yet recognize the necessity of religion for the
general interests of a complex society—finds its natural
home in a Church Establishment with the peculiar conditions of our own. Affecting sacerdotal pretensions, yet
compelled by the law of its tenure to draw all its spiritual
nourishment from the civil power, for the sake of the
emoluments bestowed on it and the social importance
accruing to it from the connection, this concrete representative of things invisible presents a spectacle of Erastianism
attractive, no doubt, to the statesman and man of the
world, satisfying to the needs of artistic culture, which
seeks in external symbols alone the spring of its devotional
ardour, but fatal to all sense of respect for the theological
positions it may assume. And the inevitable effect on a
man of fine intelligence and sensibility of belonging to a
religious body which makes political convenience the
measure of its doctrinal progress—preaching to-day as
truth what in the mutations of party or the vagaries of
judicial interpretation it may have to denounce to-morrow
as error—is nowhere better exhibited than in the case
of Bolingbroke. In his heart, he rejected all the dogmatic
beliefs which the Church prescribed. In his life, he treated
with contempt the moral precepts she enjoined. Yet he
was to the last one of her most loyal and devoted adherents.
As a statesman, he laboured to exclude from their civil
rights all who openly dissented from her communion. As
a minister of the Crown, the one measure of domestic

* Hume to Colonel Edmonstone, March, 1764 (Burton's "Life of Hume").

legislation associated with his name was an attempt to secure to her priesthood an exclusive dominion over the mind and training of youth. In his own person he made no scruple about conforming, or publicly asserting in the most solemn and ostentatious manner the orthodoxy of his religious professions. In his correspondence, he claims it as the part of a "wise and honest man" that if unhappily forced, after examining her theological pretensions, to "remain incredulous," he should not disturb the peace of the world by exposing them, but content himself with privately sorrowing "to see religion so perverted from its true design, and Christian ministers exercising over their fellows such an insolent and cruel usurpation."* Nay, in the very philosophical letters in which, being no longer on English soil, he held himself free to depart from this charitable dissimulation, so far at least as to record in writing his own heretical and schismatical opinions, he eloquently vindicates the claim of the privileged Church to put down with the severest penalties all heresy and schism which does not formally acknowledge her authority, and subscribe, when called upon, her doctrinal creeds and formularies.†

If we turn from the historical development of Bolingbroke's philosophy to examine its intrinsic merits, we shall hardly feel surprised that the simple and rational form of Theism in which he took delight—this worship of Nature and natural law personified—should, notwithstanding its first successes, have failed to win lasting converts. It had

---

* Bolingbroke to Swift, September 12, 1724.

† See the second letter to M. de Pouilly.

In justice to Bolingbroke, it should be remembered that Sir Walter Scott warmly commends him for thus conforming to the Anglican system, notwithstanding that he rejected its whole theological position, and reserves his condemnation for what, to a person not brought up in the ethics of an Establishment, will seem one of the most honest acts of Bolingbroke's life—the tardy acknowledgment of his infidelity.

its salutary effect even in England in liberalizing the
ethical system of the Anglican divines, and in purifying
and exalting their conceptions of the Deity. It had its
effect, too, in confirming the latitudinarian spirit in the
parliamentary Church, of which it was itself a product,
in extending it till its absurdity became self-evident, and
in so preparing the way, indirectly, for the Evangelical
and High Anglican reactions. But it presents, in the
absence of all supernatural explanation in the past, no
coherent theory of man's relation towards God, which will
subjugate his hard rebellious spirit, which makes "the
buds unfold and the flowers bloom within him, and his
moral being rejoice." It is based on a conception of
human life, and of the modest part assigned to it in the
ascending order of creation, which the self-love of man
instinctively rejects. Inculcating self-sacrifice and self-
devotion as his highest duty, it yet offers him no spiritual
crown, transcending earthly happiness, for his reward.
Nor does the refined abstraction proposed to be substituted
for the Christian Deity, as the result of an unaided mental
process, possess the inherent attractive power which the
God of Scripture, the glorified image of whatever is greatest
and noblest in man, exercises on vulgar minds. By Bolingbroke, and even by the arch-iconoclast Voltaire, this *fainéant*
divinity, absorbed in epicurean contentment with the universe at large, sheltering himself from responsibility for
individual failures under the general harmony of his providential scheme, delegating all his divine prerogative in
morals and religion to ministers planted in the intelligence
of his reasoning creatures, with attributes to be investi-
gated by collating the works of his hand, and laws that
result from the eternal fitness of things, was retained as
an object of reverence and worshipped till the last. But
their more logical and thorough-going disciples, instinct

with their reforming spirit, soon deposed this titular sovereign, swore allegiance to his omnipotent mayor of the palace, and made Reason itself no longer the vicegerent of God, but an independent prince with an indefeasible title and a regal power.

CHAPTER VII.

I.

THE "Dissertation on Parties," the most elaborate and complete of all Bolingbroke's indictments against the policy of Walpole, had been composed as a formal appeal to the nation on behalf of the Patriots or National party. Its object was to show that the division of Parliament into two hostile sections, the one opposing, the other supporting the responsible ministers of the Sovereign, was always the symptom of a diseased condition of the body politic; that in the natural and healthy state of that body the policy of the Crown, instead of resting on drilled and interested support, would meet with universal and cordial acceptance; and that, just as before the Revolution an abnormal and mischievous growth of the royal prerogative had produced the evil of a systematic resistance to the royal authority, and the necessity of stringent limitations being applied to it, so now the recurrence of the same phenomenon of a standing parliamentary opposition was in itself an unmistakable sign that under the reformed government new dangers to public liberty had arisen which required in their turn new remedies. The argument of these letters is based on the assumption that the Revolution involved no constitutional change in the English polity, which remained, as before, a personal monarchy advised and assisted by three co-ordinate estates; and the whole Dissertation, under its general charges of governing by party management, of subordinating national to sectional objects, of overriding the deliberate judgments of a disinterested minority, is, in fact, an attack on the fundamental principle and recognized methods of our modern parliamentary system.

In his contributions to the *Craftsman*, Bolingbroke had confined himself to pointing out the nature and cause of the national distemper. The remedies to be applied for restoring the State to health, "the manner in which the noble work of the Revolution was to be made complete, and its real ends attained," these things it was for Parliament and the "wisdom of the nation assembled there" to determine. For a private man even to suggest a solution to such high problems would be "presumption." But the wisdom of the nation, so far as it appeared in Parliament on those independent and patriotic benches on which alone true wisdom could be looked for, was, in fact, the wisdom of Bolingbroke ; and the constitutional reforms which Wyndham and Pulteney urged upon the Legislature were as much the nostrums of the unseen physician in chief as the literary statement of the case had been his diagnosis.

What Bolingbroke recommended was no new policy. It was the revival of those radical principles which, more than thirty years before, in their joint opposition to the Whig junto, the Puritan Harley had engrafted on the Toryism of the Jacobite squires, and which, on coming into power at the close of King William's reign, he had attempted to carry out in the democratic restrictions of the Act of Settlement. Bolingbroke pressed for more frequent and purer elections, guaranteed by the Triennial Bill and the ballot and the disqualification of interested voters ; for the greater "independence" of the House of Commons, guaranteed by the exclusion of pensioners and placemen and the multiplication of county constituencies; for the right of the Sovereign freely to choose his advisers and determine his own policy, subject to the right of Parliament—a free territorial Parliament, consisting exclusively of landlords though chosen by the widest suffrage, —to have the different resolutions of government stated at length on the minutes of the Privy Council, and signed by the ministers assenting to them.

The effect of this series of reforms, if completely carried out, would have been, as Bolingbroke foresaw, to re-establish the old constitution in its integrity. They would have made the Revolution Sovereign virtually independent of parliamentary control, except in those extreme cases in which gross and scandalous maladministration in some particular department of his affairs would have justified the impeachment and penal condemnation of the minister responsible for it. They would have made the House of Lords, as before, the principal branch of the Legislature. All pensioners and placemen being excluded from the popular chamber, the House of Lords would then have contained, with a few trifling exceptions, all the leading authorities in matters of government and legislation, all the great officials, all ministers of State, all the chief orators, politicians, soldiers, diplomatists in the kingdom. In that House would have originated all legislative changes introduced by Government. To that House all ministerial statements of policy would necessarily have been made. The House of Lords would have been charged also with the supreme and momentous duty of sitting in judgment upon and giving practical effect to all accusations brought by the representatives of the people against the constitutional advisers of the Crown. It would have been subject to no sense of individual responsibility to public opinion. Yet, in its collective capacity, it would have been liable at any moment, through the unlimited right of creating peers vested in the Crown, to have its opinions and its judgments turned against the popular body, and brought into harmony with the personal wishes and political interests of the Sovereign and his chosen advisers. The power of the House of Commons as a governing assembly would have been destroyed. Instead of being, as now, the fountain of political honour, the source of government, the seat of administration, the moving spring of an imperial polity, it would have been reduced to its old position of a subordinate estate of the realm, a checking body composed entirely of private gentlemen, honourable and independent but unfamiliar with affairs, disconnected from the practical work of politics, incompetent through want of knowledge effectually to control the course of business, meeting simply to present grievances and authorize expenditure.

There was, however, little probability of this Tory-radical programme in anything like a complete form being carried into effect, unless the nation could be roused in its favour. Even the most modest and unexceptionable of Bolingbroke's remedies, the bill for excluding pensioners from the House of Commons, though merely intended to strengthen the existing law, and though three times passed by the representative body with the scornful acquiescence of the minister, had on every occasion been thrown out by the Whig lords, avowedly on the ground frankly stated by Bishop Sherlock, that the power of rewarding parliamentary service was an essential condition of sound parliamentary government.[*] The bill for excluding placemen, though no longer drawn in the extreme form of the limitation in the Act of Settlement, but in the milder shape

---

* By 6 Anne, c. 7, and 1 George I. c. 56, all pensioners during pleasure or for terms of years were rendered incapable of sitting in the House of Commons ; but the Acts were inoperative through the difficulty of proving the offence.

in which Sandys afterwards carried it, had been rejected in the House of Commons by substantial majorities.* The attempt to disfranchise revenue and other government officers, even when carefully respecting existing interests and simply confined to those charged with new duties, had found little favour in either assembly, and this notwithstanding an eloquent and really powerful protest by Bolingbroke inserted in the Lords' Journals over the name of his friend Lord Bathurst.† As to the proposed return to Triennial Parliaments, which was Bolingbroke's favourite specific for the State distemper, it was not cordially liked, even by the Patriots themselves. Passed by Lord Townshend's Government in the session following the rebellion, the Act of 1716, extending the duration of Parliaments from three years to seven, had been defended not as a mere temporary expedient made necessary by the disturbed state of England, but as a reform of general advantage, designed to give greater freedom to the parliamentary executive, greater steadiness and continuity to the action of the State. As such a reform, though of course perfectly legal and even in the strict sense of the word constitutional, it ought undoubtedly, according to our modern notions, to have followed and been the recognized result of a preceding appeal to the constituent bodies. In Bolingbroke's estimation, it was the most flagrant instance of that contempt for constitutional liberty and for the time-honoured rights and privileges of the people which he attributed to the Whig statesmen. Unluckily, the ostensible leader of the Patriots had been a distinguished member of the Government which passed the Act ; and though a morbid sense of political consistency was not amongst Pulteney's failings, he was slow to admit that the evils and calamities afflicting the nation, which he and his literary friends were painting

---

* "Parliamentary History," xi. 328.   † Ibid, viii. 1058.

in such gloomy colours, were the direct result of a measure
for which he was himself personally responsible. It was
with great difficulty and by the utmost exertion of Bolingbroke's influence that this difference between the Whigs
and Tories in opposition, which threatened at one moment
to sever the party, had been smoothed over sufficiently
to allow of bringing this vital question to the test of a
parliamentary vote. At length, in the session immediately
preceding the dissolution of 1734, at the instance of the
son of his old colleague, the Jacobite Bromley, a motion
for repealing the Septennial Act, and re-enacting the more
radical measure which it replaced, had been formally made,
and definitely rejected, giving rise to a debate not more
remarkable for the famous passage-of-arms between
Wyndham and the minister than for the ominous silence
of the leading Patriots, and the unmistakable signs it
exhibited of the hollowness of their alliance.

II.

And now the time arrived when this elaborate prescription for a restored and renovated monarchy, after being
rejected in its several details by Parliament, was to be
presented on appeal to the national judgment. The
Patriot leaders entered on the election of 1734 under the
glamour of a great party triumph, sufficient, it might be
thought, to outweigh the strength of the Whig organization
and the prestige of an established Government. In the
session of the preceding year, Walpole, carried away by
financial enthusiasm, had committed the one serious tactical
blunder of his career. He was not, indeed, unconscious of
the vast amount of prejudice which his measure, if rightly

understood, would excite against him, and, after his invariable custom, when proposing any considerable innovation, concealed so far as he possibly could the real nature and intended scope of the reform he meditated. Forty years before, the Bank of England, the greatest commercial institution of modern times, had been created, as it were, behind the back of the commercial public, as one of the details of a financial measure which, for its ostensible object, simply imposed new duties on tonnage for the benefit of certain persons agreeing to advance money to the Government ; and so Walpole, encouraged perhaps by this striking instance of the success of his favourite methods, first attempted to establish the "greatest reform ever introduced into the commercial policy of England "*—the practice of warehousing goods in bond—under the provisions of an Act of Parliament of which the ostensible object was merely to transfer two commodities already subject to taxation from one revenue department to another. These two commodities were wine and tobacco ; and the avowed purpose of the minister in abolishing the duties on importation in favour of others to be levied in future on the consumption of the goods was, according to his statement, simply to protect the revenue, to prevent the extensive frauds then practised, as he showed, to an enormous extent by smuggling dealers. But his reform, though limited at first to these two articles, and defended on this special ground, was to have been the preliminary, if successful, to much larger operations, which, taken in conjunction with the bonding system (introduced with characteristic wariness in one of the minor clauses of his bill), would have gradually confined import duties to one or two kinds of carefully selected goods—luxuries, chiefly, of the most general use and consumption, and have ultimately exempted the neces-

---

* M'Culloch, in Smith's " Wealth of Nations," iii. 471.

saries of life and the raw material of manufactures from all taxation whatever. Since the time of Walpole, his scheme has in all its essential parts been successfully carried out ; and it was, in fact, a bold attempt to anticipate in a manner as quiet and unostentatious as possible the enlightened principle which has, ever since the complete triumph of free trade, guided the operations of English financiers.

But, as an economist, Walpole was altogether in advance of his age ; and the result showed that, with all his foresight and caution, he had failed either to measure or to disarm the strength of national prejudice. The nature and effect of the fiscal revolution which he meditated was not thoroughly understood. But it was understood quite sufficiently to arouse against it every commercial monopolist in the kingdom. The very notion of a general Excise, awaking as it did memories of martial tyranny and republican double-dealing, was hateful to the common people. Through the exertions of the trading interests, whose illicit profits would have been destroyed, and of the political agitators, who used them as their tools, a storm of outraged patriotism was roused throughout the country as violent, as unreasoning, as baneful in its effects, as that which twenty years before had followed the similar attempt of Bolingbroke to establish free commercial intercourse with our "natural enemies "—the French. Protection reared its head against any relaxation of duties by which the " foreigner " would benefit. The city, in the person of the Lord Mayor, Aldermen, and Common Council, appeared at the Bar in formal protest. The minister was burnt in effigy. Riots, growing in some places into open rebellion, broke out in the chief seats of commercial industry. The supporters of the Government were mobbed and hustled in the very precincts of the House of Commons, and the Sovereign was solemnly warned that the obnoxious scheme, even if passed by Parliament, could only be carried out by military force.

The measure was withdrawn. The minister, with his usual worldly wisdom, emphatically declared that never again, however much the change might promote the interests and welfare of the nation, should he be so mad as to suggest any extensions of the Excise. And the indignant Patriots, improving the victory which chance had given them, continued as emphatically to declare their disbelief in this assurance, and their conviction that if the country, after such an experience, should, at the approaching elections, entrust their interests to his care, they would find this invasion of them renewed in a still more sinister and deadly form.

Pulteney and his Whig followers assailed the Excise scheme with every artifice of rhetoric and argument, mainly for what it undoubtedly was—a violation of the time-honoured principle of protection to native industry ; and in doing so they were perfectly consistent, taking their stand on the recognized traditions of Whig policy which Walpole, moved by wider considerations, was neglecting. But Bolingbroke—Bolingbroke the free-trader, the patron of Arthur Moore, the anticipator of Peel and Cobden, the harbinger of a golden age, when

> " Free as seas or wind
> Unbounded Thames should flow for all mankind "—

was Bolingbroke to join in attacking a beneficent reform, conceived in the enlightened spirit of his own commercial policy, or was he to support an unpopular measure proposed by a detested rival ? He succeeded in finding a middle course. He did not deny that the change would be attended with some economical advantages ; but he main-

tained that these advantages would be small, when compared with the political evils that would accompany them.
He opposed the measure on what he calls " the true principles of public freedom."   He reminded his readers of the
origin of that impost which it was now proposed to extend
and perpetuate—how it had been borrowed from the Dutch
financiers by the saints and tyrants of the Long Parliament.   He reminded them that every extension of the
Excise system would require for its execution a larger and
larger staff of revenue officers, a constantly increasing
standing army of Whig placemen, Whig election agents,
men invested on specious pretexts with the right of entering every elector's home, and certain not to leave it without
the promise of the elector's vote.   He affected to treat the
whole scheme, in short, as an electioneering stratagem,
devised to preserve a dissolving majority, the bitter pill
of political subjection being in this case gilded by the
prospect of a growing revenue and lessening public burdens.
He asked of what avail would be cheaper necessaries of
life, diminished cost of production, a wider market for the
manufacturer, a larger choice of goods for the tradesman
and the consumer, if these blessings were purchased at the
cost of higher things, of the " immemorial liberties " won
by ancestral valour and bequeathed from historic times.
And he appealed to every Englishman who valued the
ancient franchises of his race to reject the proffered bribe,
and to mark at the polling booth his sense of the briber's
conduct.

But the appeal failed.   The deluded nation proved
deaf to the voice of the charmer.   " They acted on this
occasion," said Bolingbroke afterwards—"they acted the
part of a patient who, knowing the nature of his distemper,
and having a certain cure guaranteed to him, chose rather
to bear his constitutional malady than undergo the remedies

prescribed by his physician." *   The Excise scheme having been frankly and apologetically withdrawn, the tempest which it had excited lulled, passing over with the suddenness of a squall in summer seas ; and in the genial glow of returning sanity the exaggerations and sophistries of Bolingbroke and Pulteney, and the crowd of distinguished writers whom Walpole's patronage of Grub Street had elevated into Patriots, were seen and condemned.   They failed to make much impression, even in the more open and popular constituencies.   In 1734 the country was prosperous and contented.   It was not yet suffering, as it was seven years later, from the effects of bad harvests and under the humiliations of an unsuccessful war, trials quite potent enough to create a wave of democratic enthusiasm, before which many of Walpole's breakwaters and sluice-gates gave way.   It was not dissatisfied with constitutional changes, of which as yet it felt only the advantage ; and it was quite sensible of the personal objects and sordid desires out of which Patriotism was formed.   When the returns came in, it was found that the "seeds of liberty"—to quote another illustration used on the occasion by Bolingbroke—that the "delicate seeds of liberty had been choked in their growth by the rank, luxuriant weeds of selfishness and apathy." In plainer language, the majority supporting ministers, though somewhat reduced from its original dimensions, was still overwhelming.

It was then that the discomfited Patriots took to quarrelling amongst themselves, and that that famous schism in their ranks was formed which ended in Bolingbroke's elimination from the party.   The younger Whigs, or Boys, as Walpole called them—the men of native virtue and untainted mind, according to Speaker Onslow—continued for a while to dream the old dreams and pursue the

* Bolingbroke to Sir William Wyndham, October 3, 1737.

old phantoms. But Pulteney and Sandys and the malcontent Whig place-hunters, who had professed the principles of Patriotism mainly as an electoral cry, began to
meditate a change of tactics. The general election had
opened their eyes as to the feeling of the country towards
them, had shown them the strength of the Whig organization and the inefficacy against it of weapons purely
literary and oratorical. They had by this time been
reinforced, moreover, by many of Walpole's most eminent
colleagues and supporters, whom his arbitrary temper and
personal unpopularity had estranged ; and they imagined
themselves strong enough in his growing isolation to make
terms with the Mammon of unrighteousness. As one of
the most distinguished of their recent converts, Lord
Chesterfield, afterwards expressed it, " they were desirous
now to get in with a few by negotiation, and not by
victory with numbers." Influenced by such views, the
presence amongst them of Bolingbroke, the Jacobite conspirator, the proscribed Tory leader, the bitter assailant,
not of Walpole only, but of the whole Walpolean system,
was at once unnecessary and inconvenient. They looked
about for some pretext for getting rid of him, and found it,
according to the common story, in certain charges which,
in the great debate on the Septennial Act, Walpole had
brought against him of caballing with foreign ambassadors
against the Government which had treated him with such
lenity. How far these intrigues, if intrigues there were, had
gone ; whether they were such as to justify a patriotic
opposition in recommending him (as we are assured they
did) to leave England ; whether they would have justified
the minister thus assailed in formally withdrawing, had he
remained at home, that royal pardon which alone prevented,
it must be remembered, the penalties of his attainder from
still operating ;—all this is unknown. What is certain is,

that in the summer of 1735 the political connection between
Pulteney and Bolingbroke suddenly ceased ; the establishment at Dawley was broken up ; and Bolingbroke, for the
second time, withdrew to France.

When a perfectly rational, simple, and honourable
explanation of a man's conduct can be given, it is unwise
to try and trace it to obscure or discreditable motives.
There is really no reason for doubting the truth of Bolingbroke's own story, or for supposing that his retirement
to France at this time was anything but a voluntary act
on his part. He fixed his residence abroad because in the
embarrassed condition of his affairs, financial as well as
political, he lived there with greater ease and satisfaction
than at home. But he never considered himself as under
an enforced exile. He visited London without scruple
whenever private business called him there, or an opportunity seemed to offer of improving his public fortunes.
To his closest personal friends he had, long before the step
was taken, alluded to the irksomeness of his mode of life,
and stated his fixed intention of withdrawing from it as
soon as the issue which he was then putting to the country
had been fairly tried. " Disarmed, gagged, and almost
bound as I am," he had written to Pope in 1733, whilst the
hopes of the Patriots were high, before the elections had
shown the weakness of their cause, and the debate on the
Septennial Act the hollowness of their alliance—" disarmed,
gagged, and almost bound as I am, I shall continue in
the drudgery of public business only so long as the integrity
and perseverance of the men who, with none of my disadvantages, are co-operating with me make it reasonable
to me to engage in it. Further than that no shadow of
duty obliges me to go. Plato ceased to act for the commonwealth when he ceased to persuade ; and Solon laid
down his arms before the public magazine, when Pisistratus

grew too strong to be opposed any longer with hopes of success." *

To Sir William Wyndham, again, the most intimate of his political associates, the trusted depository of all his political secrets, he repeated, after the step was taken, precisely the same statements in explanation of it which he had made to Pope two years before as likely in the circumstances to cause it. "I have no excuse," he wrote in the winter of 1735—"I have no excuse for choosing to be at home but two: an opportunity of being useful to my friends and country, or the means of completing that restoration by frequent, solemn, and unsolicited promises of which the late King drew me into England. The opportunity is over; the means are not in my power; and, in the present state of things, the end is no longer desirable." And more than ten years later, after Wyndham's death, in the instructive series of letters in which he aimed at directing the political conduct of a younger friend, Lord Marchmont, and in which he explained, without reserve, the objects of his policy and the motives determining him at the most important conjunctures of his life, he expressly asserted that he did not leave England in '35 till some schemes that were then on the loom, though they came to nothing, made him "one too many" to his political friends—words which, though they have been otherwise explained, undoubtedly refer, not to any intrigues of Bolingbroke's own, but to the base intention ascribed to Pulteney of abandoning Patriotism and himself continuing Walpole's plan of government as the agent of the Whig oligarchy by the help of Walpole's colleagues.† "Is it not manifest," he had before written to Marchmont in 1740, when these schemes at length were on the eve of succeed-

* Works, iii. 316.
† Bolingbroke to Marchmont, July 24, 1746.

ing—" is it not manifest that two or three men have been labouring some years to turn a virtuous defence of the constitution into a dirty intrigue of low ambition, that they are only waiting the opportunity of pursuing the old system, and that the sole object of their pretended Patriotism is to deliver over the government of their country from faction to faction ? " *   It is no imputation on Bolingbroke's public spirit that he desired, by a formal and ostentatious retreat from active politics, to disavow all complicity in these designs, and to mark his indignation at such treachery.   On the whole, it is most reasonable to conclude that Bolingbroke's withdrawal to France was due neither to the expostulations of his friends nor to the menaces of his foes, but to those mixed motives, all personal to himself, which generally determine a man's conduct— pecuniary embarrassments from which, whilst his father lived, he was never free, and which now made the sale of Dawley inevitable ; vexation at the complete failure of efforts from which he had anticipated so much ; the determination to be no longer the catspaw of the discontented Whigs, and the consciousness that neither in his political nor in his personal views had he anything to hope from their triumph.

III.

He retired to Chanteloup, in Touraine.   In this historic chateau, built by the Princess Orsini as a retreat for her declining years, or at the smaller hunting-lodge of Argeville near Fontainebleau, where the official post held by Lady Bolingbroke's son-in-law enabled him to use at his pleasure the forest and royal stables, Bolingbroke lived, with only occasional visits to England, till the death of his father,

* Bolingbroke to Marchmont, January 1 and 25, 1740.

Lord St. John, the fall of Walpole, the failure and disgrace
of Pulteney, and the bursting of the bubble of Patriotism
again changed the conditions of his life. He had ceased
to be the connecting link between the two branches of the
Patriot opposition. He had withdrawn into foreign retirement partly to mark his formal abandonment of further
efforts in their cause. But he continued, nevertheless, to
preserve an interest in their proceedings. He corresponded
regularly on current politics with his friend Sir William
Wyndham, and with some of the younger members of the
party which Wyndham led : Lord Cornbury, the last male
descendant of the great Lord Clarendon; William Chetwynd,
member for Stafford, and afterwards master of the mint
in Pelham's ministry; Hugh Lord Polwarth, member for
Berwick-upon-Tweed, afterwards Earl of Marchmont, the
grandson of that Sir Patrick Hume who, fifty years before,
had been the marplot of Argyle's rebellion. Through these
men he still advised and directed at critical conjunctures
the policy of the democratical Tories. From Bolingbroke's
pen came most of those terse and vigorous protests which,
during the last six years of Walpole's government, they
inserted in the Lords' Journals. The motion made by
Wyndham in 1738 for the free publication of the debates
and division lists, a motion which caused almost as much
embarrassment amongst the Whigs in opposition as it did
on the Government benches, and which, when ultimately
carried, did more perhaps than any other reform to restore
public confidence in Parliament and the just authority over
it of the constituent bodies, was taken at Bolingbroke's
instance. And it was Bolingbroke who first recommended,
as a formal appeal to the nation from Parliament, the
secession of the following spring, in which the Patriots,
following the example which he had personally set them,
marked by a general withdrawal from Parliament their

sense of the inefficacy of mere argument on a party majority, and of the uselessness of attending debates when the conclusion was foregone.

Current politics, however, filled up only a small part of Bolingbroke's time. His chief occupation and solace as before were found in study and in the composition of works only slightly tinctured with party asperities. In a little pavilion which he had fitted up in the garden of the Abbey of Sens, and to which he would retire with a single attendant when the conversation of his guests became oppressive, he composed and addressed to his friend Lord Cornbury those eight letters on History, of which the last two contain an elaborate and powerful vindication of his own conduct when minister. It was then that he completed his philosophical essays, and meditated rearranging and expanding them into an exhaustive metaphysical treatise. It was then, too, that he wrote his characteristic epistle to Lord Bathurst on the true " Use of Retirement and Study," his account of the " State of Parties at the Accession of George I.," his " Idea of a Patriot King," together with that fine essay on Patriotism of which I have already spoken, and which contains in the famous digression on oratory perhaps the most eloquent passage in writings unrivalled for eloquence. But the great work of his leisure, a full and complete history of his own times, a detailed review of the whole state of Europe from the Pyrenean Treaties and of the natural and incidental interests of each kingdom, setting forth the true objects of the several Powers in entering on the Succession War, the subsequent change in their views, the motives and measures by which the contest had been protracted, the real reasons why it ended in a manner not proportionable to its success, and the new political state into which Europe was thrown at its close,—this great monument of Bolingbroke's industry, for which he had long been diligently collecting matter, he was forced unhappily by repeated disappointments to abandon.

In the spring of 1742, two events occurred which seriously affected Bolingbroke. The death of Lord St. John at near ninety, in putting him in possession of the family inheritance, relieved him from his most pressing embarrassments. Almost at the same moment the fall of Walpole, brought about at length by the slow accumulation of personal and political resentments, removed the great organizer of parliamentary government, and the great obstacle, as Bolingbroke thought, to the revival of personal monarchy. During the year and a half that followed, his visits to England became more frequent ; and in the closing months of 1744 he ended his long wanderings, and took up his final abode at Battersea in the old manor-house where he was born.

A cheerless prospect lay before him. He found the party which he had formed with so much labour dissipated, and the name of Patriot, which he had made so famous, dishonoured by Pulteney's defection. He found his country involved, largely through his own exertions, in an unjust and unsuccessful war. He found the Whig power, which he had striven to subvert, firmly refixing itself after Walpole's fall in the hands of Walpole's most trusted colleagues. He found his own domestic affairs in disorder, early friends dead or estranged, the infirmities of age, aggravated by past imprudences, fast seizing upon him.

But no accumulated misfortunes could break the spring of that vigorous and elastic mind. Almost at the moment of his return—the opportunity offering for a political manœuvre—he took a leading share in the party struggle which ended in the overthrow of Carteret, the most distin-guished of Pulteney's lieutenants, and in the reconstruction on a wider basis of the Pelham ministry, which thenceforth included most of his personal and political adherents. He succeeded in revenging himself on the statesmen who had betrayed him. But in the act of doing so he contributed to the reunion and consolidation of the Whig power ; and he failed in the higher object which at one moment, hoping against hope, he had thought to combine with the gratification of his resentment—the establishment of a Government based avowedly on the principle of comprehension, combining all political parties under the personal direction of the Crown, and changing its policy to suit the changing requirements of Parliament. In spite of all his advice and exhortation, the Tories proper, the half-converted Jacobites, the men to whom six years before he had vainly offered Prince Frederick as a Messiah, remained sullenly aloof, content, as he scornfully said, to be hewers of wood and drawers of water, aliens in the land of their birth, proscribing all Government in their obstinate refusal to co-operate with any ; and the so-called " broad-bottom " ministry, instead of exhibiting in practical operation the principles which Bolingbroke advocated, was destined to confirm through the connivance of his own followers the constitutional methods which he had denounced.

This was the final disappointment of Bolingbroke's public life. Before the reaction set in which was to give personal monarchy, under the veil of the party system, a new hold on the nation, he was himself withdrawn from the scene ; and nothing at this time portended the posthumous triumph in store for him. To his friend Lord Marchmont, who had warned him of the uselessness of his efforts, he made no concealment of his chagrin, or of his feeling that his part in the world was over. " The men who leaned upon me in their days of lameness," he writes, " have laid me by as a useless implement since the angel stirred the waters, and they got into the pool and were cured." " It is time that I should retire for good and all from the world, and from the very approaches to business, *ne peccem ad extremum ridendus."* He learned backgammon to amuse his solitude, and enable him to swallow down the dregs of life with more complacency. To divert his thoughts from present and recent events, he resumed the historical studies in which he had formerly found relief; applied his mind to the transactions of former times, which, if not more pleasant in themselves to contemplate, affected him at the moment with a less poignant sense of failure. On the general affairs of Europe, indeed, his knowledge and judgment, his experience as a diplomatist, and the great part he had formerly played, made his opinions still matter of interest; and in the months which preceded the pacification of Aix-la-Chapelle, his solitary mansion by the Thames was a favourite resort of rising politicians, who sought to draw from the negotiator of the Peace of Utrecht lessons that might be useful to them in the task of extricating England from the German entanglements in which her connection with Hanover was involving her. At the close of the war he wrote, with a view of enforcing a favourite dogma of his school, some " Reflections on the Present State of the Nation," especially with regard to her Debts and Taxes, intended to show that on the reduction of her monetary engagements depended the future existence of England as an independent Power ; and this little unfinished tract, aptly typifying its author's broken career and fortunes, brings to an end the long list of Bolingbroke's political writings.*

The last three years of his life were passed by Bolingbroke, so far as his health permitted, in preparing these works for publication. It was when engaged in this task

---

* Bolingbroke to Lord Marchmont, July 24, 1746, October 30, 1742, February 19, 1747.

that the old man's vanity and petulance betrayed him into
an unworthy action, and exposed him to a stinging rebuke.
He employed as his literary assistant and executor David
Mallet, a Scotch philosopher and poetaster of some note in
his day, a Patriot in politics, a Rationalist in religion, recommended to Bolingbroke by community both of political and
theological opinions. In 1749, with Mallet as editor, he
issued a small volume containing the letter on the " Spirit of
Patriotism," the "Idea of a Patriot King," and the "Account
of the State of Parties at the Accession of George I. ; " and
in the preface to the edition inserted, under the cloak of
Mallet's name, a bitter reflection on Pope, for having
secretly printed from the original draft in his possession
a number of copies of the " Patriot King," with alterations
and omissions suggested by his own fancy. This charge,
altogether unjust if implying any design on Pope's part
to injure the reputation of his friend, and expressed in
what, considering their long and close connection, were
most unseemly terms, roused from his lair at Prior Park
Pope's own literary henchman, Warburton, who vindicated
with complete success and with unwonted dignity the
memory of his dead patron. The public voice warmly
applauded the divine. Bolingbroke found, to his chagrin,
that in thus traducing the illustrious writer whose fame
is inseparably associated with his own, and by whom he
was loved and honoured beyond all created things, he
had committed not only an offence but a blunder—had
stirred up a hornet's nest about his own ears, and arrayed
against himself, as his friend Lord Chesterfield expressed
it, a coalition of Whig, Tory, Patriot, Jacobite, and
Trimmer.

It is charitable to hope that increasing infirmities,
exacerbating a temper always fretful and exacting, may
be held responsible for this last indiscretion ; for he was

now fast sinking under the weight of bodily and mental
troubles. A cancerous humour appeared in his jaw; and
the unskilful treatment of his surgeon aggravated the
dreadful malady. Rheumatic pains, which no healing
waters could assuage, tortured him night and day. Nor
did he escape the savage Roman curse, *ultimus suorum
moriatur.* Early in 1750, that faithful and tender companionship which had cheered his exile and been the
solace of his life, as he fondly said, in all its· melancholy
scenes, became for him a memory of the past—a precious
argument of those eternal truths which every loving life
helps to demonstrate. His wife's relations, disputing the
validity of her marriage, obtained from the French Courts
a judgment assigning to them the property which she had
left in France. This judgment was, on appeal to the
Parliament of Paris, reversed. But Bolingbroke did not
live to witness the restoration of her good name. In
December, 1751, after a probation of cruel suffering, God
opened to him the real purpose and ultimate destiny of
mankind.

He died childless, and was succeeded in his title and
estates by his nephew, on whom the peerage granted to his
father in 1716 had already devolved. The great city in
its relentless flow has obliterated most of the traces of his
life at Battersea—the antique manor-house, where his
Puritan grandmother preached to him, and his gloomy
childhood was spent; the cedar parlour, where Lyttelton
and Marchmont, Murray and Pitt, Stair and Chesterfield,
met together; the terrace by the river-side, where the
copies of the Patriot King which Pope had surreptitiously
printed were solemnly destroyed. But the schools which
Sir Walter St. John founded still survive to mark the
family's connection with the spot; and in the parish church
are stately monuments of Bolingbroke and his second

wife, with marble busts by Roubiliac, and epitaphs which Bolingbroke himself drew up.   The statesman lies in the vault beneath the altar-piece, by the relics of his ancestral home, and with the memorials of his race about him.

THE END.